ROSES
REDHEADS
— *and* —
TRUCKERS

ROSES
REDHEADS
— *and* —
TRUCKERS

HERBERT DURBIN

TATE PUBLISHING
AND ENTERPRISES, LLC

Published by Tate Publishing & Enterprises, LLC
127 E. Trade Center Terrace | Mustang, Oklahoma 73064 USA
1.888.361.9473 | www.tatepublishing.com

Tate Publishing is committed to excellence in the publishing industry. The company reflects the philosophy established by the founders, based on Psalm 68:11,
"The Lord gave the word and great was the company of those who published it."

Published in the United States of America

ISBN: 978-1-63268-242-0
Family & Relationships / Love & Romance
14.06.18

To Kathleen, who has always made me proud

CONTENTS

ROSES FOR JEANIE

HERBERT DURBIN

The old man tediously trimmed the dead leaves and faded blooms from the rose bushes in the side yard. As he did this, he was remembering how Jeanie always seemed to have a more beautiful and vibrant garden. This bush with the violet roses had been one of her favorites. He finished his chore and took the few blooms he had cut into the house. He placed them in a vase and put the vase on the fireplace mantel next to her picture. He stood for a long moment, smiling, as he studied this picture of her taken so many years ago.

In the kitchen, he poured himself a glass of iced tea and took it out onto the front porch. He sat in his rocker, took a long sip, and let his mind take him to a similar summer day many years ago. He was deep into a daydream of yesteryear when he heard, and then saw, the young girl on the bicycle take a tumble on the sidewalk just in front of his gate. The young lad accompanying her ran up and helped her to her feet.

The old man saw she had skinned her knee and that she was holding her elbow and crying softly. "Come here and let me see what you did!" he called to the young people as he arose from his chair.

The boy held the gate open as the young girl walked through it and up to the old man. Her knee was skinned, but not as badly as the elbow, which was oozing blood.

"Let's get you inside where I can clean that up," the old man said, "I have some Mercurochrome and bandages. What's your name, sweetie?"

"Eugenia," the girl said, as she brushed a tear from her eye. "Eugenia Webb. This is my friend, Herbie."

"Well, Herbie, while I fix Eugenia's scrapes, you go get your bicycle off the sidewalk. Then come in and get a couple of Pepsis out of the icebox for the two of you. There now, Eugenia. How does that feel?"

"It still stings!"

"That will pass in time. How old are you, Eugenia?"

"Ten."

"I'm eleven," Herbie stated with pride.

"Why were you trying to ride a boy's bike, honey?"

"It's Herbie's, and I made him let me ride it. He was supposed to keep me from falling!"

"You were going too fast," Herbie told her. "She was going too fast," he said again, looking down at the floor. "I'm sorry that you got hurt, Eugenia."

"It's okay. It wasn't your fault."

The young people were seated on the settee facing the fireplace and picture wall as they drank their colas. "Who are all of those people?" Herbie asked.

"That's my family," the old man answered with pride.

"Who's the beautiful lady in the picture by the roses?" Eugenia asked. "Is that your daughter?"

"No," the old man answered softly while smiling at her. "That's my Jeanie! She was just twenty-three when that picture was taken. It was right after we were married back in 1959. That picture there is of us on the day we were married. That one is Jeanie and our daughter, Roseanna, when Roseanna was about two. That one is of both our girls, Roseanna and Rosemarie, and that one is of Jeanie and our son, Ross. You two remind me of when I first met Jeanie. We were about the same age."

"Did you always know you were going to marry her someday?" Herbie asked while glancing quickly at Eugenia.

"Not always," the old man said, "but I always knew that I loved her. The first time I saw Jeanie was at the city pool. She was eleven, and I was twelve. I had gone there with my brother and sisters. Jeanie was there in a bright pink one-piece bathing suit. She was showing off, jumping from the side of the pool, and I dared her to jump off of the high board. I remember to this day what she said."

The old man took a sip from his tea. "'Darers go first!' That's what she told me. I was frightened, so I hesitated, and she called me a fraidy cat as she marched to the high board ladder, climbed to the top, and jumped off and into the water some ten feet below. I just had to follow! It's amazing what a man in love will do. I only saw her a few more times at the pool that summer. She would always challenge me to do new things. And I would do a lot of dumb things just to impress her.

The old man sat silently for several minutes just staring at the picture of Jeanie. He had a smile on his face as he remembered some of the foolish things he had done.

"When school started that year," he continued, "she was in the seventh grade, and I was in the eighth. We rode the same bus to school, and we would usually get to sit together. When I started high school and she was still in junior high, things started to be different. In high school, I was in a band and FFA. She was in almost everything. I think it was my junior year—her sophomore year—that she started going out with a classmate, Kenneth Richards. He was an athlete. He lettered every year in everything. He was the star quarterback. He was the MVP every year but one in basketball, and the star pitcher on the baseball team. I played trombone in the band and had a show pig. Kenneth had his own almost-new pickup, and I had to borrow my family's very used station wagon. Every time I saw Jeanie with Kenneth Richards, I would die a little inside. I figured I couldn't compete, so I just continued to worship her from afar.

Once again the old man paused collecting his thoughts. It was as if he was looking at a movie of his past life.

"In my senior year, her junior year, Jeanie and I were in three things together—student council, yearbook committee, and study hall. It was one day in study hall that she passed a note to me. In it, she asked me if I was going to the junior/senior banquet. I looked over to where she was seated and found her looking at me, eyebrows raised questioningly. I shrugged as if to answer, 'I'm not sure.' She passed me another note. This one said, 'Will you take me?' I looked over at her, and she had that same questioning look. I nodded. Her third note said, 'I'll meet you after school by the bike rack.' After school that day, we talked so long that Jeanie missed her bus, and I got to take her home in the old station wagon."

"What about her boyfriend?" Herbie asked. "Didn't he get mad?"

The old man took another long drink of his tea. "You're wondering about Kenneth Richards. Well, that day he was at after-school football practice. I went on to take Jeanie to the banquet that year. We had what I thought was a very good time. On the way home, we parked out on a lovers' lane, and she gave me my first real kiss. Oh, I'd kissed her before when we were much younger, but this was something very different and very special! I wanted to propose marriage right then and there. She was a lovely mature woman of seventeen. I was a naïve boy of eighteen."

The old man paused, staring long and lovingly at the picture beside the vase of roses on the mantel.

"Did you ask her to marry you? Did she say yes?" Eugenia wanted to know.

"No, as a matter of fact, I didn't. We didn't go out again that year at all. After my graduation the next spring, I went off to State University where I eventually got my degree in petroleum engineering. Jeanie went to Northwestern College the next year where she got a degree in education. We didn't see each other again for almost five years."

"I guess I'd been working for Phillips for almost a year, when one day, a coworker was telling me about this school teacher he had met. He said she would only go out with him if he would bring along a friend for her roommate. She promised him that the roommate was pretty, was fun to go out with, and that she loved roses. He begged me to go along. I kept telling him no, but he was so smitten by this teacher that I finally said I would go. I was sure her roommate would be a dog and thought about backing out several times before Saturday night finally got there.

"I got a small bouquet of lavender roses, dressed in my only suit, and hoped for the best. I thought if this old maid school teacher was too ugly, I would just hide behind the roses. When we got to their apartment, I walked behind my friend hesitantly. My friend's date let us in, explaining that my date was in the bedroom doing some last minute touch-up. I was standing there in doomed anticipation, waiting for the roommate to open the door and let the dog out. Instead of a dog, what I saw emerging from that doorway that night was the most beautiful woman I have ever seen. My mouth dropped open, and my feet felt like they were glued to the floor. The vision of loveliness glided across the floor toward me. 'Are these roses for me?' she asked. Finally, I got my voice back. 'Yes, Jeanie,' I told her. 'I got them just for you.' Her roommate was about to introduce us, but we told her we had known each other for many years. That was our only double date. The following June, we were married."

"And you lived happily ever after!" Eugenia smiled.

"Well, not exactly," the old man said, taking on a somber look. "You see, life isn't always sunshine and roses. Sometimes, you get a little rain and weeds. How's that elbow, Eugenia?"

"It seems to be a lot better. It isn't hurting right now."

"Good. Shouldn't you kids let your folks know where you are?"

"No, we don't have to be back home till four o'clock." Eugenia said.

"Are you kids hungry? Would you like a sandwich?"

"I'm a little hungry," Herbie admitted.

The old man fixed some peanut butter and jelly sandwiches and invited the two young people to join him at the table. He poured each of them a tall glass of cold milk.

"Tell us about the rain and the weeds," Eugenia prodded him.

"Well," the old man continued, "Jeanie loved children and loved her teaching job at the elementary school. She was teaching kindergarten when she found out she was pregnant. She was excited as she could be over the prospect of her own child to teach. I guess all that standing and stress must have been bad for her. She had a miscarriage of a tiny baby boy while in her seventh month. The baby couldn't be saved. I thought she would surely die. She grieved so much and so hard. I was moved into the guest room for over a year while she cried herself to sleep almost every night."

The old man sat silent for a while, staring at the pictures. "Then one day," he suddenly continued, "the sunshine came back into her eyes, and she let me hold her and love her again. She was teaching fourth grade when she found out she was pregnant again. This time, everything went well, and soon, our daughter, Roseanna, was born. She was every bit as pretty as her mother and just as busy. Three years later, our daughter, Rosemarie, was born, a tomboy from top to bottom. They were still in the lower grades when Jeanie became elementary school principal. But Jeanie still wanted a boy.

"She was the principal at the junior high school for a number of years and then went on to be the high school principal. Then one day, I think the girls were in their teens, Jeanie discovered she was pregnant again. It wasn't an easy pregnancy, her being in her late thirties, but she was stubbornly determined to have that baby. 'Maybe this one will be a boy,' she would say.

"Our son, Ross, was born just before her fortieth birthday. And like so many babies born to older women, Ross had Down syndrome. She clung to that baby boy like he was her very life. She knew he had probably no more than thirty years to live, and she wanted to make every one of them the very best for him. About a year after he was born, Jeanie became the school superintendent for all schools in this ISD. She made a way for all Down syndrome children to be educated in our school system. It became her life's work. After she retired, she went all over the country, giving speeches about Down syndrome children. Ross would always travel with her."

The old man stood up and picked up one of the pictures from the mantel. "That's a picture of Jeanie and Ross taken when they were in Washington, DC. Jeanie spoke about children with Down syndrome before a congressional committee."

The old man sat back down. He had a strange smile on his face as he concluded his story. "Jeanie was just sixty-one, and Ross was twenty-one, when their plane went down near Pittsburg. I still try to bring her roses when I can." Herbie and Eugenia looked at each other in silence for several minutes. Then looking back at the old man Eugenia said, "It's almost four o'clock. Thank you for the sandwich and for fixing my elbow and knee."

"Yes, thank you for everything!" Herbie said as he followed Eugenia to the door.

As they looked back, they saw that the old man was standing at the mantel, holding his picture of Jeanie.

THE BUMP

HERBERT DURBIN

CHAPTER 1

Petty officer, second class, Harold R. MacDonnell, stood behind the helm of the warship, peering out through the pilothouse windows at the angry seas. He could feel the up and down movement of the destroyer as it plowed through the white caps and the sudden shudder of the ship as a large wave pounded against the bow and the salty spray hit the windows of the flying bridge. The evening sky was overcast, causing the deep blue of the Pacific Ocean to look almost black. He was on the second leg of the dogwatch and was looking forward to a warm shower and bunk. He had seen tonight's movie so many times that he had no desire to watch it again.

"Right to zero-nine-three!" The conning officer called from the door to the flying bridge. His voice was barely audible over the noise of the wind.

"Zero-nine-three, aye!" Harry responded.

The ship and crew had been away from their home port of San Diego, California, for just under seven months this time. They were returning from another tour of the Western Pacific where, among other duties, they had patrolled the waters of the Formosa Strait. The ship was making turns for twenty knots and was about two days out of Pearl Harbor, heading east on its way home.

This would be Harry's last cruise, as his enlistment would be up in just over ninety days. He was not thinking of that, however, he was concentrating on the compass in front of him as he steered a considerably straight course for such heavy seas. Harry was considered one of the best helmsmen aboard the USS *Rochelle*, and because of that, he was also assigned as sea detail helmsman.

That responsibility required him to always be on the helm when his ship was going into a port and out of a port or was alongside a supply ship for refueling or taking on stores or ammunition.

Harry was liked by most of the crew, but some of them thought him an oddball. At twenty-three, he did not drink, smoke, or have any tattoos. In foreign ports, he was never seen visiting brothels, or flirting with B-girls. He was a conscientious worker but shy and introverted. He had been raised in a Pentecostal Church, and his father, back in Tennessee, was still the pastor of a small congregation. Harry didn't force his beliefs onto others. He just lived a clean, celibate life, hoping someday to meet that one girl who would make his life complete.

"Steer zero-nine-zero!" the conning officer shouted over the noise of the wind.

"Zero-nine-zero, aye," Harry shouted back.

The boatswain of the watch came into the pilothouse just then and passed the word over the 1MC, "Now lay before the mast all eight o'clock reports."

Just fifteen more minutes, Harry thought, feeling the stress of keeping the ship on a steady course in his back and neck muscles.

It was now dark out, and the winds and the seas seemed to be calming. The conning officer came in off of the flying bridge and walked over to Harry. "Keep her steady on zero-nine-zero. Good job tonight, MacDonnell."

"Aye, aye, sir. Thank you, sir," Harry answered.

The conning officer, Lieutenant Junior Grade James Cobb, was one of Harry's favorite officers. They had served together now for over two years and had made two cruises to the Western Pacific together. During that time, they stood many underway watches together. Since Mr. Cobb first came aboard as an ensign, he had taken a liking to Harry and had given him many impromptu lessons in algebra during the long boring condition 3 watches while the ship was on Formosa patrol.

"We'll be in San Diego in ten more days," Mr. Cobb addressed Harry, "Do you have any special plans?"

"No, sir. I just have to go down to Palm City and pick up my old car. The Clawsons, some friends from church, have been keeping it for me."

"You're not going home to Tennessee to see your folks?" Mr. Cobb asked.

"Not right away. I get out in three months. I'll wait until then to go home."

"Is that right? Your enlistment's almost up?"

"Yes, sir, I'm a short-timer," Harry replied.

Mr. Cobb smiled. "So am I. I have less than one year remaining on my ADOC."

"What's that mean, sir?" Harry asked.

"That's my active duty service obligation. Of course, if I'm advanced to lieutenant this time, I'll have to continue on active duty for a little while longer."

"Well, good luck on that, sir."

"Good luck to you in civilian life, MacDonnell."

"Thank you, sir."

Two days later, somewhere around 1000 hours, the ships of DESRON 3 were lined up single file as they prepared to enter the mouth of Pearl Harbor. Once again, Petty Officer MacDonnell was the helmsman. Off to the right, he could see the unmistakable shape of Diamond Head as they neared the island of O'ahu. Farther away and to the left, a plume of smoke from the volcano Kilauea was rising high into the midmorning sky. The USS *Rochelle* was third in line, and he had been given the order to steer by seaman's eye. This meant that he drew an imaginary line from the forward jack staff, dissecting the other two ships directly down the middle. This was a more accurate and less time-consuming way to steer the ship than that of the conning officer having to give constant incremental course change orders.

The destroyers were soon tied up, four abreast. The US customs officers came aboard immediately and checked all the declaration slips. A short time later, liberty call was sounded, and many sailors headed ashore to celebrate being back in US territory again. Harry was content to sit in his radar room and write letters to his folks back home.

He thought about a pretty little freckled-faced girl back there in Tennessee who had once promised to marry him when he returned from his service to his country. He still had her picture in his wallet and all her letters, including the last one where she told him she had found someone else. He even considered writing her a friendly letter, but he couldn't think of just what to say.

He remembered Peggy Baker just like he had last seen her, standing at the bus station in downtown Cookeville, waving a handkerchief while tears filled her pretty blue eyes. Harry had loved her since he was in the seventh grade and she was still in grade school. Her family attended his father's church. At first, they would sit together on the steps of the church before evening services. When he was thirteen and she was just twelve, he recalled that he held her hand for the first time. Harry remembered the thrill he had felt from just touching her hand on that occasion. They had dated all through high school.

He remembered the time when he was a senior in high school and Peggy was a junior, they had driven down by the river. During a period of heavy petting, Peggy had wanted to go all the way. Although extremely aroused, Harry had stopped them, and to be safe, had taken her home. There were those few weeks, while she was angry with him, that she had dated a classmate of his, Dennis Johnson, but she and Harry were soon back together. Although they had discussed marriage at times, he hadn't actually proposed.

Upon graduation from high school, Harry found it almost impossible to find and keep a good job because of his 1-A draft status. When it appeared that he would soon be drafted into the army, he discussed his options with Peggy, and they decided their chances would be better if he enlisted in the navy and got his military obligation out of the way. He had a brother-in-law who had served in the navy and some uncles who had served in the army. Their dislike for the army played a significant part in his decision to join the navy.

He spent twelve grueling weeks in boot camp in San Diego, California, before graduation and assignment to a ship. On boot leave, he gave Peggy an engagement ring, and she promised to wait for him. However, the wait had become too long for Peggy. When Dennis Johnson returned from his twenty-one months of active duty with the army and began to show interest in Peggy, he finally won her affection.

Harry still loved her deeply and would take her back immediately. He would have been the first one off the ship in Pearl Harbor and on the first flight back home if his mother hadn't sent him that wedding picture and announcement from the hometown newspaper. "Johnson-Baker Nuptials," it read. Peggy, in a white dress and a shiny tiara in her golden blond hair, had never looked more beautiful.

Harry finished his letters and decided to take in some of the Honolulu sights. He went below and put on his dress whites. At the quarterdeck, he requested permission to leave the ship. He saluted the colors as he departed. At the end of the pier, he caught a taxi to Honolulu and Waikiki Beach.

As Harry walked along the beach between Fort DeRussy and Kuhio Beach Park, he thought about Peggy, and an old country song came to mind. "I've got my angel on my mind, that's why I'm walkin'. There's such an ache down deep inside, now I ain't talkin'. The little hand that held mine tight, just waved goodbye tonight…"

Sad and depressed, Harry found a bench in front of a large hotel on the beach, sat, and watched the surfers for a while before heading back to his ship.

A few days later, the USS *Rochelle* arrived at San Diego and tied up at the destroyer piers at the naval station directly west of the Thirty-Second Street gate. Harry, on the helm as they came in, looked at the crowds of people without so much as a hint of emotion. He knew no one was there to greet him. When they passed the word *shift colors* and he was eventually excused from his helmsman duty, he took his time before going below. He wanted to stay out of the way of his shipmates as they hurried to change into liberty uniforms so they could go meet their loved ones.

Midafternoon, after all the married crew members and most of the others in liberty status had departed the ship, Harry also departed. At the main gate, he shared the cost of a taxi ride with two other enlisted men going to the downtown area of San Diego. Harry rented a locker in a locker club, changed into his civilian clothes, and picked up a corsage in a first-floor flower shop. He caught the bus going south to Palm City, walked the five blocks from the bus stop to the Clawson home, and arrived at their door just about four-thirty in the afternoon.

Natalie Clawson, a pretty dark-haired girl with big brown eyes and youthful feminine figure, answered the door. She was delighted to see him and greeted him with a friendly hug. Her father wasn't home as yet, but her mother greeted him warmly. Harry had often been a guest in their home, spending many hours in Natalie's room where they talked or practiced a special song together. Harry was totally comfortable in Natalie's company, and considered her a dear friend. Natalie, just four years younger than Harry, secretly wished for a more romantic relationship with him.

"Here, Nat," Harry told her, "I brought you a flower."

"Thank you. It's beautiful!" Natalie responded.

"And where is mine?" Mrs. Clawson teased.

Harry blushed. "I only got the one. I'm sorry. Do you want me to go get you one?"

"Of course not, Harry, I was only teasing. Here, come in and have a glass of lemonade. Frank will be home in about half an hour."

"I really just wanted to pick up my car," Harry told her as he took the lemonade from her hand.

"Daddy is restoring a World War I biplane in an old hanger at Brown Field," Natalie told him. "He has your car out there in the hanger to protect it from the elements."

"We'll take you out there to get it as soon as Frank gets home," Connie Clawson assured him.

"Haven't you been driving it for me like I asked you to do?" Harry quizzed Natalie.

"I did for a while, but Daddy thought the tires were a little too worn for me to be safe in it."

"I guess I'd better buy a complete new set before I head out for Tennessee," Harry told them. "I get out of the navy in less than three months. I guess I'll be heading back home then."

Soon, Frank Clawson came home and greeted Harry. While Connie Clawson remained at home, Frank took Harry and Natalie to the hanger to get Harry's car.

"I want you to see this old biplane I'm fixing up," Frank told Harry. "It's in very good condition, considering how old it is. I already have the engine running. I just have to replace some silk, and I'll be able to take it up!"

"What kind is it?" Harry asked, as he slowly walked around the plane.

"1917 Sopwith Camel!" Frank answered enthusiastically. "It has a twenty-eight-foot wing span, and the nine cylinder Clerget rotary engine produces one hundred and sixty horsepower."

"How fast will it go?"

"The maximum speed is about one hundred and fifteen miles per hour."

"It really is a beauty," Harry told him. "But it looks awfully small!"

"It only has the one seat for the pilot. That was to save weight for additional armament and ammunition. You should get your pilot's license. I'll let you take it up."

"Maybe someday I will," Harry replied.

They all went over to the corner of the hanger where Harry's yellow 1954 Oldsmobile Rocket 98 hardtop convertible was parked. He removed the canvas, and he and Frank folded it before Harry climbed in and started the engine.

As the big V8 roared to life, Harry remarked, "It seems quieter and smoother than I remember."

"I tweaked it a bit when Natalie was driving it," Frank told him. "It should get you another hundred thousand miles. But you need new tires on her, son, and very soon."

Natalie climbed in beside Harry for the ride home. As soon as they were out of Frank's sight, Natalie slid across the seat to sit close beside Harry. He didn't discourage it, but he didn't invite it either. To him, she was just a very dear friend. Their conversation was casual and friendly. They drove to the Clawson home without incident.

It was very late before Harry was able to say his good-byes. He had declined to eat anything at the Clawson's, and now, he suddenly felt the desire for one of Oscar's famous double-decker cheeseburgers. It was almost closing time at Oscar's Drive-In as he drove into the carhop area.

The carhops had all been called inside, and they were about to lock the door when Harry quickly entered the café. The staff in one part of the restaurant was closing down. A pretty auburn haired girl behind the counter to the right of the door motioned for him to sit down.

"Can I get a double-decker cheeseburger to go?" Harry asked her.

"Sure," she said, checking her watch. "Anything to drink?"

"Chocolate shake. Are you new here?" Harry asked her after she had turned in his order.

"No, I've worked here almost two years," she answered.

"I come here a lot when my ship is in port. I've never seen you before."

"I've seen you." she said, "At least I've seen that yellow Oldsmobile here before."

"My name's Harry. What's yours?"

"Suzanne," she said, pointing to her name tag.

Harry noticed she had beautiful green eyes. "Nice to meet you," he said.

By the time his order was ready, it was past closing time. He paid his bill, and as he picked up his burger and drink, she suddenly said, "Darn, I just missed my ride!"

"I'd be happy to take you wherever you're going," Harry told her sympathetically.

"That's okay," she told him. "I'll just walk."

As Harry sat in his car in Oscar's Drive-In parking lot eating his delicious cheeseburger and sipping his chocolate shake, it suddenly started to rain heavily. The lights inside the restaurant went out one by one as they closed the drive-in down. He saw Suzanne step outside the door and try to stay dry as someone locked the door behind her. He started his car and drove it as close as he could to where she was standing. He rolled the window down on the passenger side and shouted over the noise of the cloudburst, "Get in out of the rain."

She looked at him and at the rain coming down and decided to take a chance that it was safer in Harry's car than walking home in a downpour. She grabbed the door handle and climbed in. As she shut the door, Harry rolled the window back up. "Thank you," Suzanne said tentatively.

As she settled into the seat, Harry noticed that she was pregnant. "Does your husband have the duty tonight?" he asked.

Suzanne didn't answer his query.

"Which way to your house?" Harry asked.

"Just back out and turn right. Follow Broadway to Twenty-Eighth. Turn left to the Mar Vista Apartments."

"That's a long way to walk even in good weather." Harry said, trying to break the tension he felt from the pretty girl. "Like I told you, my name is Harry—well, it's actually Harold Ray MacDonnell. I'm stationed on a tin can here. We just got back from a Westpac cruise. I'm getting out in about three months."

"This is Twenty-Eighth. Turn left here," she said. "The apartments are right there on the right."

As Harry pulled into the area beside the apartments near the covered parking, he couldn't find a place to get his car out of the rain. Suzanne started to open the door and make a dash for the stairway to her second-floor apartment. Harry put his hand on her arm. "I'm in no hurry," he said. "Why don't you wait for a break in the rain?"

"Are you sure?" she asked, looking at him quizzically.

"Really! I am in no hurry to go back to my ship! I just spent more than six months confined to it."

As they waited for the rain to stop, Suzanne became more at ease and found it was easier to talk to this stranger than to any of her friends. She explained that she was here from Boulder, Colorado, going to San Diego State College. She was five months pregnant. She had met the father, Will Jones, at a USO dance. He was charming, seemed nice, and was about to go on another Westpac cruise. She had let her guard down just that once. She and Will wrote to each other for several weeks. When she discovered she was pregnant, she wrote to him telling him about it. After waiting several weeks for his reply, his letter came back saying he was sure the baby wasn't his and not to expect anything from him because he was married. She had not made any other attempts to contact him. She had called her mother and confided in her, only to be disowned by her parents. Her father was so angry and disappointed that he called her a whore. Her voice broke and was almost a whisper as she sighed. "I'm not a whore. We only did it that one time."

Harry was listening in silence, looking at her as she talked. He saw the hurt and sadness in her eyes. He didn't know how to respond. He reached over and patted her softly on the shoulder. It was like he had touched a switch. She suddenly began to cry uncontrollably. Harry just sat there, softly patting her shoulder occasionally for what seemed like an hour before she finally gained control.

They were sitting on opposite ends of the front seat of the car, just looking at each other. It had stopped raining. Suddenly, Suzanne wiped her tears, smiled broadly, and announced she had to go in. Harry waited in the car until he saw her enter her apartment before he started his car and drove away.

Harry thought about Suzanne all night. He couldn't seem to get her story out of his mind. *She has a lot of problems*, he thought. *She has no husband or father for her baby. Her folks have disowned her and won't help. How will she be able to work, go to college, and take care of an infant?* Toward morning, he finally drifted off to sleep.

Sunday reveille wasn't until seven, but Harry was already up, shaved, showered, and dressed in his liberty uniform by the time it was sounded. After a quick breakfast, he drove to the locker club, changed into civvies, and headed to Palm City for Sunday services. He was one of the first to arrive and sat down near the front. He was thumbing through the hymnal when Natalie sat down beside him.

"Let's move closer to the back," she whispered.

"Why?" Harry asked.

"Come on!" she said, pulling on his hand.

She led him all the way to the last pew and went in first. Then giving him hardly enough space to sit down, she smoothed her skirt and sat down, pulling Harry down next to her.

Harry squeezed in beside her on the pew. She leaned hard against him. "Move over," he said, "I can't even move my arms."

After Sunday services, Harry drove Natalie to the Clawson's and stayed for the noonday meal. As they sat around the table, Frank Clawson asked, "When are you planning to head out for Tennessee? You must be anxious to get back to your fiancée!"

"I'm not going back home until the end of my enlistment. I have less than ninety days left before I get out." Harry paused. "Anyway, I don't have a fiancée anymore."

"What happened?" Connie asked softly, concern in her eyes.

"I guess four years was just too long for Peggy to wait. I didn't feel like I could marry her and bring her out here on my pay until I made second class. I didn't make second class until this last cruise." He paused, sighed, and went on. "Peggy is married now. My mom sent me a picture from the paper of her and her new husband. I guess I shouldn't have expected her to wait."

"That's just a shame," Connie told him, patting his hand.

Natalie was smiling broadly, realizing that at last her competition had been eliminated. She was anxious to get Harry alone so she could show him how much she cared for him. "Let's go to the beach this afternoon, Harry. I have a new suit that I've been dying to wear!"

"I don't think I should be driving you around too much until I replace the tires on my car," Harry said. "Maybe I can get that done Tuesday. Besides, there's more rain in the forecast for today."

Not to be pushed aside, Natalie pressed him. "We'll be at the beach. It won't hurt to get wet! You can drive really slow to save your tires."

"Looks like she has an answer for all your arguments," Frank teased. "You have something else you have to do this afternoon?"

"Natalie has talked of nothing else but, 'When Harry gets back.' I think you two should go enjoy yourselves," Connie urged him with a crafty smile.

Harry had nothing pressing, so soon, the two were on their way to Silver Strand State Beach. Harry pulled his shoes and socks off and rolled up his trouser legs. The nineteen-year-old Natalie pulled her shoes off, pulled her dress up over her head, and revealed an attractive one-piece suit. She dropped her dress on the front car seat and sprinted for the water. "Come on!" she called.

Harry walked obediently behind her. She was extremely attractive, but because of Harry's recently bruised emotions, he hardly took notice. To him, she was no more than a close friend.

For the rest of the afternoon, Natalie flirted shamelessly with him. He smiled, enjoying the attention and nearness of someone of the opposite sex after having just spent so many months in the company of only men. Yet he was unable to show her the same kind of attention.

Early in the evening, he drove her to her home, told her and the Clawson's good night, and headed back to San Diego. Once again, he stopped at Oscar's Drive-In for his favorite meal. He looked around for the girl he had met the night before but didn't see her. When the carhop brought his order, he asked her about Suzanne.

"Oh, you mean the pregnant girl? She doesn't work here anymore. They let her go when she came in to work today."

Harry ate his meal slowly and methodically. *Why would they fire her?* he wondered. *Did I get her in trouble by getting here so late last night?* He finished his meal and headed for the Mar Vista Apartments.

Harry stopped at the office and asked for the number of Suzanne's apartment. "She's a pretty red-haired girl. She lives on the second floor. She's about four months pregnant."

"We can't give you that information, but I can send a messenger to tell her she has a visitor," the office manager told him. "What is your name?"

"Harry MacDonnell."

A few minutes later, Suzanne entered the office. When she saw Harry, she smiled widely. "Hi," she said to Harry. Then turning to the manager, she continued, "It's all right. He's a friend of mine."

Harry followed Suzanne to her second-floor apartment overlooking the pool. She let him in and showed him around the apartment. It was small with a kitchen and dining area, a bathroom, one bedroom, and a living area. The settee, coffee table, and chair almost filled the small living area. In the center of the coffee table was a fishbowl containing two small goldfish. Suzanne motioned for him to take a seat in the chair before she sat down on the settee.

"That's Mutt and Jeff," Suzanne told him, indicating the goldfish. "The one with the black on his tail and fins is Mutt, and the solid gold one is Jeff. My best friend in high school gave them to me just before I left Boulder. They keep me company. I can talk to them whenever I feel lonely."

Harry smiled at her. "They told me at Oscar's that you aren't working there anymore. Did I get you into trouble by being so late the other night?"

"No, I'm just too pregnant. In fact, my manager's exact words were, 'You no longer look cute and sexy in your uniform.' He was also worried about Oscar's image because I'm not married. So," she went on sadly, "I'm not only going to be an unwed mother, but one without a job. And just when I need it the most."

Harry didn't know why, but he felt an uncommon desire to help this young woman whom he had just met. "You shouldn't be all that stressed at a time like this. I'd be glad to help you in any way I can. I've been saving my money for when I get married, but now, that isn't going to happen. So I-I just don't want you to worry anymore."

Suzanne looked at Harry. She could see the sincerity in his blue eyes. "You're sweet, Harry, but this isn't your problem."

"I'd still like to help you if I can."

"How old are you, Harry?"

"Twenty-three. How about you?"

"I'm twenty. Are you going to make a career of the navy?"

"I don't think so. Right now, I haven't got a plan. I was going to get out and head back to Tennessee, but I'm not so sure about that anymore. I got a Dear John letter while I was overseas."

"I know how you must feel. My plans all fell apart when I found out I was pregnant and the baby's father didn't want me or the baby. I had to withdraw from college." She smiled and shrugged her shoulders. "I don't even have next month's rent. But I've been looking in the paper for another job."

"Should you even be working when you're—I mean, in your condition?"

"I'm pregnant. I'm going to have a baby, Harry! Don't be afraid to say it." She smiled. "And there are a lot of things I can do without jeopardizing the baby's health. Besides, I'm not due to deliver until the last of September or the first of October."

The young couple talked long into the night. Near midnight, Harry said good-bye.

Harry had duty on Monday, the fifteenth, which was also payday. The first thing he did after liberty call on Tuesday was drive to the locker club and change into his civvies. Next, he drove to Sears where he had them put on a new set of wide whitewall tires. Then he drove to the Mar Vista Apartments.

Suzanne greeted him at the door with a big smile and invited him in. She had just made some tea. She handed Harry a glass, poured herself one, and asked him to sit down.

"How did the job search go?" Harry asked her.

"Nothing yet. Once they get a look at this big belly"— Suzanne smiled—"they suddenly say the position is filled. They can see I'll only be temporary help. How have you been?"

"To tell the truth, I didn't get much sleep last night. I've been thinking about your situation a lot." Harry looked first at her, then at Mutt and Jeff, swimming placidly in their bowl, before he continued. His speech was slow and deliberate. "I have an idea that could solve a lot of your problems," he said.

"I'm all ears!" Suzanne said cheerfully.

"Listen, I'm not very good at explaining things, so bear with me, okay?"

"Sure!"

"Okay," Harry started slowly. "I'm an E-5 now. That makes me eligible for military housing if I was married. Or if they don't have an opening in military housing, I would get $77.10 per month BAQ. That's the allowance for housing. Right now, my base pay is $180 per month. It will go up to $205 per month in three months if I decide to stay in. If I was married, my wife and children would be eligible for medical services, commissary, and exchange privileges. The baby could be born right here in Balboa Hospital. Lots of guys on my ship are married and getting by pretty well." He paused and took a sip of his tea before continuing.

Suzanne was looking at him intently as he continued. "I think we—you and me, that is—should find a JP and get a marriage certificate. That way, you would be eligible for all of those things. That might take some of the stress off of you."

"That is so sweet, Harry, but I hardly know you, and I don't feel that way about you."

"Look, I'll be gone a lot of the time anyway. It won't be like we'll be married like that. We'll just do all the paperwork so you won't have to worry about rent or a job and the baby would have a last name. You wouldn't mind if it had MacDonnell, would you?"

"You have given this a lot of thought. And you have given me a lot to think about."

"There's kind of a time limit on my offer," Harry said. "Since the baby won't be here before my enlistment is up on the ninth of September, I'll need to know your decision before then in order for me to have time to reenlist. If I do re-up, I can collect the reenlistment bonus. That's another $300 right there."

"You would even reenlist for me and my baby, Harry?"

"Uh-huh."

Suzanne began to cry softly. Harry went over to the settee and sat beside her, patting her on the shoulder. "I didn't mean to upset you," he said. "Does crying upset it? The baby?"

Suzanne dried her eyes. "I need to do my walking," she told him, rising from the settee. "Do you want to come along?"

They walked without talking. Suzanne, deep in thought, would glance at Harry's face every so often. Harry was just walking obediently beside her. He felt a strange calm now that he had given Suzanne a solution to all her problems. People they met smiled and nodded as if in agreement with his proposal. Near the top of a rise on Broadway, she turned and headed back downhill toward her apartment.

As they entered the apartment, Harry remembered she had said she didn't have next month's rent. "How much is your rent here?" he inquired.

"Forty-seven fifty."

"When is it due?"

"The first of July. No later than the tenth."

"Don't worry. Even if you don't take me up on my offer, I can get you the rent money easy. I've been leaving my pay on the books for months now. Yesterday was payday. I drew enough money to buy me a new set of tires. I have enough left to pay your rent and get you some groceries."

"Why are you doing this, Harry?"

"I honestly don't know. I just feel like it's the right thing to do. I think I'll be able to get to sleep tonight and not worry about you so much."

With her hormones all out of balance, Suzanne looked like she was going to cry again. Instead, she took control of her emotions. "Let me fix you some supper," she offered. "Waffles and eggs, okay?"

"I thought you said supper." Harry grinned. "Is there something I can do to help?"

"No, thank you." She smiled. "The only thing I have to drink is milk. Is that okay?"

"Sure," Harry said, changing his seat to a dining room chair so he could watch her.

He realized how comfortable he felt when they were together. As he watched her prepare the meal, he realized for the first time just how attractive she was. She was wearing little or possibly no makeup. Her auburn hair was pulled back into a ponytail, and there seemed to be a glow of healthiness about her. Although she had told him she was in her fifth month, she had purposefully kept her weight down so that the contour of her stomach hardly cried pregnant.

"Would it offend you if I told you I think you're very pretty?" Harry asked.

"Why thank you, Harry! What a liar you are!"

"No, I mean it! I try not to say things I don't mean."

"Will you stop being so sweet to me! If you keep it up, you'll have tears in the waffle batter!"

They ate, and later, talked long into the night, Suzanne wanting to talk about anything that would keep her from thinking about Harry's proposal. Around midnight, Harry reluctantly said good night and returned to his locker club and ship.

On Wednesday at liberty call, Harry was at the head of the line. He hurried to the locker club, changed into civvies, drove to Oscar's Drive-In for two double-decker cheeseburgers, two orders of fries, and two milkshakes to go. Thirty minutes later, he was bounding up the stairs to Suzanne's apartment with his hands full. Suzanne met him at the door with a friendly smile.

"I brought supper," Harry said excitedly. "You won't have to cook teary, watered-down waffles." He grinned.

"Umm, I'm starving!" she said, digging into the bag for a french fry. "The baby's hungry too!" she said as she got another.

"Here," he said, digging plates out of the cupboard and putting them on the table. "You don't have to eat out of the bag!"

He unwrapped the burgers and placed one on each plate. He dumped both packages of french fries on her plate. "Strawberry or chocolate?" he asked as he took the shakes from the bags.

"Strawberry!" she answered.

Harry ate slowly and methodically while watching her eat with the vigor of a starving person. She finished everything on her plate, excused herself, and went to the bathroom. Harry cleaned off the table, picked up the plates, washed them, and put them away. Suzanne came out of the bathroom as he finished.

"I need to do my walk," she told him.

This time, they walked around several blocks that included the perimeter of the apartment complex and a neighborhood park. They sat for a few minutes on a bench in the park, talking. Suddenly, she took his hand and placed it on her stomach. "Feel that?" she asked. Harry nodded. "That's the baby kicking."

Harry leaned his head near her stomach as if he could hear the baby kicking. "How neat!" he said. "What are you wishing for? A boy, or a girl?"

"I'm trying not to be for one or the other," she told him, "but sometimes, I wish for a girl, and other times, I wish for a boy." She gently lifted his hand from her stomach.

"I'll bet that's normal," he said. "I've heard people say they don't really care as long as it's healthy."

As they walked back to the apartment, Harry reminded her he had the duty the following day and would not be able to bring her anything to eat until Friday. At the apartment, he gave her the keys to his car and $20 for food. He asked her to drive him to his locker club and the base. At the Thirty-Second Street gate, as he got out of the car, he asked her to pick him up at the same spot at 4:00 p.m. on Friday. "Be safe," he told her as he waved good-bye.

Harry stood and watched her disappear from sight before he turned to go through the gate leading onto the naval base.

CHAPTER 2

Suzanne Abbott felt the power of the big V8 engine in the mammoth-sized car under her control as she sped away from the base. She drove south on National Boulevard into Chula Vista, feeling a sense of freedom as she maneuvered the Oldsmobile around slower traffic. For a few minutes, she let the feeling of being behind the wheel and in control of such a large automobile overcome the lack of control in her own life. She even contemplated the devilish idea of continuing south to Tijuana and on into Baja California, where she could hide from the truth of her present predicament.

After about ten minutes of this temporary imaginary euphoria, she slowed, circled around, and headed back toward her apartment and reality. She had some serious thinking to do. She had to weigh the advantages and disadvantages of Harry's proposal. He had given her some very serious options. *But I don't know this man,* she thought, *and I certainly don't love him. Isn't marriage supposed to be based on true love? Then again, I once thought I loved Will Jones, and I had only known him for a few weeks. Will told me he loved me, yet when I told him I was pregnant, he treated me with scorn and contempt. Harry has never mentioned love to me, yet he always treats me with respect.*

She wondered if she could marry a man she did not love just for security and for the sake of her unborn child. She didn't know if she could or even if she should.

She stopped at the supermarket to get a few groceries with the $20 Harry had given her. Lately, she always seemed to feel hungry. Still, she didn't know just what to buy. She eventually bought some fruit, some milk, a dozen eggs, some small cans of tuna, some cheese, and bread. In the bakery section, she also picked up a package of cinnamon rolls.

Suzanne occupied the next two days with housework, laundry, and thoughts of the future. The lonely hours seemed to drag by. On Friday morning, she drove to Oscar's Drive-In to pick up her last paycheck and say good-bye to some of the other carhops. One of them recognized the yellow Oldsmobile.

"You dating that quiet handsome guy?" Sheila asked her. "Oh, is that his baby? I thought, because he is so quiet, and you never see him with a girl, that maybe he was queer."

Suzanne just smiled and ignored her questions.

"I know this is his car," Billie, a friend of hers, said to her quietly.

"If you must know," Suzanne told her, "Harry is a friend of mine. He had to stay on his ship yesterday, and he loaned me his car. I'm picking him up at his ship later today."

"Really?" Billie asked her. "Are the two of you dating?"

"No, we have never had a date! Harry is just a friend!" Suzanne told her emphatically.

"I bet if you weren't pregnant he'd want to go out with you. Well, since he's just your friend, how about fixing me up with him?" Billie requested.

"I like him too much to do that to him!" Suzanne said with a toss of her hair.

"Oh, you are just awful!" Billie scolded.

Harry was outside the gate at four o'clock as promised. He stood and waited at the bus and taxi stop, watching intently for Suzanne. Finally, he saw her coming down Harbor Drive driving the yellow Oldsmobile. He stepped out of the crowd of sailors into the Street, just off of the curb, and flagged her down. He got into the passenger side of the car and asked her to take him to his locker club on Broadway.

Suzanne made a U-turn at Thirty-Second Street and headed back up Harbor Drive toward downtown San Diego. She found a parking space around the corner from his locker club.

"Wait," she told Harry as he started to get out. "Why don't you bring some of your civvies to my apartment? You can change there and save these trips to the locker club."

"Are you sure?" Harry asked. "I don't want to put you out none."

"I'm sure. Bring your shaving kit too," Suzanne instructed him.

Harry cleaned out his locker and put the bag into his car. Suzanne was waiting for him in the passenger side of the seat. "Do you want to stop at Oscar's?" he asked as he pulled away from the curb.

"Absolutely!" Suzanne said. "The baby is starving!"

"That little bump is always hungry," Harry replied. "Is he still kicking you?"

"All the time! Here, feel." She took Harry's hand and guided it to where she had felt the last kick. The baby did not cooperate.

A few minutes later, they were pulling into Oscar's Drive-In. "Do you want to go inside?" Harry asked her.

"No, I want a carhop to bring me my food for a change. Park in Billie's area there." She pointed. "I was here this morning to pick up my check. When they saw your car, some of the girls made insinuations. They think we are going steady."

Billie came out almost immediately. She hurried up to his car and began to flirt with him to observe Suzanne's reaction. Suzanne ignored her and just ordered. "You want your usual?" Billie asked Harry.

"Yes," he replied, "but this time, with an order of fries."

As Billie hurried to turn in their order, Suzanne said, "I thought you didn't eat fries."

"I don't. They're for the bump."

She looked at him, smiling. *He is always so thoughtful of others,* she thought.

When their order came, Harry put his bag of fries on the seat beside her. They sat eating and talking. With each passing hour, Suzanne was feeling more at ease with Harry, more relaxed and more ready to let him take care of her. She was beginning to like the feeling of being dependent on someone else. With both her hunger and that of the baby's appeased, she felt more carefree and happier than she had felt in months.

"Let's go to Balboa Park to do our walking today," she said.

Harry drove them to Balboa Park and parked in an area that was shaded by the huge eucalyptus trees. They walked for over an hour. By the time they returned to the car, it was late afternoon, and the long shadows caused by the setting sun were everywhere. It was dusk before they got back to Suzanne's apartment.

"Do you drink coffee?" Suzanne asked Harry as she busied herself in the kitchen. "I think I'd like a cup."

"That sounds good," he answered. "But are you sure coffee is okay for the bump?"

"You worry too much. Coffee in moderation is okay. I have some books I've been reading."

She finished the coffee preparation and poured each of them a cup. "Come sit with me in the dining area," she told him.

Harry joined her. They both sat sipping coffee for some time. The only thing said during that first cup was when Harry told her how good it tasted. She poured them both a second cup, emptying the pot. She rinsed the pot out before returning to her seat. She studied Harry's face. He was very good-looking, bright, intelligent, but very naïve. His innocence and honesty intrigued her. Finally, she spoke.

"I've thought a lot about what we discussed before. You know, getting married and all? I don't think it would be fair to you. I think you would get to a point where you would detest me and blame me for your unhappiness. There will be plenty of sleepless nights with a baby crying all night or needing feedings and its diaper changed. I will probably get fussy too and take my frustrations out on you. That kind of thing happens in marriages where they get married for all the right reasons. Are you sure you are ready for all of that? Is that what you want?"

Harry was sipping on his coffee. He set his cup down and looked at her. "Are you saying you don't want us to get married?"

"No." She smiled. "I'm trying to let you know it won't be all that much fun at times. I'm giving you a chance to withdraw your offer."

"No, thank you," Harry said. "Then I'd still be worrying about you."

"Okay, I offered. Now here's what I think we should do. First, we'll get a marriage license and a certificate of marriage for you to show to the navy. Then you'll move in here with me until we can apply for navy housing. In every aspect except one, we will live as man and wife. After the baby's born and I'm back on my feet, we'll get a quickie divorce, and you'll be released from your contract. What do you think?"

Harry sat awhile, thinking. "What if I don't want to be released from my contract?"

"Oh, you will!" Suzanne stated positively. "Don't worry about that. I can be a real bitch sometimes."

"I can't even imagine that," Harry said, smiling. "You are always so sweet and nice to me."

"Well, you've always been sweet and nice to me too. Now come with me. I want you to see something. In anticipation of what you would say, I've rented a foldaway bed for you to sleep on. You can put it in the living room at night and roll it back into my bedroom in the morning. I'm sorry, but right now, I need the big bed for myself and my big belly. You can hang your uniforms and civvies in this closet. For now, you'll have to keep your undies and socks in your duffel bag. Just until we can get you a bigger chest of drawers. The bathroom is quite small, but I think we can manage with a few rules. The main one being, if you make a mess, you clean up the mess! Have you ever had a female roommate, Harry?"

"No," he said, looking at her inquisitively. "I don't have to be back to the ship until seven o'clock Monday morning. Are you saying I can use the foldaway bed tonight, tomorrow night, and Sunday night too?"

"Um…yes, I guess that is what I'm saying. So you can stay here every night. You don't have to be on your ship until…whenever."

Harry had been taking orders from someone every day for the past forty-five months. Now, it seemed he had another officer-in-charge. This one, however, was the cutest one he'd ever had, and she smelled nice too. She was supposed to be dependent on him, but it felt like it was the other way around. If he was going to have her apartment as his base of operations, that meant he would need to include her in all his plans. "Would you like to go to church with me Sunday?" he asked.

"I guess so. We should probably be seen in public together."

"Do you want an engagement ring?"

"No. I think that would be a little much. But I do think a small wedding band would look correct. Don't worry. I'll buy that for myself after the ceremony."

"If I got you one now, it might keep people from looking at you curiously."

"I'm used to that, Harry. Besides, a ring won't change the past."

They talked far into the night. Finally, Harry rolled the folda-way bed into the living room and helped her make it up. He had showered on the ship, so he only had to be in her bathroom for a short period of time. He settled down in the strange bed in the strange place and listened to the running shower as Suzanne bathed. Many hours after she had gone to bed and turned out her light, he was still lying awake, trying to imagine a future with her.

On Saturday morning, they went to the supermarket. Harry couldn't get Suzanne into the commissary without a military dependent's ID card. They bought what few groceries they thought would be needed to last for about a week. They took the groceries home and put them away. Harry then took her onto the naval base, showing his ID card and claiming her as a visitor. He pointed out the commissary, the exchange, the library, the swimming pool, the enlisted mens' club, and the movie theater.

"The movie will only cost us a dime each for admission," Harry told her. "As soon as I can get you a military dependent's ID card, you'll have access to everything I've shown you."

"Where is your ship? Can I see it?"

"I can drive us down onto the pier next to it, but if you'd like to go aboard, I have to go put on my uniform. Only officers are allowed on board in civilian clothing."

"You can take me aboard some other time. I'd just like to see your ship up close."

Harry drove them onto the pier and stopped opposite the quarter deck, with her side of the car closest to the ship. She opened her door to get out and get a closer look. Harry got out as well.

The officer of the deck recognized Harry and called, "Good afternoon, Petty Officer MacDonnell, Mrs. MacDonnell."

"Afternoon, sir," Harry answered, without correcting him. "Suzanne just wanted to get a look at the ship."

"I wish I could let you aboard, Petty Officer, but you know the regulations."

"Yes, sir, I do. Maybe tomorrow afternoon."

Harry drove them away from the ship and off of the base then headed south toward Imperial Beach. Suzanne had told him she wanted to do her walking on Silver Strand Beach. It was a warm day, but the cool breeze off of the Pacific Ocean made it more comfortable.

Suzanne was walking at a brisk measured pace. Harry was walking quietly along beside her, carrying both his and Suzanne's shoes. He paced himself to match her shorter strides.

"How tall are you?" he asked.

"The last time I was measured was in high school. I was five feet five inches tall. I played forward on the high school basketball team. I don't mean to brag, but I was very good at my position. I was high scorer in a lot of our games. How tall are you?"

"At my physical exam, when I joined the navy, I was five feet eleven inches tall. I figure I'm still about the same. I wear a size nine shoe. I have a twenty-nine-inch waist, a thirty-four-and-one-half-inch inseam, and wear a size seven and one-quarter hat. Anything else you'd like to know about me?"

She turned toward him, smiling. "Do you shave at night or in the morning?" she teased.

"Mornings usually. But if I go on a date, I shave before I go. I guess my answer is both."

"You are too serious!"

Her pace began to slow, and they turned around and headed back toward the car. She was young and healthy, but the added weight on her abdomen was causing a strain on her back.

"I wish we hadn't walked this far," she complained.

"Here, let's sit down for a minute," Harry said as he helped her to a seated position. "I can go get the car and bring it closer. Will you be all right here by yourself until I get back?"

"I'll be fine if I can just rest a minute."

"I'll be right back," Harry told her, handing her shoes to her. "You wait right here."

Harry took off in a swift run toward the parking lot. He stopped at the curb just long enough to slip into his untied shoes then trotted to the car. Shortly, he was pulling the car off of the highway and onto the shoulder in a direct line to where she was seated on the beach. He kicked off his shoes and ran to help her to her feet. By now, she had regained her energy. As they walked back to the car, she was laughing and teasing him about his amateur attempt to rescue "a beached whale."

It was the first time they had really laughed together and had so much fun. Suzanne thought to herself that maybe being dependent on Harry wouldn't be such a bad thing. She couldn't remember ever having this much fun with Will. In fact, Will had spent much of their time together trying to seduce her while her only physical contact with Harry was when she let him feel the baby kick or when he took her hands to help her in some way.

They arrived at her apartment about sundown. Suzanne was the first in the shower to wash the sand and salt away. Harry followed a few minutes later. When he was dressed, he found her in the kitchen, cooking.

"Will you watch these chops for me for just a minute? I need to check my dress for tomorrow. I'm not sure I can still get into it."

When she returned a few minutes later, she had such a sad look on her face that Harry had a difficult time not caressing and consoling her.

"It's just as I thought," she said, "I have nothing to wear!"

"It's a good thing San Diego is a sailor town and a lot of the shops stay open very late," Harry said optimistically. "We'll go get you something right after we eat. You should have a new Sunday go-to meeting dress if you're going to be Mrs. MacDonnell."

At a maternity clothing shop, they found a women's dress suit. The top had pleated sides, so it could be worn no matter how big she got, and the skirt had an expandable elastic insert right in the front. It was fashionable and attractive.

"We'll need matching comfortable shoes and a purse," Harry told the saleswoman.

"You'll want new hose to wear with these shoes!" the saleswoman told Suzanne.

"Of course," Harry answered for her.

"And what about a nice hat?" she asked, holding up a very pretty one.

Suzanne looked at Harry. "Of course a hat would make the outfit complete," she said as she tried on the hat. "But can we afford all of this, Harry?"

"You have to get that hat!" Harry said.

As they drove back to the apartment, Suzanne was not unhappy, but still she admonished Harry. "You just spent over $23 for just one outfit!" Suzanne told him, frowning disapprovingly. "I'm going to have to put you on a budget!"

"Are you good with figures?" Harry asked her.

"Yes, I've had to budget my whole life. And my major at college is accounting. After we've been to the JP, I'll get all the information from you about your pay and allowances, and we'll figure a budget based on that." She paused, looked at Harry for agreement, then continued, "If you want me to, that is."

"I think that would be a good idea," Harry agreed.

"We'll need a checking account," Suzanne went on, "and maybe a savings account. We'll need to determine how much cash either of us needs to carry."

They had reached the apartment, and talk of a budget turned to the new clothes again. Eventually, Harry rolled the foldaway bed back into the living room, and they were soon fast asleep in their separate rooms.

As usual, Harry was early to church on Sunday morning, but this morning, he had brought a visitor with him. They sat down near the front. Suzanne was lovely in her new clothes. Her long luxurious auburn hair was combed out, flowing from beneath her hat and hanging down her back in curls.

Soon, the Clawsons entered, and Natalie, looking over the congregation, eventually saw Harry. She didn't even notice the woman beside him as she had eyes only for him. Once again, she went to him, took his hand, and tried to persuade him to go with her to the back pew.

"Natalie," Harry said, "this is Suzanne, a friend of mine." Then addressing Suzanne, he said, "This is Natalie, a friend of mine."

Natalie looked at Suzanne with suspicion while Suzanne looked at Natalie with a knowing smile.

"Well, if you won't go to the back with me, at least move over so I can sit down," Natalie demanded.

Frank and Connie came over to them as Harry and Suzanne stood to move over so Natalie could join them on their pew. Harry shook hands with them both and introduced each to Suzanne. Connie, noticing the obvious, asked, "How long have you and Harry been friends?"

"Not long," Suzanne answered her, smiling sweetly. "We just met a few days ago at the place where I used to work."

"Welcome to our service," Frank told her, smiling. "Natalie, you should come sit with us and leave Harry and his friend alone."

"No," Natalie said stubbornly, "I'm going to sit with Harry and Suzanne. It's okay with you, isn't it, Harry?"

"Sure." Harry shrugged.

All through the service, Natalie kept crowding Harry; he moved closer to Suzanne to get away from it, and Suzanne moved over when Harry crowded her. This procedure continued until, by the end of the service, they were almost sitting in the center of the pew.

On the way back to the apartment, Suzanne remarked, "That must have been uncomfortable for you. That young lady has a major crush on you and isn't afraid to show it."

"Natalie?" Harry asked. "She's just a kid. I met her here when she was fifteen or sixteen. I think she just turned eighteen, but I have never had any desire to go out with her."

"She is very pretty, Harry. You mean you haven't noticed that?"

"Oh sure, but I've spent so much time with her in her room and all. She's more like a sister to me."

"In her room?" Suzanne asked, her eyebrows arched questioningly.

"Yes." Harry then explained, "We used to do duets at the church, and we'd practice our songs in her room on Sunday afternoons."

"Where were her parents when all of this was happening?" Suzanne wanted to know.

"I don't know. Around the house somewhere, I guess," Harry said.

"You had the door open, of course!"

"No, the noise would have bothered them."

"I cannot believe you, Harry!"

"Why?" he asked. "It's the truth."

"Oh, I believe it's the truth, I just can't—" She looked at him as he drove along, concentrating on his driving. "Yes, I can believe that's the real Harry," she said softly. "I think it would be very easy for a young woman like her to fall in love with you."

On Monday morning, Harry put in for early liberty. He left the ship just before noon. He and Suzanne went to city hall and obtained a marriage license. During the three-day waiting period, they continued to live a meager existence in Suzanne's apartment. Harry had the duty on Wednesday. On Thursday morning, June 25, he put in for early liberty again and arrived at the apartment just after noon.

Suzanne was dressed in her Sunday go-to meeting suit; Harry was in his dress whites when they left her apartment. They stopped at a jewelry store where they purchased a small yellow-gold wedding band.

They then went to National City to the justice of the peace, Clyde P. Dipple, where they were joined as man and wife in a very short and simple civil ceremony. Harry put the ring on her finger, they smiled shyly at each other, and Harry paid the JP before they walked out.

They walked silently back to the car and drove to the apartment without saying a word. Suzanne glanced occasionally at Harry, then down at the tiny gold band, then back at Harry. She thought to herself, *This is it. We've really done it. Who is this stranger that I have just committed my life to?*

Harry was thinking, *I'll get the paperwork for Suzanne's dependent ID card in the morning. Then she'll have access to all military dependent privileges. She won't have to worry about anything anymore. I'll take good care of her and the bump.*

CHAPTER 3

Suzanne Marie Abbott, age 20, current address Mar Vista Apartments, 2835 Broadway, Apartment 26. Harry printed the maiden name of his wife on the form for a dependent ID card. He continued with the required information before attaching a copy of the marriage certificate and submitting it for approval. The yeoman typed it up and told Harry he would have the XO sign it. He told him that he could pick up the approved form before he departed the ship at liberty call that afternoon.

This evening would be the last time Harry would see his new wife for two weeks. He had the weekend duty, and the ship was getting underway early Monday morning for two weeks training in the Pacific. They would pull into San Francisco the next weekend and be back in San Diego late Friday evening, July 10. Harry had thus far failed to inform Suzanne about the underway training and needed to give her the information that night.

Harry waited outside the gate until almost four-thirty before he saw Suzanne coming down Harbor Boulevard in the yellow Oldsmobile. He climbed in and immediately asked about her health and that of the unborn baby's.

"We're fine." She smiled. "Don't you even want to know why I'm late?"

"Yes, of course," he said. Then changing his voice to that of a scolding parent's, he said jokingly, "Why were you late, young lady?"

"I was talking to the landlady about a job!" she said excitedly. "My college courses may pay off after all! She wants to hire me part time to keep her books! Isn't that great, Harry?"

"Well, things are really looking up for you! First, you marry this great guy, and now, you have a great job."

"Wait a minute," she joked. "I married a great guy?"

"Well, at least you got a great job," Harry said submissively.

"That remains to be seen. But Mrs. Reynolds told me she'll pay me a dollar an hour."

Suzanne pulled into one of the covered parking spaces at the apartments. "I also got her to assign us this parking space, and we are on the list for a two-bedroom! When it comes through, you'll have your own bedroom, Harry! Come on, I got supper almost ready!"

Harry had never seen her so happy and energetic. He felt happy just watching her being happy. It was as if they were really man and wife. *So this is what it feels like to be married,* he thought.

He laid the form for the ID card on the small dining room table and went to change into his civvies. When he came back, she had set the table and removed the form.

"Did you find the request for a dependent ID card?" he asked her.

"Yes, what do I do with it?"

"Your first test as a Navy wife. Monday, you need to take it to the base personnel office. They'll issue you an ID card. Once you have that, it's like a free pass to all the dependent support facilities. The things I showed you the other day—base dispensary for your medical checkups, base commissary for discounted groceries, base exchange for discounted clothing and sundries, base banking, base swimming pool, base movie theater, and enlisted men's club."

She placed her hands on his shoulders, turned him toward the dining room table, and pushed him gently toward his chair.

"What is this?" Harry teased.

"This is your first official meal as a married man. We start with a salad then spaghetti and sauce. You can have the garlic bread with both the salad and the pasta. Here's a plate of black and green olives as garnish. The red drink in the wine glass is really just Kool-Aid. I hope that's okay."

"This is great," Harry praised her. "If you weren't off-limits, I'd have to kiss you!"

She smiled, blushed, and giggled. "What kind of dressing do you want on your salad? I have Thousand Island and french."

"I guess I'll have the Thousand Island please."

She took off her apron and joined him at the table. They enjoyed their meal and light conversation. Afterward, Harry helped her clean off the table and wash the dishes.

"Did you use every pot and pan you own?" Harry teased.

"Uh-huh."

As he washed and she dried, he told her he had the duty the next day and the ship would to be gone for the next two weeks. He told her he was leaving all the funds that he drew last payday for her to deposit in a checking account. "I think you can bring a card home for me to sign to get my signature on the account. You need to memorize my service number because that's the number they need on any business you transact on the base. It's on the request for the dependent ID card that I left on the table. It will also be on your ID card."

Suzanne found the form and read it over. The joyful excitement of the day had suddenly dissipated when he told her he would be gone for two whole weeks. There was sadness in her voice as she told him, "I'm going to miss you, Harry."

"I got serious and ruined everything, didn't I?" Harry asked. "I'm really sorry, Suzanne."

"Do you realize that's the first time you have ever used my name when addressing me? It's like you're afraid to say my name."

"Really? I didn't realize that. No, I'm not afraid to say it. I think it's a beautiful name. Suzanne, Suzanne," he repeated.

The night went by too swiftly, and soon, it was morning and time to return to the ship. Suzanne drove him to the gate, neither one of them saying much. As Harry climbed out of the passenger side door, he looked over at her. She was in her housecoat, her hair done up in rollers, absolutely no makeup. He should have been repulsed, but he found her to be enticingly beautiful. For the first time in a very long time, he didn't want to leave someone.

"Bye, Harry," Suzanne said. "I'll see you in two weeks."

"Good-bye, Suzanne, my wife," Harry said, smiling. "I'll call you just as soon as I get back."

Suzanne pulled into traffic and sped away. Harry stood watching until she was out of sight then plodded to the ship's gangway and went aboard like an emotional zombie.

As Suzanne turned the Oldsmobile into traffic and headed back to the apartments, she was feeling new emotions. *He called me his wife,* she thought. *How sweet. Am I falling for that big lummox?*

Weekends aboard a destroyer in port are long and boring, with at least two four-hour watches each day. By 2100 hours on Saturday, Harry was so bored and homesick for Suzanne that he obtained permission to go to the head of the pier and make a phone call. He called the apartment office and asked Mrs. Reynolds if she could get a message to Suzanne and have her call him back at the phone booth. Mrs. Reynolds took the number and told him she would deliver the message to Mrs. MacDonnell. Harry waited patiently, guarding the phone booth until the phone rang.

"What's wrong, Harry?" Suzanne asked as soon as her voice came on the line.

"Nothing now. I was just missing you!"

"You haven't been gone long enough to miss me," she teased. "It has hardly been twelve hours."

"More than thirteen actually. So I guess you don't miss me. Does the bump miss me?"

"Harry, please. This is ridiculous."

"Are you going to church tomorrow? You could hold my place for me on our pew. I don't think Natalie would try to sit on your lap."

"Yes, I thought I'd go. Do you want to send anyone a message?"

"No. I just wish I was going with you. I'd better go now. There are several other guys waiting for the phone. Bye, Suzanne."

"Bye, Harry."

Suzanne turned to Mrs. Reynolds. "We just got married two days ago, and it's his first night away from me. He's like a little boy!"

Mrs. Reynolds laughed. "Tell me, dear. Is he the father?"

"No, but he has promised to take care of us both just like he was."

"I can see that he truly loves you."

Suzanne didn't dispute the assumptions of Mrs. Reynolds. It wouldn't prove anything. In fact, it might help people accept her situation if they thought they were in love.

On Sunday night, Harry made a similar call to Suzanne. She told Harry that when she had arrived at church without him, the Clawsons had asked about him. She said she had told them that he had the duty. When Mrs. Clawson saw her ring, she had asked her where her husband was, and she had told her he had the duty. When Mrs. Clawson asked if he was on the same ship as Harry, she had told her, "Yes, he was," and that, in fact, her husband's name was Harry MacDonnell. She said the Clawsons had looked shocked, and Natalie had left the church, she thought, crying.

"I was afraid it would affect Natalie that way," Suzanne said, "but I don't think I should be lying about it. Especially in church. I'm not ashamed of being married to you, Harry."

"I'm proud to call you my wife also, Suzanne." After a short pause, Harry continued. "I won't be able to call you before I get back. I think we should look into getting a telephone in your apartment. I miss you. I'll see you in two weeks."

Even the long hours of arduous underway training couldn't keep Harry's mind off of his new wife. He had been lonely before but had never experienced homesickness like he was feeling now. He determined he would have to find another way other than military service to provide for his wife and child. He would stick it out until September 9, his discharge date, then find a civilian job. He had taken Suzanne's problems as his own, only to find that in doing so, he had complicated his own life in ways he had never imagined. He wasn't in the habit of asking anyone for help, so as he struggled with his dilemma, it didn't enter his mind to discuss these things with Suzanne.

When the ship returned to San Diego midday on Friday, July 10, Harry was exhausted physically, mentally, and emotionally. He was in the liberty section that had a long weekend and could hardly wait for them to tie up so he could change into his dress uniform and go call his wife. As soon as he was relieved from his helmsman duty, he hurried below to change.

As he was standing on the quarterdeck in the liberty party, a shipmate called out, "Hey, MacDonnell, I heard you got married. I guess we can't call you Cherry Boy anymore!" Several of the men in the liberty party laughed and jeered.

Harry blushed. He was still very much a virgin. *They must think that's the only reason for a person to get married,* he thought. He ignored them as much as he could.

When the liberty party was allowed to leave the ship, Harry raced to the phone booths at the head of the pier. He had to wait behind several other sailors before he could make his call to Suzanne. He left a message with Mrs. Reynolds that Suzanne should pick him up as soon as possible at the main gate in the usual spot.

Harry waited for what seemed like hours before he saw the yellow Oldsmobile coming down Harbor Boulevard. When Harry climbed into the car and saw his lovely bride, he wanted to pull her into his arms and kiss her tenderly. Instead, he looked at her with a smile and said, "Hello, Suzanne. How have you been?"

"Just fine," she told him. "I've got so many things to tell you! I hope you aren't hungry, I didn't expect you home until around four-thirty. I got my ID card. Do you have the duty this weekend? Mrs. Reynolds pays me every Friday. I got paid for fifteen hours last week, and I already have twelve hours this week. I found a service station on Nineteenth Street where they only charge twenty-two and nine-tenths per gallon. Why are you grinning, Harry?"

"I'm just very glad to be home."

"Oh, I forgot the biggest thing of all. We got a two-bedroom. I've already moved us. It's just two doors over from our old place. I think all of the rooms are bigger, and the furniture is a lot newer. You're going to love it, Harry. It's only $10 a month more than the old one. You have your own bedroom and your own closet, and a chest of drawers to put your underwear and socks in. The bed in your room is just a three-quarter bed. I hope it will be big enough for you. Selfish me, I took the bigger bed."

They were pulling into their parking space. Suzanne was driving the Oldsmobile like she had been doing it for years. She opened the trunk, and Harry saw several bags of groceries from the commissary. He picked up the two largest ones and followed her up the stairs to their new apartment.

"So you've been to the commissary. How did you like it?" Harry asked her.

"It's great! Everything is so much cheaper than the supermarket. There were a lot of navy wives there. Many of them pregnant just like your wife." She smiled, jabbing at him playfully with her keys. "Well, what do you think of our new place?"

Harry set the groceries down and followed her throughout the apartment. He would have commented, but he was enjoying her continual chatter and didn't want to interrupt it. Harry realized he loved to hear her voice. It filled the empty spaces in the apartment and in his lonely life. What Harry didn't realize in his simple, naïve way was that he was slowly falling deeply in love with Suzanne.

At the same time, Suzanne was experiencing the joy brought about by the innate maternal and spousal necessity to be home-maker. She was, as explained in the psychology books, nesting. Harry was just happy she had left room for him on the limb.

After his tour of their new apartment, Harry carried up the remaining groceries and the packages from the exchange.

"I need to take all of these new bed linens to the laundry before I make up your bed," she told him, continuing her happy chatter. "See, I bought you a new pillow. Is it okay?"

"Sure, it looks fine. Let me change my clothes, and I'll go down to the laundry with you. Do you have enough change?"

"I've never seen men in the laundry room, Harry, are you sure you want to go with me?"

"I waited two long weeks to be home with you. I'm not letting you out of my sight now!"

Harry proudly walked along beside her, carrying the basket of linens. He felt a glow of happiness and contentment being in her company. He helped her load the machines. While they sat and waited for the machines to finish, they went over the remainder of the past two weeks and their immediate future plans. Harry told her he had the weekend off, that his next duty day would be Wednesday and then he would have the duty weekend. He told her they had been tied up at a pier in San Francisco on July 4 and that he could see the fireworks display from the ship. She explained how she had gone to Balboa Park and witnessed the fireworks display there.

"Next year, we'll watch them somewhere together," Harry promised. "You, me, and the bump."

"But I thought we agreed on a quickie divorce after the baby is born," Suzanne reminded him cautiously.

"You agreed to it. I never did. We'll just have to wait and see."

Harry put the wet clothes in the dryers as she instructed while she dropped in some nickels. Later, he helped her fold the clothes and load the baskets for the trip back to their apartment. As she passed a small rose garden in the center of the apartment complex, Suzanne had to stop to admire the beauty and the aroma. As Harry watched her, he was thinking, *There is never anything insincere or distasteful in her actions.* Harry felt as if his heart was smiling.

He helped her make his bed, and later, after a leisurely meal, Harry cleaned up the kitchen while she got ready for her walk. They walked about an hour, making a sort of rectangle around several blocks of the area and arriving at the apartment with an hour of summer sun left. They sat on their balcony overlooking the apartment swimming pool and watched some of the residents splashing in the shallow end.

Harry wanted so badly to just reach over and take Suzanne's hand and hold it, but his shyness prevented it. As the sun dipped behind the eucalyptus trees, he saw her shifting in her chair. "Are you cold?" he asked her.

"No, it's just uncomfortable holding this baby on my lap this way."

Harry arose, took her hands, and helped her to her feet. "Let's go in where it's more comfortable sitting."

The remainder of the night went by without incident. Saturday afternoon, they drove to Silver Strand Beach and walked in the sand and surf. "I'm in my sixth month," she told him. "My calculations put the birth around the last of September. I sure do wish it was over. Sometimes, it feels like I've been pregnant my whole life. Would you believe I once had a very nice figure?"

"You know what I wish we had?" Harry asked her. "A camera. We could take pictures of you now, and later, when you get your figure back, you can compare."

"No! I don't want pictures of me like this!"

"Why? I think you're beautiful!"

"Oh, you do not! I thought you always tried to tell the truth."

"I am telling the truth. Your beauty just flows from every pore."

"Oh, stop it, Harry!" She giggled. "Your nose is growing!"

The young married couple continued to enjoy the miracle of youthful companionship as they learned more and more about one another. They were beginning to really enjoy each other's company and friendship. It was obvious they truly liked one another. Their burgeoning love was expanding as quickly as the life growing inside of Suzanne.

Sunday morning, they once again went to church in Palm City. They sat with the Clawsons, and even Natalie sat in the same pew on one side of Harry. This day, however, she did not crowd him. When they were invited to go home with the Clawsons for Sunday lunch, they agreed to go along.

All three ladies were in the kitchen and dining room, preparing everything. Harry and Frank Clawson were in the living room. "So you are an old married man now," Frank stated. "We were sure surprised to learn about that. How long have you been planning it?"

"Not long," Harry told him. "I just met Suzanne the day after I got back from Westpac."

"I guess one could say, when you make up your mind to do something, you do it."

"Yes, sir."

"Are you planning to take your new wife to Tennessee when you get out of the navy? I'm sure you'll want her to meet your folks."

"No, sir, I don't think so. Not right away at least. I think I'll stay around here and look for work. There must be something I can find to do."

"It's odd you should say that," Frank said seriously. "They're hiring truck drivers up where I work in El Cajon. Have you ever driven a semi, Harry?"

"Yes, sir, I've driven all kinds of trucks. I had a number of temporary truck driving jobs before I enlisted, but I don't have a chauffeur's license anymore."

"You should make an application at J & J right away. I don't know how long they'll be hiring."

"I'll do that. Thank you, Mr. Clawson."

"It's Frank, Harry. Call me Frank."

"Okay, Frank."

"Everything's ready," Connie called from the dining room door.

"Everything smells delicious!" Frank said, praising his wife's cooking.

There was fried chicken, corn on the cob, mashed potatoes, chicken gravy, sliced tomatoes, green beans, and hot rolls. Harry sat quietly, eating in his usual slow and methodical way. Suzanne ate like a farmhand. She noticed Connie watching her with raised eyebrows.

"This bump, as Harry calls it," Suzanne said, indicating her stomach, "is always hungry!"

They all got a good laugh.

"May I inquire as to when the bump will be joining us?" Connie asked.

"In about eleven weeks."

"So you're in your sixth month, you're carrying high. You're going to have a girl!" Connie predicted.

Harry looked at Frank, who was about to make a pronouncement. "Don't doubt her kids. She's never been wrong! Except for Natalie, that is."

Another round of laughter.

"If it's a girl, what will you name her?" Natalie wanted to know. "Harriett?"

"Maybe," Suzanne said, looking at Harry fondly.

"To name her after me, it would have to be Haroldette," Harry corrected.

Another round of laughter.

During the after-dinner cleanup, Natalie excused herself from the kitchen and asked Harry to join her outside. They walked slowly around the yard while Natalie quizzed him.

"Why, Harry? Why did you marry her? I know she's pretty and nice and all, but for goodness' sake, Harry, didn't you notice she was just a little bit pregnant? And, I'm sure, with someone else's baby! I thought that when your fiancée dumped you, it would be you and me. Didn't you ever love me, Harry?" She started crying softly. "Didn't you love me just a little?"

"I loved you," Harry answered. "I still do. I always will. Only with you, Nat, it has always been like you were my little sister. I can't be romantic with my little sister."

They were standing close together. Natalie clenched her hands into fists and hit him in the chest, shoving him away. "Oh, just get away from me. I don't want a brother. I hate you, Harry!" She ran into the house.

Suzanne and Connie had witnessed the scene from the kitchen window but couldn't hear the conversation. As Harry entered the house with a look of dejection on his face, Connie was knocking quietly on Natalie's bedroom door. Suzanne came to Harry's side. "Everything okay?" she asked tenderly.

"Nat hates me."

"No, she doesn't. Tomorrow, she'll feel differently. Right now, she's hurt."

"You know I never meant to hurt anyone, don't you?"

"Yes, Harry, I know."

Frank came in from the bathroom, noticed something was wrong, and asked, "What happened? What did I miss?"

"Just the main bout," Suzanne told him. "Harry and I are about to go. We really enjoyed the meal and the hospitality. Thank you for having us. Please tell Connie thank you for us. Come on, Harry. I'll drive."

"Don't forget what I told you," Frank called after Harry. "Give me a call if I can help in any way."

"No, sir, I won't forget. Thank you again, Frank," Harry replied.

As Suzanne drove the car away from the Clawsons', she asked Harry, "What was Frank talking about?"

"Mr. Clawson works for J & J Trucking in El Cajon. He's a diesel mechanic there. He's one of the best. Anyway, he told me they are hiring semi drivers."

"How does that affect you?"

"Well, I used to be a truck driver before I enlisted in the navy. I've been thinking I may not reenlist if I can find a job that won't take me away from home so much. I hope you won't think I'm a big baby, Suzanne, but the past two weeks when I couldn't be with you, I was terribly homesick."

Suzanne looked at him and smiled. "That is so sweet, Harry. I missed you too!"

"What do you think I should do? Stay in the navy or try for the truck driving job?"

"I think you should make that decision. It's something that could affect the rest of your life. You're only committed to me until the baby comes. You probably shouldn't be making decisions based on how it will affect the baby and me."

"But you and the bump are the reasons for all of my decisions." He paused, waiting for her to respond. When she didn't, he continued, "Well, if it's going to be left up to me, then I'm going to get out of the navy. I have more than sixty days' leave on the books. I'm going in Monday and asking for a terminal leave."

"What is a terminal leave, Harry?"

"Basically, it's like a paid vacation. I'll still be in the navy until September 9, with all pay and allowances, but I'll not be required to go in to the ship. What have you planned for Monday while I'm at the ship?"

"A couple of hours with Mrs. Reynold's books. Why don't you take the car? You might get off early."

"Okay, I will. But what I was going to suggest is that we try to get a telephone in our apartment. Could you call about that?"

"Oh, Harry, really? Our own telephone? Can we afford it?"

"I don't know. Maybe we should wait to see if I get the job with J & J. What do you think?"

"I think we should see about a telephone. I can pay for it with the money I earn."

Suzanne parked in their covered area. They climbed out and went inside. She told Harry she didn't feel like walking today because her feet and ankles were swollen and hurting. Harry told her to take off her tight clothing, put on a loose-fitting gown, and lie down on her bed. He took one of the cushions from the couch and the pillow from his bed and propped her feet up. He took her shoes and stockings off and began to rub her feet and the calves of her legs. She tucked her gown between her legs like shorts.

"Can you do the lower part of my thighs too?" she begged.

Harry spent more than thirty minutes gently massaging her feet and legs before he realized she had dozed off. He put a single sheet over her legs, covering her to about the middle of her lower abdomen. He stood for a long moment, watching her sleep and listening to her soft breathing. He was tempted to leave a soft kiss on her cheek. He breathed a big sigh before quietly leaving her bedroom.

Monday morning, Harry submitted his chit for terminal leave. His division officer signed it and told him to walk it through to the XO. He found his department head in the ward room with several other officers.

"May I speak to you, Lieutenant Blundell?" Harry asked.

"Come in, Petty Officer MacDonnell," Lieutenant Blundell said. Then, seeing the chit, he asked, "What do you have there?"

Harry handed the chit to him. "I'm requesting terminal leave, sir."

"You've decided to leave us?"

"Yes, sir, I may have an opportunity for a good job, if I act quickly enough."

Lieutenant Blundell signed the chit and, handing it back to Harry, said, "Good luck, sailor, we'll miss you around here, especially on the helm."

"Thank you, sir," Harry told him. Then he put on his hat and saluted him, turned, and walked out of the ward room.

Harry's next stop was the XO's stateroom. Harry tucked his hat under his arm and knocked on the door. "Come in!" Commander Cramer called.

"Good morning, Commander Cramer, I've been instructed to walk this chit straight through to you for your approval or disapproval."

Commander Cramer took the chit and looked at it. He checked the approval box and scribbled his signature on it. He turned in his swivel chair, handed the chit back to Harry, and stood up.

"Permission to cover, Commander!"

"Permission granted!"

Harry put on his hat and saluted the XO, who returned his salute uncovered. "I won't tell if you don't." He smiled and shook Harry's hand. "Good luck, shipmate! It has been a pleasure serving with you."

"Thank you, Commander."

Harry took the ladder to the main deck in one step, sliding with his hands on the rails. He bounded into the ship's office and handed the approved chit directly to the Chief Yeoman who was at the coffee pot. "What's this MacDonnell? More early liberty? I know you just got married, but at this pace, you're going to wear out your welcome. That little wife of yours may want some time to herself."

"It's for terminal leave, Chief. I have more than enough leave on the books to take me all the way to the end of my enlistment. Do you think you can get me off of the ship today?"

"Go pack your sea bag, MacDonnell," the Chief said as he handed the chit to a personnelman second class. "Let's get on this, Brewer."

By 1400 hours, Harry had packed up everything from his locker and radar room. He had checked out with all the required places and was just waiting on his orders. He was in the berthing compartment, exchanging sea stories with a couple of his division shipmates, when the messenger of the watch came to get him.

"The CO wants a word with you," the messenger informed him.

Harry went hurriedly to the captain's cabin and knocked on the door.

"Come in!"

"You wanted to see me, Captain?"

"Yes, come in, Petty Officer MacDonnell. Commander Cramer tells me you're leaving us. That was very short notice. I'll have a time replacing you on the helm. We—you and I—were a good team. We brought her in alongside smartly many a time. I really hate to see you go. Fair winds and following seas, shipmate," the captain said. He stood up and shook Harry's hand then saluted.

Harry, taken aback, returned his salute while still uncovered. "Thank you, Captain," he answered.

CHAPTER 4

The one-story building housing the offices of J & J Trucking in El Cajon, California, was located inside a large fenced area. Harry noticed many walnut-brown semitractors, with the J & J logo painted prominently on the side, parked in rows along one fence. Along the opposite fence was a row of shiny stainless steel trailers. Behind the office building, along the back of the complex, was a huge garage area having multiple large doors. This was where Frank Clawson and the other diesel mechanics plied their trade.

A gate guard waved Harry into a parking space outside the fence. In the guardhouse, he filled out a short form and was given a visitor's pass and directions to the employment office. "Ask for Mr. Rawlings," the gate guard instructed him. "Your car will be safe where you parked it."

Harry walked purposefully across the pavement to the door marked Employment Office. There were three other applicants ahead of him. A receptionist gave him a clipboard with a three-page questionnaire. In the former employer section, Harry didn't have enough space to list them all, so he decided to just list the ones pertaining to truck driving. Shortly after he handed the clipboard back to the receptionist, he was called in for an interview.

"Mr. MacDonnell," the man said, shaking Harry's hand, "my name is Dan Rawlings. Have a seat please. I'm very impressed with your résumé." After a short interview, Mr. Rawlings said, "We'd like to give you a chance to become a driver for J & J. Do you have a commercial driver's license?"

"No, sir, but I'm sure I can get one."

"Come with me. I'd like you to demonstrate you driving skills," he said as he picked up a set of keys and handed them to Harry. "You see that last tractor over there? I want you to go start it up; drive it over to the trailers; pick out one of the trailers, not the one on the end; hook up to it; drive around the complex one or two times just to get the feel of it; then back it into the space where you found it; unhook it; and return the tractor to its original spot. Think you can do all of that?"

"Yes, sir."

Harry had never driven a Mack Truck before, but he liked the feel of all that power. He performed the required task, as prescribed, with skill and precision. Handling machinery had always come easy to him.

"Very well done," Mr. Rawlings told him. "Let's go inside, and you can give your particulars to our office staff. We'll order you some uniforms. What name do you want on you name patch? Harry or MacDonnell? Or you could choose just Mac."

"Harry will be fine."

"We have so many drivers taking the test for a commercial driver's license that the DMV sends a person out each Wednesday to test right here at our facilities. Be here at eight o'clock tomorrow morning. We'll put you on the payroll then. We pay $2.25 per hour, time and a half for all over forty hours, double time for holidays and Sundays. Congratulations and welcome to J & J Trucking, Mr. MacDonnell!"

"Thank you, sir."

Harry could hardly wait to tell Suzanne of his good fortune. He had gotten the job so easily, it surprised him. If he passed the tests tomorrow, he had the job. His heart was light as he wheeled into their parking space at the Mar Vista apartments.

As he approached their apartment, he noticed the door was open. He could faintly hear conversation coming from inside. "Suzanne!" he called.

"In my bedroom," she answered. "Look, Harry, I decided to put the phone in here by my bed. This is Dick from the telephone company."

"I just have to install this cover, and you're in business," Dick said, looking at Harry from where he was kneeling beside Suzanne's bedside table. He stood, picked up the receiver, dialed a number, and spoke briefly to someone on the other end of the line. "There you go," he said. He picked up a couple of tools, had Suzanne sign his work order, and he was gone.

"That's our very own telephone number in the center of the dial!" Suzanne told him excitedly. "He left us a phone book too."

"What is our number?" Harry asked.

"Riverside five-four-two-three-four!" she told him enthusiastically.

Harry took a small piece of paper and wrote the number on it—RI 5-4234. He placed it in his wallet. "You can look forward to many calls from your husband, Mrs. MacDonnell," he said. "I really do feel safer with you having a phone right next to you when I'm gone."

"Gone, Harry? Where are you going?"

"I got the job with J & J Trucking. I start tomorrow. I just have to pass a couple of tests in the morning to get my commercial driver's license. I'll be making long hauls all over the western part of the United States, as far east as St. Louis and north to Seattle. I'll be gone some, but I'll also be home more than when I was aboard ship. No six-month Westpac cruises. The pay is pretty good too. Two dollars and twenty-five cents per hour for the first forty hours. Mr. Rawlings said you hardly ever get just forty hours. But if I never get more than forty hours, that would be $90 a week. I think with your budgeting, we will do very well."

Harry suddenly realized Suzanne was lying on the sofa, her head on one arm, trying to put a pillow under her legs. He hurried to help her. "With all the excitement about my stupid job,

I forgot to ask you how you are feeling. Are you okay? Is the bump okay?"

"I'm having a circulation problem, Harry. My legs keep going to sleep, and now they are throbbing."

"I'm going to go get the lotion. While I'm gone, fix your skirt so I can get to as much of your legs as possible. I'll be right back."

Once again, Harry spent a considerable time rubbing Suzanne's legs and feet. After which, he elevated them to a higher position, with her knees bent slightly. He then went into the kitchen to fix some tuna salad for their lunch. He fixed her a plate and took it into the living room.

"How are your legs?"

"Much better, thank you." Suzanne smiled up at him.

"Think you can sit up and eat?"

"Thank you, Harry, but I don't think the baby wants tuna salad. We're more in the mood for liver and onions."

"We don't have the fixings for that here. You better get up so I can take you to a restaurant."

Suzanne got up, fixed her hair and makeup, changed into something more dressy, and they were soon pulling into a restaurant parking lot.

When their waitress came to their table, Harry asked if they had liver and onions and was relieved to find they did. "We'll have a large order of the liver and onions for the lady. I'll just have a cheeseburger."

"Get some fries too," Suzanne urged him.

"And a large order of french fries," Harry said.

When their orders finally arrived, Suzanne took about two bites of the liver, ate all of Harry's fries, and all the bread with lots of butter. She asked Harry to get more bread. He signaled the waitress and ordered more bread.

While they were waiting for the waitress to bring the bread, she reached across the table and took the last half of Harry's cheese burger and ate it. She ate only one piece of the second order of bread before announcing she was full. The large plate of liver and onions was still sitting on the table, hardly touched, when they left.

I thought pregnant women only craved pickles and ice cream, Harry thought.

Suzanne continued to take her afternoon walks around the apartment complex. When he was at home, Harry dutifully walked beside her. By now, they were a regular sight in the neighborhood. People in their yards or sitting on their porches smiled and nodded and sometimes waved as the young couple passed by. Some even greeted them.

The bump was doing some fast growing in these last few weeks, and Suzanne seemed to be getting larger by the day. Harry thought she was also getting prettier by the day and told her so.

"How can you say that when you know I'm fat and ugly?" she whined. "God, I wish this baby would get here!"

Harry's truck driving job took him away from home for as long as five days at a time when he made the round trip to St. Louis, but he got to take the next three days off after he returned. A round trip to Phoenix could be done in less than twelve hours, so the driver who took that trip didn't get the next day off. Other destinations like Seattle and Fort Worth required four days to make the round trip and purchased the driver two days off after the return trip. A round trip to Albuquerque purchased the driver one day off. With all the hours of overtime and double time, Harry was making them a very good living. Still, he detested anything that kept him away from Suzanne.

Harry returned from his trip to Phoenix one evening later than normal, and it was already dark out when he arrived at the apartment. Suzanne didn't meet him at the door as usual, and the apartment was dark. Concerned, he hurried inside to look for her. He found her sitting alone in the dark living room, a box of tissue by her side. Her eyes were red and swollen, evidence of long periods of crying. Harry pulled the chair close to her and sat down, facing her taking her hands gently in his.

"What's wrong, Suzanne?" he asked, concern and urgency evident in his voice.

She hadn't been crying when he first found her, but now she began again. "It's Jeff!" She sobbed. "I found him dead and floating on the top of the fishbowl this morning. What kind of a mother am I going to be when I can't even take care of Mutt and Jeff?"

Harry stood up and eased himself down on the settee beside her. Cautiously, he put his arm around her shoulders. With his other hand, he softly caressed and smoothed her hair.

He didn't have any idea of what to say to comfort her, so he didn't say anything. He just held her close to him while she finished her cry. She was leaning against him, her head resting against his shoulder. She could feel the strength and comfort of his strong arm around her, the tenderness of his hand on her hair—a rare and tender moment of caring in their otherwise seemingly dispassionate relationship.

Suddenly, she began to struggle to lift herself up from the settee. Harry quickly helped her to her feet. She dried her eyes and announced, "I need to fix you some supper!"

July turned into August and, before they knew it, August into September. Harry was on a two-day break, having just made the Fort Worth run. With just days left on his terminal leave, when he would be transferred to the naval reserves, Harry and Suzanne decided to make one last trip to the commissary to stock up on groceries.

They had their basket about half full, slowly going down the canned goods aisle, when all of a sudden, Suzanne looked up, sucked in her breath noisily, and seemed frozen in her tracks. Harry looked to see what had caused this reaction. He saw only a man and woman. The man was in uniform. The woman with him was holding his arm in such a way that Harry assumed she was the man's wife. Suzanne hastily turned the cart around and held tightly to it.

"What is it?" Harry asked her, very concerned.

"That's Will Jones," she whispered. "And that is *not* his wife!"

Harry was concerned for Suzanne. The look on her face was not one he was familiar with—a combination of hurt and shock.

Suzanne was feeling several emotions—betrayal, loss, sadness, regret, and hatred. "Let's go, Harry," she pleaded, "before I make a scene."

In the car on the way home, Harry listened to Suzanne as she tried to explain away her emotions. "That was Sally Bower! She's a known Westpac widow. Every time her husband goes overseas, she's out barhopping and picking up lonely sailors. So he lied about being married too! He never loved me! That was a lie! You know what else, Harry? He's not even that good-looking!"

Harry tried to console her but found the best way was to stay close to her so he could listen while keeping his thoughts to himself. By the time they had put the groceries away, she was quietly humming to herself.

Harry had the strongest urge to caress her and try to make her feel better, but he dared not. He looked at her longingly. She was now only about three weeks away from delivery. The fact that the life inside of her was started with Will Jones must have some effect on her emotional stability. There was nothing Harry could do to change any of it. He wondered if his marrying her had only complicated her life rather than solving her problems. He felt frustrated and totally left out of an important part of her life.

"Time for our walk," Suzanne suddenly announced. "Come on, Harry."

Harry obediently followed her out the door. They were quietly walking side by side down the sidewalk near the park. Suzanne reached over and took his hand and interlaced her fingers with his. Harry's heart skipped a beat as he felt the warmness of her hand in his. He smiled approvingly.

"We need to think about a name for the baby," she said, smiling up at him. "We can't keep calling him or her the bump after it's born."

Harry, trying to lighten her mood, said, "No, I think Bump would be a great name for a boy or a girl. Can't you just picture it? Years later, a sports announcer saying, 'The next batter is Bump MacDonnell! Bump is batting eight hundred this season,' or 'That's pretty Miss Bump MacDonnell modeling the spring ensemble.' Can't you just hear it?"

Suzanne was actually laughing at Harry's silliness, still holding his hand tightly. "If it's a boy, I want to name him after you," she replied, trying to be serious. "If we have a girl, I think Mary is a very good name."

"I'm very partial to the name Suzanne," Harry told her, looking at her adoringly. "What about Mary Suzanne?"

"I like it. Then is Harold okay if it's a boy?" she asked.

"Harold Bump MacDonnell. I like it."

"Oh stop, Harry." She laughed. "I think he should be named Harold Ray Junior."

"That was too easy," Harry said. "I've always heard that settling on a name for a baby was difficult!"

They stopped on the sidewalk, and she turned to face him, still holding his hand. "That's because we make such a great team! Don't you think we make a great team, Harry?"

"Yes. Yes, I do," Harry replied, looking down at her adoringly. The urge to hold her close to him was almost overpowering. He had now been married nearly eleven weeks and had never held and kissed his wife. Their eyes met as they stood there facing each other. Harry thought he felt and saw an emotional bond between them. Just as he thought the moment was right for a tender kiss, Suzanne turned to continue their walk. Harry obligingly walked beside her, happily holding her hand.

Before leaving work on Friday, Harry had invited a young driver by the name of Bobby Scott to go to church with them on Sunday. Bobby was a handsome young man, twenty-one years of age. He was originally from Corpus Christi, Texas. When not dressed in his trucker's uniform, he wore Levi's, western shirts, cowboy boots, and a Stetson hat. He had wavy dark brown hair and brown eyes.

Bobby knocked on the door of their apartment on Sunday morning as they were finishing breakfast. Harry and Suzanne invited him to ride to church with them, but he wanted to drive his own vehicle and just follow them. He had recently purchased a new 1959 Buick LeSabre convertible. A beautiful car, it was white outside with red interior.

They arrived at the church, one after another. Harry and Suzanne were standing by Bobby's car, talking to him, when the Clawsons drove up. Harry did the introductions and noticed how Natalie was immediately attracted to the handsome Bobby. The attraction seemed to be mutual. They all sat together on the same pew in church, and somehow, Natalie managed to seat herself next to Bobby. Harry grinned to himself. Natalie had gotten over being angry with Harry several weeks back, and they had resumed their friendship.

It had not gone unnoticed by the pastor that Harry and Suzanne's tithe envelope was a lot fatter since Harry found the new job. The pastor, wanting to give subtle recognition to Harry, requested that he and Natalie sing a duet that Sunday. After some persuasion, they agreed. Someone loaned Harry an acoustic guitar, and he and Natalie sang "Peace in the Valley," one of their better harmony pieces.

At the end of the song, Harry quietly eased himself into the pew beside his wife. Suzanne took his hand, squeezed it, and smiled admiringly up at him. "I didn't know you could play and sing like that," she whispered.

As it was now almost a ritual part of Sunday, the MacDonnells had the noon meal with the Clawsons. However, today, there was another person at the table. Natalie arranged things so that she and Bobby were directly across from one another. Although they didn't talk much, their eye contact was almost constant. Harry watched with amusement.

In the afternoon, as they were all starting to go home, Natalie followed Bobby to his car for what looked like some intense conversation. Suzanne was already in their car, and Harry was about to get in as Natalie came hurriedly by, eyes on the ground, deep in thought.

"Not even a good-bye?" Harry teased, grinning. "Didn't take you long to replace me!"

Natalie looked up and smiled. "Good-bye, Harry!" She turned and ran into the house.

"They make a cute couple," Suzanne told Harry as they were on their way home. "Almost like they were made for each other. What do you know about him?"

"He's a darn good semi driver! He's from Texas. He's twenty-one years old. That's about it."

"I'll bet Natalie already knows more about him than that," she teased. "Ow! Harry, I'm having pains down there! Can you stop the car?"

Harry pulled into a store parking lot. Suzanne lay down with her head in his lap. She stuck one foot out of the window and the other over the back of the seat. "What can I do?" Harry asked, almost in a panic.

"I don't know!" Susan told him through clenched teeth. "I think I'm going to have this baby right here, right now!"

Harry held one of her hands and smoothed her hair. He could tell by the way her fingernails dug into the palm of his hand that she was hurting badly. "Do you want me to try to get you to Balboa Hospital?" he asked, trying to keep the panic out of his voice.

"No! I don't know! Oh, Harry!" she moaned, looking up at him through frightened eyes.

Harry backed the car out of the parking area and sped to Balboa Hospital. Suzanne was admitted to emergency. The pains gradually subsided, and as they didn't reappear, they were told by hospital staff that they believed she had just experienced what was described as false labor pains. Eventually, she was able to sit up again, and Harry took her home.

For the next several days, when Harry was on the road, he made calls to Suzanne every time he pulled off the road long enough to do so. Every time, she assured him she was okay and had no new problems. When he was at home, he never left her side, even waiting outside the bathroom door any time she was in there.

"Why don't you just come in and hold my hand while I pee?" she scolded, when finding him stationed outside the bathroom door one time.

It was after they had gone to their separate rooms Tuesday night, just before midnight, that Suzanne woke Harry. "It's time," she said. "I need you to take me to the hospital."

Suzanne was in labor for nearly six hours while Harry paced the hall just outside the delivery room. Just before 7:00 a.m. on September 30, 1959, Mary Suzanne MacDonnell was pushed into the world with hardly a whimper. She weighed in at 6¾ pounds. A nurse stuck her head out and told Harry he could see his daughter through the nursery window in about ten minutes.

"Mrs. MacDonnell will be in her room in just a little while," she told him.

Harry stood outside the nursery window until a nurse held Mary up for him to see. A tear of happiness ran down Harry's cheek. The baby was squinting against the lights and wrinkling her brow. When she opened her eyes, he was sure she recognized him as her daddy. Harry was too naïve to understand that newborns couldn't focus on anything that far away. The nurse put her back into the baby bed, and Harry hurried off to see Suzanne.

"Did you see her?" Suzanne asked Harry as he entered the room.

Harry was bending to caress her and kiss her when he caught himself and returned to a totally upright position. "Yes, I saw her. She's beautiful! She looks just like her mother!"

"Then she can't be very beautiful. Look at me, Harry. I'm a mess!"

"Well, then you're a beautiful mess, and I'm proud of you. The nurse said you were very brave this morning. She said it was a natural birth, whatever that means."

"It means they didn't give me any shot in the spine to deaden the pains."

Just then the nurse came in with baby Mary. "Time to try to feed her," she announced. "Do you want to stay and watch?" the nurse asked Harry.

Harry, having never seen his wife's bare breasts, didn't want to embarrass Suzanne or himself, so he excused himself and waited by the nursery window until he saw them bring Mary back. He then returned to Suzanne's room.

"It felt strange," she told Harry, "but she took to the breast immediately. She is so tiny and perfect. Did you see her tiny fingers and toes?"

"No, I didn't get to see her that close up."

"You should have stayed, Harry."

"I thought it might embarrass you—me here, staring at your naked breasts."

"I think you would have been staring at Mary, not at me."

Harry didn't answer. He just sat and looked at Suzanne for a long time. She was smiling at him, trying to read his thoughts. Finally, she said, "It has been a long night. I think I'll get some sleep now."

Harry divided his time between the nursery and Suzanne's room. He made one phone call to J & J Trucking to tell them he would be in as soon as possible and the reason for his missing work. His supervisor congratulated him on the birth and told him to take the time he needed.

Suzanne was able to return home two days later on Friday, October 2. On Sunday morning at church, Mary MacDonnell was the center of attention. Harry had always known he came second to Suzanne, but now, he had been moved to third place. Nevertheless, he was beaming with pride as he took his place beside his family on the church pew. Taking care of a new born was a full-time job, and they declined an invitation to take Sunday dinner at the Clawsons.

Suzanne was the very best of mothers. Mary was not a difficult baby and soon learned to sleep through the night. When Harry was not on the road, he took over all the care of the baby, except for the feeding. This gave Suzanne time to get some rest and accomplish some household chores. Theirs would have been a totally happy home, except for the absence of a physically demonstrated love.

Mary's baby bed was in the room with Suzanne, and many a night, she would witness Harry quietly lifting Mary's tiny form from her bed and carrying her to sleep on his chest in his room. Mary would babble and coo then settle down to sleep on his chest like it was a downy cloud. If during the night she needed changing, Harry always did that too.

Mary loved bath time, and Harry loved giving her baths. They would have so much fun that Suzanne secretly envied Mary's joyful times with Harry. It was plain Harry doted on this child.

Harry's pent up love for Suzanne was part of the reason he lavished so much love on Mary. He had plenty of love for both but was unable to demonstrate his love for Suzanne. This often frustrated him, and he obsessed about it while driving his rig to St. Louis one week. "You should be a man and just demand she let you show her how much you love her!" he said out loud. Then he argued with himself, "You can't force someone to love you!"

He worried that any day now, she would want to discuss the quickie divorce she had promised. He didn't think he could live without her and Mary. He knew he had to discuss it with her soon. They were living in such harmony now that he thought maybe he should just ignore the inevitable. Finally, he decided he had to face it and that he would broach the issue the next time he was home.

Mary was six weeks old now. Harry prepared for bed like always, wearing a tee shirt and boxer shorts. He slipped into Suzanne's room to take Mary to sleep with him. Mary wasn't in her bed.

"Harry," Suzanne whispered softly, "if you want to hold Mary on your chest tonight, you'll have to do it here in my bed."

"Where are you going to sleep?" Harry asked innocently.

Suzanne was lying on the opposite side of the bed, with Mary in the middle. She sat up and patted the other side of the bed. "Here, Harry. It's time my husband shared the same bed."

Harry looked at her in the faint glow of a night light. She was as sincere as she was lovely. He sat down carefully on the edge of the bed and lay back rigidly. Slowly, he began to relax.

Suzanne picked Mary up and cradled her to her breast. "Come closer, Harry. You're about to fall out of bed."

He moved closer. Suzanne moved close enough to place Mary in his arms then snuggled against him. A thrill ran through his body. He held Mary on his chest with one hand and arm then carefully placed his other arm around Suzanne's shoulders. Was he finally going to be able to caress his wife? Harry felt a glow of happiness fill him as he realized the truth of the moment. She seemed smaller and softer than he had imagined. He had never been this happy. Suzanne only stirred one time during the night to cover them all with a blanket. They were still in the same positions when Mary sounded reveille at 5:00 a.m. She was wet, and she was hungry!

Harry awoke to sounds of his daughter's unhappiness. He slowly realized where he was and how he was still holding his wife with his other arm. Once again, a thrill ran through him as he realized the implications of it all. For a split-second, he thought about not moving, but Mary was persistent. Quietly, he removed his arm from around Suzanne and slipped out of bed. He changed Mary's diaper and put her on his shoulder. As Mary snurffled into his neck, he went into the bathroom and wet a washcloth in warm water with one hand while holding Mary on his shoulder with the other. When he came out of the bathroom, Suzanne was stirring.

"Somebody's hungry," he told her softly, handing her the warm washcloth. Harry averted his eyes while she bathed her nipples then traded her a hungry Mary for the washcloth. He took the washcloth to the bathroom where he absentmindedly rinsed it thoroughly before he brushed his teeth and washed his face. As he hurried out of the room to fix them some breakfast, Suzanne called to him.

"Come here, Harry. Sit down here on the side of the bed. Don't you want to see your daughter nurse?"

Harry dutifully did as his wife instructed, trying not to stare as he watched Mary work her tiny mouth to get her nourishment.

"Bring me another warm washcloth please," Suzanne asked as she moved Mary from one breast to the other.

Harry was in awe of nature's wonders as he watched the relationship between his young daughter and her mother. He thought it was the most beautiful thing he had ever witnessed.

Soon, Mary was asleep, so he took her to her crib while Suzanne went to bathe. Harry fixed them both breakfast before he shaved and took his own shower. He dressed in his trucker's uniform and picked up his lunch. He was about to leave for work when Suzanne came up to him.

"Don't you kiss your wife good-bye?" she asked.

Harry felt a blush in his cheeks and ears. It was as if she could read his mind. "Of course," he replied. He clumsily kissed her on the mouth and hurried out the door.

Harry thought about his wife and daughter every second of every day. Today was no different, except now, his mind kept replaying the clumsy way he had kissed Suzanne good-bye. When he had thought about what it would be like to kiss her, it had always been more like Errol Flynn and Yvonne De Carlo, not Goofy and Yvonne De Carlo. He blushed again as he thought about it.

Harry was making the Albuquerque run and would not be home for two days. He had plenty of time to plan a more romantic encounter. But, he thought, regardless of his plans, he was so inexperienced and clumsy that he could never pull it off. He loved Suzanne so much. Why did it have to be so difficult to tell her and to show her how much?

After eleven hours of driving, he pulled off the road in Gallup, New Mexico, to rest for the night. The first thing he did was call Suzanne. He stood at the phone booth inside the little office of the rented cabin on Route 66 and fed nickels into the pay phone.

When Suzanne came on the line, he told her he had only enough change to talk for three minutes.

"Then you'd better talk fast, Harry."

"How are you? How is Mary?"

"We're fine. Mary is missing her daddy."

"I miss her too. I miss you even more, Suzanne. I've been thinking about you all day."

"You should keep your mind on your driving, Harry. Mary and I want you to be safe and come back home to us real soon."

"Suzanne—" Harry hesitated. "I really wanted to call to tell you I-I love you."

"I know, Harry. I love you too."

There was silence on the line as Harry tried to grasp the total meaning of her declaration. "How long have you known?"

"What? That you love me or that I love you?"

"Uh, both I guess."

"I've felt your love for me for a long time. Me realizing I was in love with you took a little longer. I've been waiting for weeks for you to make the first move. I finally gave up waiting on you. That's why I invited you to share my bed last night. We're married, Harry. It's time we started acting like it."

Harry was searching for something to say when the operator cut in to tell him he needed to deposit more money or hang up. He called, "I love you!" as the line went dead.

That night, he didn't sleep all that well and was up and on the road before daylight.

He detached from his trailer, picked up another full one, and headed back to El Cajon. In less than half an hour, he was rolling down Route 66, headed back to his family. J & J Trucking discouraged its drivers from putting in more than ten hours behind the wheel in any one day, but today, Harry was plenty wide awake. He was in Flagstaff in record time, refueled, grabbed a sandwich, and was rolling again in less than thirty minutes. It was just a little before nine o'clock when he pulled into the yard at J & J Trucking in El Cajon, California.

"You trying for a new record?" the dispatcher asked him.

"I'll see you day after tomorrow," Harry told him as he turned in his logbook. "Right now, I have a date with my wife!"

A few minutes later, Harry was entering their apartment. This time, when he kissed Suzanne, he was slower and more alert to what he was doing. She seemed to melt into his arms, her whole body pressed against him passionately yet lovingly. This was actually the first time he had kissed and caressed her properly, and her response was what he had dreamed it would be.

When she moved away, they both went to Mary's crib so he could see her. Mary was awake, and he picked her up and cuddled her to him, kissing her on the head. Harry was a very happy man.

After a hot shower and a light meal, Harry was ready for a bed. Suzanne had fed and changed Mary, who was now fast asleep in her crib. As Harry stood by her crib, about to take her to sleep on his chest, Suzanne took his hand.

"Let her sleep," she told him quietly, pulling him toward the bed, "Tonight, I want to sleep on your chest."

AFTERWORD

Although this story is totally fictitious, the author did in fact
meet a pretty young auburn-haired waitress in the late 1950s.
She was pregnant, unmarried, and worked at the San Diego,
California, Oscar's Drive-In when they met. He gave her a ride
to her apartment building after she finished her day's work, and
a similar conversation did take place. It was their first and only
meeting, and they never saw each other again. The conversation
there outside of her apartment building that night was so poignant that it stayed with him for nearly fifty-five years before he
decided to include it in this book.

PANZY O'TOOLE

HERBERT DURBIN

THE ACCIDENT

All evening, whenever she got a moment, Myrtle O'Toole worked on her application for assistant librarian. She had been interrupted many times by six-month-old Panzy needing changing, feeding, or just needing attention. Myrtle had a scheduled meeting with the head librarian at the Dexter City Library at 10:00 a.m. the following morning. She had been promised by her neighbor, Mrs. Jessup, that she would look after Panzy while she went to the library for her interview. However, just this evening, Mrs. Jessup had dropped by to say she wouldn't be able to watch her. Now that she had no one to watch after little Panzy, she was worried that she would have to miss out on the interview altogether, and she badly needed the job.

Panzy's father, Sean O'Toole, had been drafted into the navy and gone away on a tour of sea duty aboard the USS *Indianapolis* (CA-35). The *Indianapolis* was a heavy cruiser assigned to the Pacific fleet and steaming in the waters of the Pacific Ocean. Sean had never seen his daughter, Panzy. When he received the small black-and-white picture of Myrtle holding the infant Panzy, he attached it to the underside of the bunk above his head so he could look at the two of them during the rare occasions when he was able to occupy his bunk.

As a young married man, Sean had not volunteered for service in the war against the Axis powers like so many others had but had stayed on his family farm, trying to make it work. He had been caught in the draft late in 1944, when he was just twenty-two years old. He had been apprehensive about leaving Myrtle, who at the time was pregnant with their first child.

Sean's father, Shamus O'Toole, had given up on the farm three years earlier and taken Sean's mother, Mary, and his two younger siblings to Camden, New Jersey, where he found a job in the foundry at the New York Shipbuilding Corporation—the very shipbuilder that had built the warship that Sean would later be stationed aboard.

Myrtle's adoptive parents, Mr. and Mrs. Joseph McFarland, lived in the small farming community of Lowry. Lowry was an unincorporated community of less than one hundred people, located some twenty miles southeast of Dexter. Mr. and Mrs. McFarland were an elderly couple who had adopted Myrtle from the orphans' home when she was thirteen. Their reason for adopting her, they said, was their need for someone to help out around their house now that they were growing older. To them, the fully mature Myrtle was nothing more than a bondservant.

When she met the handsome dark-haired and blue-eyed Sean O'Toole at a church picnic one Sunday afternoon, Myrtle was immediately smitten. Likewise, when Sean first laid eyes on the comely Myrtle McFarland, with her wavy strawberry-blonde curls and her hazel-green eyes, he was just as taken with her. Although Myrtle was more than five months older than Sean, they were soon married in a religious ceremony at the Lowry community church only a few months after their initial meeting.

Neither Myrtle nor Sean knew what lay ahead of them. As fate would have it, near the very end of the war, Sean's ship, the USS *Indianapolis*, was designated to take the atom bomb that would be dropped by the Enola Gay on Hiroshima, Japan, to a secret place in the Pacific. On July 30, 1945, a few days after delivering their secret cargo, the USS *Indianapolis*, while steaming in the waters off of the Philippine Islands, was suddenly torpedoed by a Japanese submarine. It took less than fifteen minutes for the ship to slip under the shark-infested waters of the Philippine Sea. Of the 1,197 crew members aboard, only 317 survived. Sean was not one of the lucky ones.

When Myrtle got the letter from the war department which read in part, "We are sorry to inform you," she thought she would die of heartbreak. Panzy would now grow up without knowing her father. Myrtle was painfully aware of just how lost and alone she'd felt growing up without knowing either of her biological parents.

Sean had been sending Myrtle most of his salary of $54 a month. Thus, she and Panzy were able to get by. But now, since his death, in order to provide for her daughter and herself, she had left the house on the farm near Lowry and taken Panzy into nearby Dexter. Her aim was to immediately take any type of employment. The rooming house where they were staying had began threatening to evict her for failure to pay past due rent. The mere fact that she had a baby was the only thing that kept a roof over their heads and kept the landlord from fulfilling the threat.

Myrtle had visited Olsen's Drugstore, across from the Dexter City Library, a few times while searching for work. She sat in a booth and checked the want ads daily and made as many interviews as she could manage with a six-month-old baby in tow. The nice man behind the counter had once let her have some milk for Panzy without charging her when she told him she had just discovered she was short of money. This morning, she would ask him for one more favor. She must keep her appointment at the library.

"Please, sir, can you keep an eye on Panzy?" Myrtle asked as she set the portable crib on the end of the counter. "I just need to run across the street to the library. I'll be right back!"

Jeff Stuart looked up from his glass-washing chore just as the young woman set the bassinet on the end of the drugstore soda counter. He recognized her from the few times she had been in, but he didn't know much about her other than she was a war widow, her name was Mrs. O'Toole, and her daughter's name was Panzy. She usually occupied a booth near the wall and waited for someone to leave the paper so she could read the want ads section. Occasionally, she would buy just enough milk to fill the baby's bottle.

"I'm sorry, you can't leave her here!" Jeff called after her. "Hey! Mrs. O'Toole, come back! Please, you can't leave your baby here!"

Myrtle acted as if she didn't hear him as she exited hurriedly through the drugstore doorway and out onto the sidewalk.

On this early October morning, there was a heavy fog and a light cold mist falling. As Myrtle hurried across the street, she turned her collar up against the cold wind and misty rain. If she hadn't turned her collar up, she might have seen or heard the automobile speeding toward her. The driver was driving much too fast for the weather conditions, and when he did finally see the outline of the woman in the gray coat, it was too late to avoid striking her. Myrtle flew into the air as her résumé papers scattered. She went up and over the automobile, landing violently onto the pavement just behind it, where she was then struck by a second vehicle.

Jeff heard the sound of horns and people shouting from the street in front of the drugstore, but he couldn't leave his post behind the counter. And now he had the added responsibility of a baby as he waited for her mother to return. As he strained to see what all the commotion was about, a man rushed through the doorway and asked to use the telephone.

"There's been a terrible accident down the street near the intersection," the man said. "I need to use your telephone to call for an ambulance!"

"Do you need change?" Jeff asked him.

"No, thank you. I have a nickel. Would you happen to know the telephone number of the hospital?"

"Just ask the operator to connect you," Jeff offered.

"Oh yes, of course, I'm a little shaken from what I saw out there just now. The woman is badly mangled!"

Mr. Olsen, the druggist and Jeff's employer, came from inside the drug preparation and storage room to see what was going on.

He listened to the information about the accident from the man on the telephone. Then he noticed the bassinet with the baby.

"What's this, Jeff? Are we a nursery now?"

"I'm sorry, Mr. Olsen. Mrs. O'Toole came in, put the baby on the counter, and ran out. I told her she couldn't leave her here, but she acted as if she didn't hear me. She told me she was just going across the street to the library and would be right back."

"She's probably in that crowd of onlookers," Mr. Olsen said. "Well, if she isn't back in a reasonable time, I want you to go take the baby to her at the library!"

"Yes, sir."

Jeff had moved the bassinet from the counter onto a stool behind the counter where the baby was less obvious. Now he noticed she was awake and looking around. Jeff also noticed there were several neatly folded diapers in the bassinet, along with a bib, another dress, a full bottle of milk, and some baby powder. Jeff removed the bottle and placed it in the icebox. Panzy rolled onto her stomach with some difficulty because of the confining area of the bassinet, raised her posterior into the air, and was soon able to push herself into a seated position. Jeff realized the possibility of an accident if the bassinet should tumble off of the stool, so he lifted the tiny girl out of her bed and held her to his chest. It was obvious she was in need of a dry diaper. She reached up and grabbed his nose and smiled up at him, showing the buds of two tiny teeth on her lower gums.

"Your mommy will be back in just a few minutes," Jeff told her, bouncing her gingerly in his arms. "You'll get a dry diaper then. Now what am I going to do with you until she returns?"

"They're sending an ambulance right away!" the man at the pay telephone announced. He hurried out and soon disappeared into the crowd of spectators on the sidewalk.

The ambulance soon arrived. Several men surrounded the second vehicle and lifted it off of the woman while men in white picked up the injured woman and placed her on a stretcher. The ambulance left, with the loud wail of the siren piercing the fog and misty rain. The crowd dispersed, and still, Mrs. O'Toole did not return for her baby. Mr. Olsen came back out and admonished Jeff once again.

"Here, leave the baby with me!" Mr. Olsen said, taking Panzy from Jeff. "Now go over there to the library and find out what's taking that woman so long!"

Jeff was back in just a few minutes. "They told me at the library that they have not seen a Mrs. O'Toole today. She was supposed to be there at ten this morning, but she didn't keep her appointment. I'm sure she'll be back. She didn't look like the kind of woman who would just abandon her baby. If you'd like, I can run home and get Judy to come in and watch the baby for awhile until her mother returns."

"That's a good idea," Mr. Olsen replied. "Here are the keys to the panel truck. Please go fetch her."

Jeff and Judy Stuart had been married for over four years but were still a childless couple. They deemed it God's will since the job that Jeff had at the drugstore paid so little that they were living from paycheck to paycheck. They kept a milk cow behind their little house, and Judy sold milk, cream, and butter. With their twelve laying hens, she also sold a few dozen eggs each week. Judy was also an accomplished seamstress and made many of their own clothes. Her vegetable garden also provided much of the family fare.

Both Judy and Jeff used bicycles for their major mode of transportation as automobiles were in short supply and the wartime rationing of gasoline and tires caused a hardship on those persons who were fortunate enough to own an automobile. The Stuarts had to have ration stamps just to buy sugar, meat, fats, fish, and cheese. They had to present an empty toothpaste tube before they were allowed to buy another.

Jeff had been called up for the draft, but at his induction physical, the doctors found a heart murmur, and he had been classified 4F. He was somewhat disappointed about that because he believed his military pay and allowances would be much more than the salary he was receiving from Mr. Olsen. Although he and Judy were barely getting by, neither of them thought to complain.

Jeff pulled the panel truck up in front of the small frame house and went inside to find Judy. As always, she was delighted to see him and greeted him with a big smile, a loving hug, and a kiss.

"What brings you home in the middle of the day?" she asked. "Did you forget something?"

"I need you to come with me to the drugstore for a little while," he explained.

Judy took off her apron and dutifully followed Jeff to Mr. Olsen's panel truck. Judy was a tall frail-looking woman who seemed much older than her twenty-six years. Her brown hair was done up in a bun on the back of her head. Her blue-gray eyes seemed a little sad when not looking at her husband. She climbed into the seat and sat silently, waiting for Jeff to explain.

"A lady left a baby at the drugstore and hasn't yet returned. I told Mr. Olsen you would watch the baby until the mother gets back."

Judy intertwined her fingers and placed her hands in her lap. She didn't say anything during the ten-minute ride to the drugstore. Jeff was silent too, concentrating on keeping the vehicle below the national wartime speed limit of thirty-five miles per hour.

Judy happily cared for little Panzy for the rest of the day, waiting for her mother to return. She changed her diaper, gave her a bottle, and sang quietly to her. When she heard the gossip about the woman who had been injured in the street in front of the library, she suggested to Jeff and to Mr. Olsen that the woman and Panzy's mother might be one and the same. Mr. Olsen called the hospital and was informed that they did indeed have a Myrtle

O'Toole there. He was not told of her condition but was informed that they were interested in finding her next of kin.

"We'll keep the baby with us until her mother gets out of the hospital!" Judy stated authoritatively. "Or at least until they have located her kin. We have plenty of wholesome milk."

During the next few days, the authorities searched for the relatives of Myrtle O'Toole with no positive results. They were unaware that she had a baby that had been left homeless, and it didn't occur to Jeff and Judy to take the baby to the orphanage. Jeff made a trip to the hospital to tell Myrtle that Panzy was being cared for, but he was turned away when he told them he was not a relative.

Myrtle's shattered body remained in the hospital; she was in a coma for eleven days before she succumbed to her injuries. Unfortunately, it was this twist of fate that put Panzy O'Toole into the exact same category as that of her mother when she was this age. Panzy too would grow up without knowing her biological father or remembering her birth mother.

Judy immediately fell in love with little Panzy, with her curly strawberry-blonde hair and her deep blue-green eyes. It was as if Panzy was Judy's very own daughter. She made her frilly dresses and fixed her hair in the prettiest styles. People remarked that they had never seen a neater, cleaner, happier baby.

"She's always dressed like she's going to a party," one lady at church was heard to say.

Jeff also doted on Panzy and bored all his customers with stories of her progress. "She has five teeth now! She can pull up and stand up all by herself! She's the smartest baby I've ever seen! She calls me da da!" and so on.

PANZY'S INHERITANCE

In an effort to make everything as normal as possible for Panzy, Judy decided they should find out her exact date of birth. She not only wanted to know when to celebrate her birthday but also wanted to be able to mark her progress. One morning, they borrowed the panel truck from Mr. Olsen and drove to the county seat, some thirty-five miles away.

They carried little Panzy with them when they went inside the county clerk's office. Judy told the clerk that they were in need of the baby's birth certificate. Judy and Jeff signed all the required request forms and gave an approximate date. Judy informed the clerk that Panzy's mother had died, but before she did, she had entrusted the care of her baby to her and Jeff. Although the clerk had some difficulty and could have used an exact date, she did finally locate Panzy's birth certificate. Judy's guess of April 15 was only a few days off from the actual date of April 18. The clerk made them a copy of the birth certificate and wished them good luck.

From the birth certificate, they were able to establish that Panzy's middle name was Mae. They also found out the identity of her biological father. Judy thought that it might come in handy in the future, should Panzy ever feel the need for that kind of information.

With birth certificate in hand, they set out to make Panzy their legal ward. Jeff discussed it with Mr. Olsen who helped him retain an attorney.

The search for her father's kin or other next of kin soon began, and the attorney told them he would keep them informed.

Meanwhile, he was able to get a court-ordered temporary legal guardianship set up for the Stuarts.

During the next few days, weeks, and months, Panzy saw her first Halloween, her first Thanksgiving, and her first Christmas.

The snows of winter had just receded, only to be seen on the faraway mountains, when Jeff first saw the impeccably dressed man. He walked into the drugstore carrying a briefcase. He was short and thin. He was wearing a fedora, a suit with a vest, and he had on thick heavy-rimmed eyeglasses. He sat down on a stool at the counter and removed his fedora, revealing a balding head.

"Can I help you?" Jeff asked, placing a glass of cold water in front of him.

The man took a long drink of water before answering. "You probably know everyone who lives in this area," he said.

"Probably," Jeff replied. "Everyone needs medicine at sometime in their lives."

"My name is Clovis Lovejoy," the man said, extending his hand.

"Jeff Stuart," Jeff told him as they shook hands.

"I'm with Veterans Life Insurance. I'm looking for a war widow who is supposed to live on a farm near here. You wouldn't happen to know a woman by the name of Myrtle O'Toole, would you? And maybe you could tell me exactly how to get to where she lives?"

"I'm sorry I have to be the one to tell you this, Mr. Lovejoy, but Myrtle O'Toole is buried in the Dexter Cemetery east of town."

"Myrtle O'Toole? A young woman about twenty-three or twenty-four years of age?"

"That's the one. She was killed in a terrible automobile accident in the street right out here in front!"

Mr. Lovejoy began digging into his briefcase. He pulled out a file and began turning pages. "No other beneficiaries," he mumbled to himself. He looked up at Jeff. "I'll need a death certificate. Where is your courthouse located?"

"It's in Jackson," Jeff informed him. "That's the county seat of Morrison County. It's just thirty-five miles to the southwest down US 59. Did I hear you say 'no beneficiaries'? What does that mean? You do know that she had a daughter, don't you?"

"She had a daughter?" Mr. Lovejoy asked rhetorically.

"Yes, sir. Her name is Panzy. My wife and I are her legal guardians," Jeff replied.

"I hope you can prove all of this," Mr. Lovejoy told him seriously. "Otherwise, Veterans Life isn't obligated to pay any of the insurance money. Although not named, the heirs of the beneficiary would be in line for the insurance. Can you produce papers proving what you've told me?"

"Yes, sir," Jeff said.

"Well, this may be my lucky day!" Mr. Lovejoy said with a smile. "Would you repeat your name, sir?" He opened a notebook and took a mechanical pencil out of his briefcase.

"Jeffrey Wayne Stuart."

"Would you please spell Stuart for me?"

"S-t-u-a-r-t."

"And your address please?"

"Box 5, Rural Route 1, Dexter," Jeff informed him.

"Would you mind accompanying me to your house so I can see the birth certificate and guardianship papers?"

"I can't leave work right now, sir," Jeff answered. "But my wife is at home. I'm sure she would show them to you. You just go straight east down the highway in front of the drugstore. When the highway makes a sharp left turn to the north, just go straight ahead down the graded dirt road for another mile and a half. It's the white house with the yellow trim on the north side of the road. There's a tire swing hanging from a big chestnut tree in the front yard. You can't miss it."

Clovis Lovejoy pulled out his pocket watch and checked the time. He rubbed his chin in thought. He put the folder and notebook in his briefcase, closed it, and stood up. "How far did you say it is to your house?"

"About six miles. It's about a ten-minute drive. Maybe less now that the wartime speed limit has been lifted. May I ask how much insurance Mrs. O'Toole had coming to her?"

"Standard GI death policy, $10,000. Thank you for your help, Mr. Stuart," he said as he extended his hand. They shook hands. "I'm sure I'll be seeing you again." He put his hat on and left the drugstore.

Jeff watched from the window as the man got into a new shiny black 1946 Chevrolet, backed out, and drove away.

"Who were you talking to?" Mr. Olsen asked as he came from the rear of the store.

"He said he was an insurance man. I'm pretty sure it was about Panzy's real father. You know, the serviceman who was killed in action in the war? That man was looking for the serviceman's wife, Myrtle O'Toole. You remember, the lady who was hit by the automobiles in front of the library? He said Mrs. O'Toole had an insurance payment of $10,000 coming. When I told him that she was dead, he said if he could see proof of Myrtle's death and we could show proof that Panzy was her child, then Panzy would probably receive the insurance money."

"If that's true," Mr. Olsen said with a smile, "it looks more and more like God wants you and Judy to raise that little baby. I suppose the money will be held in trust for her until she's twenty-one?"

"I don't know," Jeff replied. "He didn't say anything about that, but it would be nice for her. Someday, she's going to find out that she's an orphan. Maybe that will help to ease the pain."

Just then, they were interrupted by James, the grocery delivery boy from the IGA up the street. He stuck his head through the open doorway and called, "Hey, Jeff, did you know you have a flat tire on your bicycle?"

"No, I didn't. Thanks, James."

"I don't have my patching kit with me," Jeff explained to Mr. Olsen. "I need a couple of minutes off to run up to the hardware store and get one."

"Sure, go ahead. I'll watch things."

When Jeff returned, he told Mr. Olsen it was the rear tire and he had no tools with him. "I'll push it up to Ralph's filling station when I get off today and borrow some wrenches from him. I can use his compressed air and save myself from having to pump it up by hand. I'm going to be late for supper tonight, and Judy doesn't like that."

"You have many goatheads at your place?" Mr. Olsen asked. "I'll bet you're going to find a goathead puncture."

"Yes, sir. I wouldn't be surprised."

Jeff's single-speed bicycle had balloon tires that had worn thin treads on them. The rubber companies had stopped producing gun mounts and started making tires again just after the war ended. The demand for new tires had priced them way above what his budget would allow.

Jeff patched the two holes he found in the inner tube and scoured the inside of the tire for goathead thorns. Ralph told him he had a couple of very old red rubber inner tubes hanging in the storeroom out back with multiple patches that he would let him have for 15¢ apiece. Jeff bought the inner tubes and cut out the valve stems. He made a single lengthwise slit around the inside and used one of them as a tire liner inside the rear tire. Then he placed the repaired tube in the tire and aired it up.

Once he had replaced the repaired tire on the rear of his bicycle, he adjusted the chain for proper tightness and connected the brake lever. He then spent an extra fifteen minutes, putting a liner in the front tire. He aired up the front tire and rode the six miles to his home as rapidly as he could.

When Jeff arrived at home, he was nearly an hour late. Judy was pacing nervously, watching out through the window in the front door until she saw him turn up the path. She sat Panzy in the homemade playpen and went to put their supper on the table.

"What kept you?" she asked as he entered the front door.

"Da da," Panzy said as he stooped to hug and kiss her. He helped Judy put the casserole on the table then gave her a kiss and a hug. As he washed up at the kitchen sink, he explained his lateness. He then lifted Panzy into her high chair before sitting down at the table. Jeff said grace over their meal and handed Judy his empty plate for her to fill. Panzy was already holding a spoon in one hand and eating with the other. Jeff accepted his full plate and set it in front of him before Judy explained about her visitor.

"I had a visit from a Mr. Lovejoy this afternoon," she said, opening the dialogue.

"Yes, he stopped by the store today," Jeff replied. "I told him to come out here and talk to you."

"He took Panzy's birth certificate and our certificate of guardianship with him. He gave me a receipt for them and told me that as soon as he can make photostatic copies of them, he'll mail the original documents back to us. Panzy really took a shine to him, and he was taken by her also. He picked her up and held her for a little while until she tried to take his eyeglasses. He said she was pretty enough to be a movie star, just like Shirley Temple."

Jeff smiled broadly. "She's a lot more beautiful than Miss Shirley Temple," he bragged.

"Mr. Lovejoy also said Panzy may be in line for a life insurance payout from her father who was killed in the war," Judy continued. "He told me he was on his way to Jackson to conduct other business but would contact us as soon as a decision is made."

"It's $10,000, Judy! We may be as poor as church mice, but someday, little Panzy here may be rich. Mr. Olsen thinks the insurance money might be held in trust for her until she's twenty-one."

"Moy," Panzy said, holding out her bowl.

Both Jeff and Judy looked at her. Her face, her hands, her bib, and her tray were covered with chicken cacciatore. She even had some of it in her hair.

"More?" Jeff laughed. "Did you manage to get any food into your mouth?"

Panzy shook her head vigorously and repeated, "Moy!"

Judy dutifully refilled her bowl. "Here, use your spoon, Panzy," she told her. Then speaking apologetically to Jeff, she said, "I'll clean her up and bathe her before I put her to bed."

"Why don't you just sit her on the floor and let Rover lick her clean," Jeff joked. "That way, we won't have to feed him later."

When Panzy was finished with her food and began to play in it, Jeff addressed Judy. "Here, let me put her in a bath and get her dressed for bed. You've had her to yourself all day."

Judy sighed deeply, got up, and started clearing the table.

"Would you rather I did cleanup while you bathe Panzy?" Jeff asked.

"No, it's fine. I'm just a little tired."

Jeff left Panzy in her high chair, took Judy by the hand, and led her into the living room. "Here," he said, "put your feet up and relax. I'll bathe Panzy, and then while you sing her a lullaby, I'll clean up the kitchen." He bent and gave her a tender kiss.

Panzy loved bath time, and Jeff let her play some while he rinsed the cacciatore off of her. He soaped her down, shampooed her curly strawberry-blonde locks, rinsed her off again, and toweled her off while she giggled. She kicked her legs in the air while he powdered her and pinned a soft white cloth diaper on her. She stood and put her hands over her head while he put her gown on her. He hugged her tightly to him.

"Umm," Jeff said. "You smell nice and clean. Now, mommy is going to read and sing to you. I love you so much!" He carried Panzy into the living room and put her into Judy's arms. "All clean," he told her. "I'll try not to make too much noise in the kitchen."

As he started toward the kitchen, they both heard old Bossy moo.

"Oh, Jeff," Judy called out to him, "I still haven't milked the cow. Do you think you could do that too?"

Jeff got the milk pail and headed outside. He put a measure of feed in the cow trough and locked Bossy's head into the stall so she wouldn't move before he was finished with the milking. He set the stool beside her and took the warm wet cloth he had brought and washed her teats. He sat, working his fingers and listening to the sound of the pail filling with milk.

Bossy was a good Guernsey cow, producing almost three gallons of milk at each milking. As his mind wandered, he thought about how Judy had so much work to do with the chickens and the cow and now with Panzy. She kept the books on the production of milk, cream, butter, and egg sales; separated the cream; churned the butter; and gathered the eggs. She was a farm girl, and this was nothing new to her, but now Panzy was walking and getting into everything. He wished he could make things easier for her. He and Judy had been dividing up the milking chore—Jeff in the morning and Judy in the evening—but still it didn't seem enough. His job at the drugstore didn't seem very important. Still, it brought in a little money each week.

The milk pail now full, Jeff released Bossy into the corral and carried the milk inside. Judy was in the kitchen, scraping the dishes into the dog bowl. Rover stood up from his spot on the oval rug in the living room and lazily walked into the kitchen to inspect his supper.

"Panzy went to sleep almost as soon as you gave her to me," Judy said.

Jeff got the milk can, put the strainer on it, and started slowly pouring the milk from the bucket into the can. "Do I need to gather eggs too?" he asked.

"No, Panzy and I did that. Thank you anyway."

They soon completed the evening chores and prepared for bed. Jeff was first in bed, and after Judy checked on Panzy, who was sleeping on a pile of blankets on the floor at the foot of their bed, she joined him.

"I've been hearing some talk at the store," Jeff started. "They're building a large number of new GI houses up in Atherton. They're paying 75¢ an hour for men who can do labor and 85¢ an hour if you know how to swing a hammer. Men are making $45 to $50 a week! Maybe I should go up there for a while and try my hand at something besides soda jerk."

"What about your heart, honey? Wouldn't that kind of work put a strain on it? And Atherton is over fifty miles away, you'd never be home."

"I know, Judy, but think bout it. It's $45 a week! That's over $2,000 in a year. Just think what you could do with that. I shouldn't let a little heart murmur keep me from doing a better job of providing for you and Panzy."

"How would you get up there and back home again?"

"I've thought about that. I can hop on the freight train that goes through Dexter twice a week, headed north. It goes right through Atherton."

"I could sure use a new sewing machine." Judy sighed. "Let's sleep on it." She snuggled against Jeff's side. He gathered her into his arms and kissed her softly. They were soon asleep.

The large Rhode Island Red rooster, known fondly to the Stuart family as Red, sounded the morning alarm. Sometime during the night, Panzy had climbed into bed with them. Jeff felt a warm glow of happiness as he cuddled the small body of his daughter against himself. She was, of course, wet and in need of a fresh diaper.

"You go take care of Bossy," Judy told Jeff. "I'll take care of Panzy and get breakfast ready."

He kissed them both affectionately before plodding off to the bathroom.

Breakfast consisted of fried eggs, fried potatoes, biscuits, creamy gravy, hot coffee, and cold milk. "I sure could use a slab of ham or some bacon," Jeff said as he wiped the last smear of gravy from his plate with a crust of biscuit. "I think I'll save up to buy us a piglet. It could be large enough and fat enough by this winter for us to butcher."

"Where would we cure it, Jeff? We don't have a smokehouse. You are always getting these ideas."

"Well, my folks always had fresh pork, and so did your folks."

Judy was busy cleaning off the table. She bent and kissed him softly on the cheek. "I need you to plow a couple of rows in the garden before you go off to work this morning. It's time to put in some spinach, lettuce, onions sets, potatoes, and peas. I'll plant some of the long white radishes you like too."

"I need to fix that section of fence where the chickens got into your garden last year. I'll do that first, and if I have enough time before I go to work, I'll make you a couple of furrows."

"Thank you, honey."

Jeff always allowed himself thirty minutes to ride the six miles to work, but he could usually make it in just under twenty minutes. Fixing the garden fence had taken him longer than he expected, and after plowing only one row for Judy's garden, he was pumping hard against a strong west wind, trying to make it to work before the drugstore opened at nine. As he pedaled, his lunch bag bounced around in the basket on the front of his bicycle. He hadn't seen Judy make his lunch this morning, but he was sure it would be a jelly sandwich made from her homemade apple jelly on her thick sliced homemade bread.

He skidded to a stop on the sidewalk just outside the drug-store with two minutes to spare. Jeff was breathing hard and per-spiring even in the forty-degree early spring weather. He hurried inside, put on his apron, and readied his cash register.

Mr. Olsen, who was always at work hours before the drugstore opened, called to him. "Is that you, Jeff? Why are you breathing so hard?"

"Yes sir," Jeff panted. "I had to ride against a stiff wind this morning."

Mrs. Olsen came in at 1:00 p.m. to spell Jeff while he ate his lunch, and Jeff took his jelly sandwich to the rear of the store so he could talk to Mr. Olsen while he ate.

"I've been thinking, sir," he began. "If you could spare me for a little while, I'd like to try to get on as a hand up in Atherton where they're building all the new GI houses. I hear you can make as much as $45 a week! Well, sir, Judy and I could sure use the extra money now that we have Panzy to think about. I wouldn't want to leave you if it will work a hardship on you. You've been awfully good to me and to Judy."

"Of course, Jeff, I understand. You've been the best employee I ever had. I'd like to give you a raise, but the 25¢ an hour I'm paying you is as high as I can go right now. When do you think you'll want to go?"

"I heard some of the men who worked for that company last year say that they can't pour concrete until after the last freeze. That's probably not before mid-April, but I also heard they are already hiring ditch diggers and steel men. They pay 75¢ an hour for ditch diggers, and I think I can dig as much ditch as the next man."

"They also work a sixty-hour week!" Mr. Olsen replied. "At least that's what I've been told. Do you think you can handle that many hours of hard physical labor?"

"Yes, sir, I believe I can."

"Well, then I'll ask Mrs. Olsen to fill in for you until I can find a permanent replacement. You can continue working here until the end of the week. I'll have your pay ready for you at close of business Saturday. And Jeff, if you don't get the job up there, please come back and tell me. I'll hold your job open for you until I know for sure."

That evening, when Jeff arrived at home, he was hesitant to tell Judy what he had done. They had their usual conversations, finished their chores, enjoyed Panzy for a while until she fell asleep, and eventually, they were able to relax in bed.

"I got a row of potatoes planted today," Judy told him. "Can you make me some more rows in the morning?"

"Of course. I'll try to finish four or five for you." He reached and took her hand, rolling onto his side so that he could look into her eyes.

She smiled at him. "I love you," she whispered.

"Don't be too hasty," he told her. "You might not feel the same after you hear what I have to tell you."

She snuggled against him, an impish smile on her face. "Go ahead," she teased. "Test my love for you."

"I'm trying to be serious here," he scolded. "I told Mr. Olsen I just can't make it on $12 a week anymore. He told me he understood, and well…Saturday is my last day."

"He fired you?"

"No it's not like that. We agreed it would be a good idea for me to try to get on with the construction crew up in Atherton. If I can't, he promised to take me back. In the meantime, Mrs. Olsen is taking my place. I'll pack a few things and take the first freight that comes through town next week."

"Jeff, do you know any of the men who are working up there?"

"Yes, John Wilbanks is working there. He went up two weeks ago as soon as the earth thawed enough so they could start digging in it. And Jack Marley will be working as a finish carpenter when they get the houses up and ready for doors and trim and the like."

"Maybe there are others. Maybe someone has a car, so you all can come home Saturday night and then you could go to church with me and Panzy on Sunday. Atherton by car is just an hour or so away."

"We'll see how it all works out. Now let's get some sleep. Oh, and Judy, I love you too."

It seemed they had hardly closed their eyes when Red sounded the morning wake-up alarm. As Jeff stumbled out of bed and headed toward the bathroom, he mumbled, "One of these days Red is going to end up in the stew pot."

After morning chores and a hearty breakfast, Jeff got to work on pushing the hand plow through the fertile soil that was Judy's garden. He managed to make her six new furrows before he had to stop and ride off to work. The spring winds weren't as strong this morning, and he was at work at his usual time, ten minutes before nine.

The remainder of the week was tediously routine, with the only highlight being the daily progress of little Panzy. She helped her mother scatter and cover the seeds. Judy kept her close by her side, teaching her what she was doing and why. It seemed like Panzy understood, although she did dig up an onion set and try to eat it.

Each morning, Jeff plowed as many furrows as he could with the old hand plow, anxious to get her garden ready for planting. Each evening, he would hurry home from work as soon as he could. It seemed he was keenly aware that he would soon be gone from his family for days at a time, and he wanted to crowd as many hours of happiness into each day as he could.

At church on Sunday, Jeff saw John Wilbanks and his family arriving and took the opportunity to address him about the job in Atherton. John told him that a number of men met at the Greyhound bus depot in Dexter each weekday morning before 6:00 a.m. They all piled onto the back of a flatbed truck, and the driver took them to the construction site in Atherton. He explained that the driver brought some of them back each night, arriving at the Greyhound depot somewhere around 7:30 p.m.

He told him that the truck driver charged each man 50¢ per round trip and explained how it was cheaper than paying for a room and better than sleeping on the ground. Jeff promised he would be there before 6:00 a.m. that Monday.

On Monday morning, Jeff climbed out of bed at 4:00 a.m. He coaxed Bossy into giving just over two gallons of milk. He ate a hurried breakfast and got 50¢ from Judy, money that she took from her milk, cream, butter, and egg sales. He then climbed onto his bicycle and hurriedly pedaled to the Greyhound bus depot in Dexter.

There were thirteen of them huddled on the back of the truck under the canvas top as it made its way to Atherton. The ride in the predawn hours was windy and cold. Jeff was wearing a work jacket over his bib overalls, but it was hardly sufficient to ward off the cold wind as the old truck sped along the highway.

When they arrived at the work site, the foreman took his name and social security number and wrote it in a book that he carried. "We work a ten-hour day, six days a week—7:30 a.m. to 6:00 p.m." he explained. "We allow thirty minutes for lunch. We pay 75¢ for every hour you work, less what the government requires that we take out for federal old age benefits. We furnish the picks, shovels, and wheelbarrows. There are no advancements on salary, no lenience for coming to work late or drunk. We don't tolerate standing around, so if you smoke, save it till your lunch break. Any questions?"

"No, sir!" Jeff told him.

He then told Jeff to pick up a pick and a shovel and follow him to where several other men were digging a foundation ditch. It was a rude awakening for Jeff. In a very short time, he had gone from a tender-handed soda jerk to a ditch digger. At the lunch break at twelve-thirty, as he wet his blistered and bleeding hands in the cool water from the water can, he wished he had brought a pair of leather gloves.

Judy had thought to put two jelly sandwiches in his lunch sack, and he was thankful for them. The sugar seemed to restore his ebbing energy. The foreman blew a whistle at 1:00 p.m., and he went back to his pick and shovel. He had torn his lunch sack into strips and wrapped his hands with the brown paper from the sack. This gave him enough relief so that he could make the rest of the day. As he climbed onto the back of the truck for the ride back to Dexter that evening, he was dirty and tired. His muscles ached, and his hands were hurting badly.

It was just after 7:30 p.m., Monday, when Judy heard Jeff's bicycle rattle up to the front porch. She opened the front door and carried Panzy out onto the porch to meet him. Even though his face and clothes were covered with construction dirt, she hugged him tightly and kissed him lovingly as he took Panzy from Judy's arms. Even in his state of exhaustion, the closeness of his family seemed to give him new strength. He tossed Panzy carefully into the air a few times, catching her while listening to her giggle.

As they entered the house, Judy took Panzy from him. "Supper is ready when you are," she told him.

Later that night, after little Panzy was in bed, Judy cleaned and dressed his palms. She put Vaseline on his sunburned ears.

"You need a hat," she told him. "That cap only keeps the sun and hair out of your eyes. Wear a stocking cap over your ears tomorrow and let your cap out to fit over it. You have that old, nearly worn-out pair of leather gloves. You'll take them with you tomorrow. With your first paycheck, we'll get you a decent hat and some better gloves."

Jeff looked at his wife lovingly as they sat on the edge of the bed beside each other. He cradled her in his arms and kissed her willing lips. They looked at each other knowingly. For the next several minutes, Jeff forgot his tired aching muscles, his blistered hands, and his sunburned ears as he tenderly made love to his wife. Later, as she wound and set the clock, she told him, "You can sleep an hour longer in the morning. I'll take care of milk-ing Bossy."

When Jeff awakened the next morning, Judy already had his breakfast ready. As they kissed good-bye at the door, she handed him his lunch and 50¢ for the truck driver. "Be careful and come back home safe to us," she told him.

Tuesday for the construction crew was similar to the day before. Jeff was able to endure it about the same as Monday; the gloves did help some, and he didn't get any more sunburn on his ears, though the back of his neck did feel burned.

That evening, he was sitting on the rear of the truck bed as it pulled up in front of the Greyhound bus depot. He jumped off before it came to a complete stop and ran to his bicycle. He couldn't wait to be in the inviting arms of his wife and to see his lovely little daughter.

Judy seemed to be in a happy, joyful mood when she met him on the porch. They exchanged hugs and kisses before he picked Panzy up in his arms to love on her.

"Da da ome!" Panzy said.

"She's been asking about you all day," Judy told him. While Jeff washed up, she put supper on the table.

"What's this?" he asked as he looked at his plate. "Where did you get the trout?"

"Panzy and I walked down to the creek this morning for a couple of hours. I caught six very nice ones."

"I'm starved!" he said as he tore into his fish, fried potatoes, corn bread, and coleslaw. "Did Panzy catch any?"

"She helped me hold the pole."

Jeff looked at his little girl with admiration. He reached over and patted the top of her head softly. "You are just a doll, do you know that?" he asked.

Panzy smiled at him as if agreeing that she did indeed.

After the supper dishes had been cleaned up, Jeff gave Panzy her bath. She was soon fast asleep on her pallet. Jeff sat down near Judy, who was putting a patch on the knee of another pair of his overalls. He stretched his legs out and leaned back against the back of his chair, just trying to relax his sore aching muscles. Judy got up, went to the side cupboard, and got something. When she returned, she handed him a small piece of paper.

"Mr. Lovejoy came by this afternoon," she informed him.

Jeff was looking at the check in his hands. He just stared at it a long time before he finally began to speak. "This is made out to us. 'Pay to the order of Jeffrey and Judy Stuart, $10,000!' That can't be right. This is Panzy's money."

Judy laid her mending down in her lap, still holding the needle in her hand. "Mr. Lovejoy told me that they can't make the check out to a baby, and as her legal guardians, we are responsible for her and the money. He suggested that we spend it on Panzy, but he said the insurance company has no say in how we spend it. He brought back Panzy's birth certificate, our guardianship papers, and a photostatic copy of the death certificate of Myrtle O'Toole. I've already put them in the cedar chest. Do you want to see them?"

"No. I don't need to see them," Jeff replied. "Now let me get this straight. We could legally go spend this money on something like a tractor or a used car?"

"That's the way he explained it."

"Put it somewhere safe for the time being, Judy. When we get a chance, we need to take it to the bank in Dexter and cash it."

"What will we do with the money then?" Judy asked him seriously.

"I don't know. My father lost all of his money in the financial crash of 1929. He always told us, 'You just can't trust banks.' But we have to do something to keep it safe."

"I'll put it in the cedar chest with the other important papers," Judy promised.

Wednesday morning, Jeff found his muscles to be very sore, and he had difficulty getting out of bed. Some of the sores in his hands were still open and oozing. All day, he fought the urge to tell the foreman he was quitting, but by the time the day ended, he had worked the soreness out of most of his muscles. His palms, on the other hand, were hurting badly and healing slowly. As he rode his bicycle into the yard that night, he found his wife and daughter on the front porch, waiting to greet him, Panzy chortling her "da da ome" refrain.

After another of Judy's delicious home-cooked meals, he got down on the floor to play with Panzy, but he asked Judy to bathe her, as he was trying to keep from putting his sore hands into water for a prolonged amount of time.

Later, Judy put some healing ointment on his hands as they prepared for bed. "Here," she told him, gently putting a mitten on each of his hands. "I made you these soft cotton mittens today. I want you to keep them on your hands while you sleep. I went into town today to the co-op gin and bought you a new pair of heavy cotton gloves that you can take with you to work tomorrow."

"Thank you, sweetheart," he said, giving her a tender kiss. "What did you do with Panzy when you went into town?"

"She rode in the basket. I told her to hang on, and she did. She thought it was a lot of fun. I took her by Olsen's Drugstore, and Mrs. Olsen just fell in love with her. Mr. Olsen wanted to know how you were doing at the new job. I told him they were really working you hard. Oh, Mrs. Hardy stopped taking milk today. She said they just can't afford to pay 50¢ a gallon right now. I let her have a gallon for free. I told her if she didn't take it, I would have to throw it out."

"Her with all those kids. Did she say where Mr. Hardy is?"

"She told me he took off awhile back to go look for work, and she hasn't heard a word from him since. She don't even know if he's still alive."

"Children need their milk to grow up strong and healthy," Jeff said seriously. "Tell her she can keep getting the milk for the kids until Mr. Hardy gets back. Tell her we'll just run a tab if you think that will make it easier for her to accept it. Of course, we won't keep tabs."

Judy kissed him good night. He held her long and lovingly. "The only time I don't hurt anywhere is when you're here in my arms," he whispered.

"Not tonight," she told him. "You need to rest and let your hands heal."

He slowly released her from his embrace and turned onto his back. In a very short time, he was asleep.

Judy was still awake. She smiled to herself. *All this hard work has made Jeff more passionate,* she thought as she turned things over in her mind. *It's probably because he feels like a real man again. He's working at a difficult job among other men, finally earning a decent wage. Maybe he feels like he can at last properly take care of his little family. Of course, that's what it is. I don't want to discourage those feelings of success. I should probably be more receptive to his advances.* She set the clock and realized just how little time she had before she needed to get up and start everything all over again. She bent and checked Panzy before finally settling down for the night.

BIRTHDAYS

Jeff began to feel stronger, and the soreness in his muscles was soon gone. His hands healed and calloused. By April 18, Panzy's first birthday, he was routinely doing his sixty hours a week. Each payday, he would dutifully give Judy his paycheck after signing the back of it. She would then take it to the bank each Monday and cash it like she had done the check for the insurance money. But instead of putting the money from his checks into the cedar chest, she kept that money in the cracker tin on the top of the icebox with the money from her sales of dairy products and eggs. Also in that tin, she kept a small ledger and a pencil. She entered each deposit and each withdrawal meticulously.

Mr. Cogswell, the banker, had argued that she should put the insurance money and the money from Jeff's paychecks into some accounts there at the bank. She had declined to do so, mostly because of Jeff's distrust of banks, which was instilled into him by his father when he was very young.

On Thursday evening, April 18, as Jeff rode his bicycle into the yard, Panzy met him dressed up in a very pretty dress Judy had made just for the occasion. "It's her birthday," Judy explained.

"Happy Birthday!" Jeff told her, picking her up and hugging her.

Judy didn't want him to soil Panzy's new dress, but she noticed he was not as dirty as usual and remarked about it.

"We have running water at one of the sites now," Jeff explained. "I was able to wash up before I caught the truck."

Judy had made Panzy a small cake. After supper, she brought it to the table. She took a wooden match, lit it, and stuck it into the center of the cake flame side up. "Blow it out," she told Panzy.

Panzy blew out the flame then clapped her hands, as if applauding her own success. Judy and Jeff, taken by her happiness, applauded with her. Jeff's heart swelled with pride. As Judy cut a small slice of cake for Panzy, Jeff stooped and kissed Panzy on the cheek.

They all enjoyed a piece of cake before Panzy had to take her bath and go to bed. As Jeff put her on her pallet, he remarked to Judy, "Next year, I hope we can have ice cream with our cake. Maybe I'll be earning enough so we can get one of those ice cream makers."

"Maybe," Judy said. "We'll see. I need you to fix the basket on my bicycle so that Panzy can ride in it more easily. She's getting so big, and it's hard for her to sit in it all bunched up like that."

"I'll see what I can do," Jeff replied, heading for the front porch. He was gone most of an hour before he returned. "You'll need to put some padding in the basket, but I think she'll be able to ride in it more easily now."

As Jeff went to get ready for bed, Judy went to look at her bicycle basket. Jeff had cut two places out of the lower wires on the front of the basket for Panzy's legs to fit through. He had filed smooth the area where he cut off the wires. Then he had attached a board to the bottom of the basket for a seat. He had rounded the forward edge of the seat board with a rasp and attached another board horizontally to the rear of the basket for a backrest. *He is so clever,* Judy thought.

Jeff was almost asleep when Judy slipped into bed beside him. She snuggled up close to him. "Thank you," she said softly.

"For what?" he asked, turning toward her.

"For everything. For being my husband and for being a father to Panzy."

He reached to caress her, kissing her tenderly. "I don't need any thanks for that. They are the two easiest things I've ever done."

They were lying in each others arms. "I love you, Jeff."

He kissed her again. "I should thank you. I've never understood why you chose me. Fate should have made you a gentleman's wife."

They were silent for a while as Judy enjoyed the nearness. She kissed him softly. "You're all the gentleman I need or want."

He held her tenderly, breathing in her aroma. "I've been meaning to ask you," he whispered. "Have you been taking some magic pills?"

"No, of course not. What are you talking about?"

"Well, every since Panzy came to live with us, you seem to be getting younger and more beautiful each day."

"Oh, Jeff. You don't have to lie to me to get what you want!"

"No lie, no ulterior motive. I mean it. There's a new glow about you."

She kissed him long and lovingly. "Get some sleep now," she told him. "It will soon be tomorrow."

On Sunday, as the Stuarts rode their bicycles into the church yard just prior to the Easter service, Jeff noticed John Wilbanks drive up in a shiny new Ford. His wife was beside him wearing a new Easter bonnet and dress. As John got out of the new car, he called to Jeff proudly, "I just got it yesterday! Ain't it a beaut?"

"It sure is! What does an automobile like this cost?" Jeff asked as he walked around it.

"It cost $1,400! The bank loaned me the money."

"Wow, $1,400? That's a lot of money. How much do you have to pay the bank each month?"

"I'd rather not say, but I won't be riding with you guys on that cold truck anymore."

"Congratulations," Jeff told him, shaking his hand. "We'll miss you and your corny jokes." He turned and hurried to take his place beside Judy and Panzy in the church.

Before riding their bicycles back home after church, Jeff wanted to ride past all the car lots to look at the new automobiles. Seeing John Wilbank's new Ford had made him yearn for some better transportation for his family.

They looked at a new Ford. The price on the windshield was $1400. Across the street was another dealer with a new Dodge sitting out front. The price tag on the new Dodge was $1,487. Just up the street from the Dodge dealer was a new cream-colored four-door Chevrolet Fleetmaster for $1,212 that really caught his eye. He made several trips around it, kicking the tires and looking under the hood.

Panzy was hungry and soon grew restless, so they began pedaling toward home. "That's more than you can earn in six months," Judy admonished him as she recalled the way he had looked over the new Chevrolet.

"I know, but—"

"You always get so impatient about things," she scolded. "Someday, we'll get us a car. We don't have to get a new one, you know. Did you notice that little Ford roadster at the Ford place? The price on the windshield was just $250. It's a 1936 model, but it looked very nice."

"Trade bikes with me," Jeff interjected, changing the subject. "I want to take Panzy for a while." They traded bicycles, and Jeff started pedaling rapidly toward home. "Hold on, Panzy," he called. "We're going for a fast ride!"

Panzy laughed excitedly, her strawberry-blonde curls bouncing about her head as they sped down the pavement. Judy was right beside them on Jeff's bicycle. They were soon on the graded dirt road that led to their house. Once inside, Judy quickly fed Panzy and put her down for a nap.

Later, she and Jeff sat at the table, eating a late lunch. Judy had fixed a delicious meatloaf. Mashed potatoes, brown gravy, canned corn, a fresh spinach salad, and hot buttered rolls rounded out the remainder of the meal. As he finished the last bite, Judy took his hand and pulled him from his chair.

"Go clean the gravy off of your chin," she joked, "and meet me in the bedroom. I want to take a nap too."

Jeff did as she asked. As he returned from the bathroom, he found Judy already beneath the sheet. As he stripped to his shorts and slid under the sheet, he noticed she was not wearing her usual gown. Further investigation revealed she was not wearing anything at all. He quickly removed his shorts and tossed them onto a nearby chair.

It was getting dark outside when Panzy crawled up onto the bed and awakened him. Jeff kissed Judy awake. "That's the best nap I ever had," he told her. He slipped out of bed, put his shorts and trousers on, and picked up Panzy.

"You need a fresh diaper," he told her, placing her on the end of the bed to change her.

"I shouldn't have fallen asleep so soon afterward," Judy told him apologetically. "But you were holding me so tenderly." She kissed him on the cheek before hurrying off to the bathroom.

"I'll take Panzy and go gather the eggs," he called after her.

When he returned a short time later with Panzy and a basket of eggs, Judy was busy cleaning up the noontime dishes. She was singing softly to herself. She smiled happily at Jeff and Panzy as they entered. "How many eggs did you find?" she asked Panzy.

"An even dozen," Jeff answered for her. "They were already starting to roost, and old Biddy didn't like us disturbing her. She really put up a fuss." He got the milk pail and went back outside.

"Your daddy has to go milk the cow," Judy told Panzy as she placed her in her high chair.

"Cow?" Panzy asked.

A short time later, Jeff came in with a full pail of milk and did the straining. As he rinsed the pail and set it down, Judy asked him, "Do you remember the blue 1936 Ford roadster we saw today?"

"Yes, I remember it," Jeff answered her. "It was a tidy little car. You know the second seat is just in front of the spare tire. It's what they call a rumble seat."

"Yes," she acknowledged, "I know. And I also noticed it had new tires all around. Here, eat your supper."

Nothing more was said about cars for the rest of the evening. Jeff helped her clean up the kitchen after supper, and they talked about routine things. Panzy busied herself stacking canning jar lids on the kitchen floor nearby, Rover lying close beside her, his chin on the floor as he watched her.

They went to bed late that night, the nap having revived them. Even so, Jeff was soon fast asleep. Judy was lying awake, wondering if what she was plotting was the correct thing to do. She loved Jeff dearly and had never done anything behind his back. She would love to surprise him with a car, but $250! Maybe if she set aside a small sum each week from her milk fund, they could afford to buy it before the cold of winter came. She had always been the frugal one, and thus, she had almost talked herself out of it before she fell asleep.

Jeff was delighted that he had a meatloaf sandwich in his lunch sack that Monday. He noticed there was a note wrapped around it in Judy's neat handwriting. He picked it up and was about to read it just as a gust of wind carried it away. John Wilbanks was able to pick it up and read it aloud for all hands to hear. "I love you, Jeff!" he almost shouted. Some of the coarser men laughed; others smiled. Jeff smiled inside and out. "I love you too," he whispered, picturing Judy in his mind.

Over the next several weeks, Judy was kept busy with handling the dairy and egg sales, doing her housekeeping, tending her garden, doing her sewing, and being a mother to Panzy. She kept Panzy by her side whenever she was awake, talking to her and teaching her constantly. Panzy's vocabulary improved with each passing day.

Panzy had been walking since she was ten months old and was soon potty-trained. The little potty-chair that Jeff made for her was sitting in the bathroom, so she could go there anytime she realized there was a need. Judy had made her some little cotton panties, sewing elastic around each leg and at the waist. Panzy was soon adept at taking them off and putting them on. She still had some trouble with her dresses. Judy watched and marveled at her progress. Soon, it was the first topic of discussion at the supper table. "Panzy helped me pull these radishes and wash them," or "Panzy held her own fishing pole today."

Jeff always patted or kissed Panzy as he heaped praises upon her. She was a happy and healthy little girl.

Thursday night, June 13, after Jeff was sure Judy was fast asleep, he crept into the kitchen and got $50 from the cracker tin. He didn't make an entry into Judy's ledger and hoped she would not notice that the money was missing for the next several days.

During the lunch break on Friday, he persuaded John Wilbanks to take him to the Sears Roebuck store in downtown Atherton. There, Jeff purchased a brand-new Singer sewing machine. It cost him $49.50. It had a beautiful wooden cabinet and an electric motor instead of a foot treadle. He and John Wilbanks loaded it into John's car, and John promised him a ride home that evening.

It was nearly dark as they pulled into the yard. Jeff was feeling a bit guilty. He wished he had taken enough money so he could bring Judy a box of candy and some flowers too. This was her twenty-seventh birthday, and he was bringing her a tool for her work. *But it will lighten her load,* he thought to himself. *She has to pump that old treadle machine so hard and so long sometimes.*

As soon as John stopped the car in front of the house, Judy wiped her hands on her apron and took Panzy outside to see who it was. John helped Jeff unload the machine there in the yard then said a few words of greeting before making a hasty departure. Jeff carried the machine up the front steps and inside of the house before stopping to hug and kiss his wife and child.

"Happy birthday, honey. I hope you like it," Jeff remarked as he lovingly hugged Judy.

Judy returned his embrace before she touched the smooth finish of the wooden cabinet. "Thank you. It's a beautiful little table. Is it for Panzy's room?" she asked.

"No," Jeff told her. "Lift the top."

Judy lifted the top and looked into the well that held the body of the sewing machine. "It's a new sewing machine!" she exclaimed.

Jeff lifted the machine into position. "The inside surface of the top now becomes your worktable," he explained.

"Where is the treadle?"

"It doesn't have one! See? It's electric!"

"Oh, it's beautiful, Jeff, I can't wait to use it!" She hugged him tightly around the neck and kissed him affectionately.

Jeff picked Panzy up and loved on her for a while as they made their way into the kitchen. "What did you and mommy fix for supper?" he asked her.

Judy's excitement lasted late into the night. As they lay in bed that night, Jeff attempted to assuage his guilt. "I wanted to bring you roses and chocolates too, Judy. I love you so very much. Are you sure you're okay with just the sewing machine? I took the money from the cracker tin to pay for it."

Instead of a verbal answer, Judy rolled on top of him, took his face in her hands, and kissed him passionately.

PANZY HAS MORNING SICKNESS?

Judy was in the garden with Panzy, gathering some spinach, lettuce, green onion tops, and radishes. The potatoes were blooming, and the corn was to her shoulder. Small nubs showed what would soon be growing into edible ears. Suddenly, Judy felt nauseated. She turned away from Panzy and lost her breakfast. She touched the inside of her wrist to her forehead. *No fever,* she thought.

"Let's go inside, Panzy," she said. "I think Mommy is having a little heat stroke."

They carried their vegetables inside and put them in a pan of water to soak before Judy sat down on the couch with a cold cloth on her brow. She tried to hold Panzy there on the couch with her, but Panzy wanted to get down and take the pots and pans out of the cabinets and put them back in. Judy could see her from where she sat. She began to search her mind. She remembered things her mother had told her and things she had heard other women say.

Could it be true? she thought. She had been so busy being a mother to Panzy and taking care of Jeff she couldn't remember if or when. She got up and went to look at the calendar hanging on the inside of the bathroom door. She had not marked anything in May or anything this month. But they had been married for more than four years without the slightest hint of a pregnancy, and she thought herself to be unable to conceive. She walked back into the living room. "That nap on Easter Sunday!" she stated aloud as she walked past the kitchen door.

"Ut, Mommy?" Panzy asked.

Judy was used to talking to Panzy like she was another adult. "I think you may be going to have a baby brother or baby sister next year," she told her. "Would you like that?"

"Okay, Mommy," Panzy replied. "I ungry."

"Put all the pots and pans back in the cabinet, and I'll fix you a sandwich."

"Okay, Mommy."

Judy had boiled some eggs earlier for egg salad sandwiches, but as she began peeling and chopping up the eggs, she was suddenly overcome by the smell and had to return to the bathroom for another bout of throwing up. Through sheer willpower, she eventually got the egg salad mixed. She cut the crust off a slice of homemade bread and fixed Panzy a sandwich. She placed her in her high chair and gave her the sandwich and a glass of cold milk. Judy herself ate some crackers with a cup of hot tea. Eventually, her stomach began to settle down.

She was delighted to see Mrs. Hardy's old Ford Model T truck pulling up in front of the house. She had her three younger children with her. As she climbed down, Judy saw that she was carrying a cardboard box in her arms. "I brought back some of your milk jars," she explained as soon as she saw Judy.

"Thank you," Judy replied. "Please come in for a minute. I'd like to talk to you."

Rover had gone to the truck, barking and wagging his tail. The Hardy children climbed down and began petting him.

Mrs. Hardy, seeing that her children were being entertained, agreed to sit and talk awhile.

"I haven't even told Jeff about this," Judy started, "but I think I may be having a baby."

"Congratulations, dear."

"The thing is," Judy went on, "I got sick to my stomach this morning. Did that ever happen to you?"

"The first two, yes. Then I was okay for the next two, but very bad again when I was pregnant with little Floyd. The thing to do is get yourself some lemons. Eat 'em, suck on 'em, squeeze 'em into your mouth. They seem to help me a lot. Keep some crackers by your bed and stay away from the spicy foods. You may have to get your husband to do a lot of the cooking. Sometimes, the cooking smells will set you off. It usually all passes by the time you get to your fourth month."

"Oh my, that's probably not until August!"

Rover started barking again, and they checked to see the reason for it. The three Hardy children were running around the truck while Rover playfully chased after them.

Judy had placed the box of empty jars on the kitchen table. "I talked to my husband about your situation," she explained to Mrs. Hardy. "He agreed you should not be depriving your children of milk. We are willing to let you have all the milk you need and let you just run a tab."

"That's sweet dear, but I may never have the money to pay you."

"That's okay. I'm sure the Lord will provide."

Judy got two gallons of milk out of the icebox and put them into the box Mrs. Hardy had brought. "Can you use a couple dozen eggs?" she asked.

"Oh, Lord bless you," Mrs. Hardy said, giving Judy a hug.

They started toward the door—Mrs. Hardy carrying the box with the four half gallon jars of milk and Judy carrying the eggs. "Now remember what I told you about the lemons," Mrs. Hardy reminded her as they reached the truck.

She got her children all settled, told the oldest child—a boy of about six—to watch the spark and throttle, then she went to the front of the truck and gave the crank a couple of quick turns. The old Model T belched to life. She climbed in, turned the truck around, and headed back toward the Hardy farmhouse.

Judy stood and watched it disappear out of sight. Panzy suddenly appeared beside her. The loud voice of the rather large Mrs. Hardy had awakened her from her nap. "I'm glad you are awake," she told her. "We are going into town to the IGA. You go to the potty while mommy fixes her hair."

At the IGA, Judy found some lemons. She also got a twenty-five-pound sack of flour and two pounds of ground beef. "That's going to crowd you out of the basket," she told Panzy.

As Mr. Simmons rang up her groceries, he remarked about how big Panzy had grown.

"Each time I see her, she seems to get bigger and prettier," he remarked.

Judy smiled with pride. "Panzy, say thank you to Mr. Simmons."

"Ank oo, me Sims," Panzy said, smiling up at him.

"How old is she now?" Mr. Simmons asked.

"Fourteen months," Judy answered proudly.

"She talks very grown-up for someone of her age. You're doing very well with her. I'm sure Jeff is just as proud."

"Yes, he is. Thank you, Mr. Simmons."

Judy raised the pillow that was Panzy's seat cushion and laid the flour sack in the basket underneath it. She put Panzy in the basket seated on the cushion above the flour and tucked the bag of lemons on one side of her and the package of ground beef on the other. "Hold on, Panzy," she instructed as she straddled the bike and started for home. As she passed the Ford dealership, she noticed the little blue Ford Roadster was still there, but the price on the window had been reduced to $235. *That's better,* she thought, *but it is still a lot more than I have been able to save.*

Judy had been putting aside $10 a week from Jeff's paycheck and her milk and egg money for the past nine weeks. As she rode home, she thought about how she might be able get the little Ford for Jeff's birthday, the tenth of August, which was now less than two months away.

Judy had never learned to drive a car, yet Mrs. Hardy seemed to have no difficulty. Judy was sure it would be an easy thing to master. She recalled people saying things like "letting out the clutch," "slamming on the brakes," or "giving it the gas." She had only wondered what those things meant. She remembered that Jeff had told her he had mastered it in one lesson. But then, Jeff was so intuitive.

Judy had first seen Jeff when she was a girl of fourteen just starting her sophomore year in high school. Jeff was a seventeen-year-old senior, very popular with all the high school girls. Judy, plain and studious, never thought she had a chance with the popular Jeff, but for some reason, he was attracted to her. She had looked up to him with a sort of hero worship at first, but soon, the attraction turned into something more. They dated sporadically for more than five years, whenever they found it possible to get together. They were finally married June 8, 1941, just before her 22nd birthday, which was on June 14. Jeff, at the time, had been twenty-four.

Judy rode into the yard and parked her bicycle under the tree. She helped Panzy out of the basket and gathered her groceries. "This is a new print on the flour sack," she told Panzy. "I think it will make you a nice new gown. Here, you want to carry the lemons for Mommy?"

It was now the later part of June, and the evening sun didn't go down until later, and it came up earlier as well. At the job site, there was talk of working twelve hours a day. Returning GIs and the expanding oil fields surrounding Atherton had caused a demand for the houses, and the construction company, Denton & Briggs, was anxious to complete as many as possible in as short a time as possible. There was some rumblings among the crew and talk of organizing or joining a union. A compromise was reached with the crewmen agreeing to work five twelve-hour days, from

6:30 a.m. to 7:00 p.m., on Mondays through Fridays and only six hours, from 6:30 a.m. to 12:30 p.m., on Saturdays. This increased Jeff's hours from sixty hours per week to sixty-six.

On the job, Jeff was eager and quick to learn. In just a few weeks, he had gone from ditch digger to steel tying, then to hod carrier, and eventually, to carpenter helper. When the foreman learned he could swing a hammer with the best of them, he was put on the framing crew. This brought with it a raise of 10¢ per hour. His ability to read blueprints and vision the results was soon noticed by the construction supervisor, and he was promoted to crew foreman with another raise of 5¢ per hour. By the time they began working the sixty-six-hour week, he was drawing 90¢ an hour and bringing home nearly $60 a week.

It was 8:20 p.m. and already getting dark when Jeff rode into the yard. Judy and Panzy met him on the front porch. He kissed them hello happily.

"Your supper is ready when you are," she told him.

"Bergstrom wants to start charging a dollar a day for the truck ride," he told her as he cut a big piece of the eggplant parmesan.

"You'll just have to pay it," Judy told him.

"I know, but I wanted you to know that I'll need more money each day. So what did you and Panzy do today?"

"Panzy picked the fresh greens for your salad, helped me carry in some groceries, restacked the pots and pans in the cupboards, and helped me gather the eggs."

"It won't be long before she'll be able to do all those things on her own." He patted Panzy on her head and leaned over to kiss her on the cheek. "My big girl," he said admiringly.

Panzy smiled at him. "Da da," she said, grabbing his hand and transferring parmesan sauce to it.

Jeff took his napkin and wiped both her hand and his. He smiled at Judy who was looking at him strangely.

"Da da," Judy said. "You really enjoy being a daddy, don't you?"

"Of course! But I wonder if I'm as good a father as her real daddy would have been. Fatherhood is an awesome responsibility."

"She's happy, healthy, and well-fed," Judy stated.

"And loved as much or more than he could have ever loved her." He touched her little back tenderly once more before falling silent.

Judy sat and looked at him. She was sure Panzy loved him as much as he loved her. *But not as much as I love him right now,* she thought.

Jeff got up, scraped his plate into Rover's bowl and put his plate into the sink. He kissed his wife and told her how good the meal had been. "Bossy need milking?" he asked.

"No, all the chores have been done. Could you bathe Panzy while I finish up in here?"

He picked up the happy little girl and carried her to the bathroom. She needed to use the potty first. After she had her bath and was asleep on her pallet, Jeff took his shower. He was stretched out on the bed just letting his tired sore muscles relax when Judy came out of the bathroom in her gown and joined him on the bed.

"I've been thinking," Jeff remarked conversationally. "I need to make Panzy a bed. She can't continue to sleep on a pallet for the rest of her life."

He reached for his wife. As he tried to put his arms around her, he accidentally, momentarily, yet roughly hit one of her breasts.

"Be careful when you touch me there, Jeff," Judy warned him in a soft voice. "They have been awfully tender lately."

"Have you hurt yourself in some way? Did Bossy butt you?"

"No." She laughed. "It's just the way they get when someone's going to have a baby."

There was silence as Jeff began to comprehend the magnitude of what Judy had just said. "Wait!" he exclaimed excitedly. "What did you just say?"

"I haven't confirmed it yet, but there are a lot of indications that you are going to be a daddy again in January."

"Is it safe for me to hug you?"

"As tightly as you wish."

He hugged her and kissed her affectionately. He put his hand softly on her lower abdomen, just below her navel. "There's a baby in there?" he asked excitedly.

"Yes, I think so. You remember Easter Sunday when we almost woke Panzy from her nap? I think that's when it happened."

"We have to say a special prayer of thanks at church this Sunday. You know, Judy, I thought there was something wrong with me. I wasn't healthy enough to go into the service. I've only recently been able to earn a decent living for us, never been able to get you pregnant, but now," he almost shouted, "now, I feel like a man!"

"Calm down, Papa Stuart." She grinned. "You'll wake Panzy."

"I wonder if it's too early to pass out cigars."

She laughed at him. "I think you should at least wait until the rabbit dies. Now hush and go to sleep."

Jeff cradled her lovingly in his arms as he drifted off to sleep.

With Jeff now getting home around 2:00 p.m. each Saturday, he was able to get some things done around the house. He built a nice bed frame for Panzy. Judy sewed a mattress tick for it and stuffed it with cotton. She fixed up the second bedroom for her while Jeff built some low shelves. He built Panzy a wardrobe with two hanger rods, one low enough for her to easily reach. One evening, he drew plans for a smokehouse and made a materials list. He built and hung a porch swing.

Judy had been putting aside $10 every week since Easter when she saw how excited Jeff had been about John Wilbank's new car.

It had been more than seventeen weeks, and her little nest egg had now grown to $170. On Saturday, August 10, she got Panzy ready early. She took $175 and put it into her purse. She placed Panzy into the bicycle basket and pedaled to Leonard Bass Ford. When she and Panzy were introduced to Mr. Bass, she smiled her prettiest. Panzy climbed up onto the chair to Judy's left and began quietly playing with her rag doll.

"What can I do for you, Mrs. Stuart?" he asked.

"I've come about the 1936 Ford Roadster," Judy began, using her most convincing business voice.

"That's a great little car!" Mr. Bass told her. "Low mileage, new tires, an almost new top."

"Yes, but it's over ten years old," Judy stated knowingly.

"Ah, yes, but it has been well-cared for. That's what we call a one-owner car!"

Judy continued to smile. "I have $175 cash that I'll give you for it right now."

"I have it priced at $235," he told her.

"Yes, sir, and you've had the price on it since early June."

Mr. Bass squinted his eyes, rolled his unlit cigar—first, against his lips with his tongue, and then between his fingers—as he looked at her and then Panzy. He returned the cigar to his mouth, took a pencil, and began to do some figuring on a large lined tablet lying on his desk in front of him. Finally, he nodded, looked up, smiled at Judy, and said, "You've bought yourself a car, Mrs. Stuart. We just have to fill out a form or two, and you can drive it home. I'll even have my mechanic see to it that the gasoline tank is full."

"I've never learned to drive," Judy told him. "Could you have someone drive it to my home for me?"

"There's nothing to it! I'll show you how to drive, and you can drive it home yourself."

They completed the transaction, Judy folded the ownership papers and put them into her purse, and the three of them went out to the car.

During her driving lesson, she let the clutch out too fast and killed the engine a few times. She revved the engine, popped the clutch, and spun the rear tires a few times, but very soon, she had mastered the clutch and foot feed interaction. She ground the transmission gears a few times before finally being able to shift smoothly. The whole process, from sales to driving, had taken just over two hours. The mechanic helped her put her bicycle into the rumble seat.

With Panzy in the seat beside her, Judy drove determinedly out of the car lot at the Ford dealership and into traffic. Fifteen minutes later, she was pulling into the yard in front of their house. She parked the car around in back near the rear door. She turned off the ignition switch and just sat there for a few minutes, listening to Rover bark at the new car. She wasn't sure if the butterflies in her stomach were from the excitement of the day or if they were caused by her pregnancy.

After relaxing a few minutes, she climbed out and up onto the rear of the car and pulled her bicycle out of the rumble seat. Then she got Panzy out of the car and took her inside. "Today is your daddy's birthday!" she told her. "We need to bake him a cake. I'll let you do some of the decorating after the cake cools."

Lately, Jeff had been catching the truck at the curve in the highway a mile and a half from his house. He had just been walking that distance, but he arrived home earlier than he would have had he ridden his bicycle from the bus station. He walked rapidly this Saturday afternoon and arrived at his front door at exactly 2:00 p.m. Panzy heard him on the front porch and ran to greet him. He picked her up, and they kissed. He hugged her and carried her into the house.

"You taught Panzy to kiss?" he asked as he kissed and hugged Judy.

"No. Why do you ask?"

"She just kissed me on the lips!"

"It was a birthday kiss. I guess she learned it from watching us."

"That's a happy thought. What have you girls been up to today? How's the morning sickness thing?" he asked, patting her expanding abdomen.

"I'm getting better at contending with it." Judy smiled.

"That was a delicious sandwich today. What was it?"

"Tuna salad. I'm glad you liked it. I nearly threw up two or three times while I was making it."

"Listen, honey, I appreciate you wanting to fix me new and wonderful things for my lunches, but don't fix them if they're going to make you sick."

Judy hugged him around the neck and kissed him again. "I do it because I love you."

Panzy was tugging on his hand. He stooped and lifted her into his arms, holding her with one arm as he put the other around Judy. "I am truly blessed," he proclaimed. "Have you gathered the eggs yet?"

"No, we haven't."

"Come on, Panzy," Jeff said, putting her down, "Go get the egg basket so we can go gather the eggs."

"I'll go with you," Judy volunteered.

Panzy was carrying the basket and Jeff was holding the door for them when he noticed the car. "Whose car is this?" he asked.

"Let's look at the title and see," Judy said, opening the car door and getting the papers that proved ownership. "Here, you read them," she said, pretending she had something in her eye.

Jeff read his own name aloud.

"Happy Birthday, darling!" Judy chortled.

"What? When? How did you do this?" Jeff asked, forgetting all about gathering the eggs.

"I bought it for you today!" Judy stated excitedly. "I paid just $175 for it! I talked Mr. Bass down from $235!"

"So how did it get here? Who drove it home for you?"

"I drove it home," she bragged. "Me and Panzy."

"Wow! I don't know what to say." He opened the driver's-side door and got in. He looked at all the dashboard instruments, checked the pedals, and looked all around. He got out and opened the rumble seat and climbed in and looked it over. "I think it will be a great family car," he said. "We should be able to fit five kids back here easily." He climbed out and kissed Judy affectionately.

"You really like it?" she asked.

"Yes, of course! Come on! Let's go for a drive."

They all three happily climbed in. Jeff had to acquaint himself with the differences from Mr. Olsen's panel truck, but soon, he was driving around and around the house while Rover chased and barked. Finally, he drove out onto the road in front of their house and spent about fifteen minutes road testing the new car and honing his driving skills. Suddenly, he remembered the fact that they were supposed to be gathering eggs. He drove them back to their house and parked in the shade of the big chestnut tree.

"We need to get those egg gathered," Jeff said, picking Panzy up and walking backward toward the house so he could keep his eyes on his new car.

Judy walked happily along beside him, her arm looped through his, a big smile on her face. *It really made him happy*, she thought. *I'm so glad it did. He works so hard for us.*

Later at supper, Judy brought out the cake she and Panzy had made. Jeff smiled as he read what was written in the icing. "Happy birthday, Daddy," it read. He turned to Panzy. "Did you write this?" he asked.

She nodded vigorously.

"I guided her finger, but she did the writing," Judy explained. "We had to stop several times and wash the finger because she kept sticking it in her mouth so she could lick the icing off of it."

Jeff kissed Panzy while Judy was cutting the cake. He stood and went over to Judy. He placed his arm around her. "Just ten months ago, I considered myself a failure and a very poor man, with just a beautiful and loving wife," he began. "Today, on my thirtieth birthday, I consider myself the richest man in the world."

"And you accomplished all of this in just ten months?" Judy asked.

"No, *you* accomplished it all! You and Panzy. Thank you from the bottom of my heart. This is a birthday I will never forget."

As they lay in bed that night and Jeff was lovingly holding his wife in his arms, she turned to him. "Jeff," she whispered, "you should have seen Panzy today. I had a bout of morning sickness, and when I stood up from the commode and went to wash my face, she leaned over the commode, holding her stomach and moaning. Then she made a noise like she was throwing up and said, 'Oh, I sick!' She was having pretend morning sickness!"

"She wants to be just like her mother." Jeff smiled. "You have a great amount of responsibility there, Judy." As he kissed her good night, he could feel the smile on her lips.

On Sunday, the Stuart family arrived at church in their new car. Jeff drove up in front as proudly as if he were driving a brand-new Lincoln Continental. He sang the hymns with new gusto. He had so much to be thankful for—his lovely wife, who was with child, his beautiful daughter, his job that was finally paying him enough so he might get a little bit ahead, his health, and his life. When the collection basket was passed around, he put an extra $2 in it along with his tithe envelope. Jeff was a happy and contented man.

PIANO LESSONS

At four months, Judy was now showing. She had designed and made a dress with a high waist and many ruffles all around. This hid her lower body, but her breasts were obviously beginning to swell. Many of the women wanted to know just when the baby was due. Judy was predicting mid-January.

Although Jeff now had his own means of transportation, he preferred to save his gasoline and leave the car for Judy to use. For the remainder of the summer and fall, he continued to ride the truck to the construction site.

One September day, as Judy was singing to Panzy, trying to teach her a new song, she was surprised by the voice of Mrs. Hardy coming from the front porch.

"Hello!" Mrs. Hardy called.

"I'm sorry, I didn't hear you. We were canning some peas and singing," Judy replied. "Please, come in."

"I heard you singing and hesitated to bother you," Mrs. Hardy said as she set the box of empty jars on a chair.

"I'm not sure we were singing true pitch. I often wished I had a piano so I could teach Panzy to sing on key."

"Umm," Mrs. Hardy replied, "I think we can fix that. I have an old upright piano in my house. It was my mother's, and it was in the house when Mr. Hardy and I moved in with her. Now that she's gone, no one ever plays it anymore. It's probably out of tune, but it's in very good shape. If you want it and can find some way to haul it over here to your house, then it's yours."

"Oh, I couldn't do that. Let me pay you something for it."

"Oh, no, dear, you and Mr. Stuart have been so generous to me with the milk and all, I want you to have it! Now that's settled!"

"Thank you ever so much, Mrs. Hardy. I'll let Jeff know, and we'll try to get some men to help us haul it up from your house this Saturday after Jeff gets home from work."

"I'll dust it off and get it ready for you," Mrs. Hardy replied. "Do you play piano?"

"Yes, a little. My mother played, and she taught me the basics, but I haven't played for years. How many gallons do you need today?" Judy inquired.

"Whatever you can spare, dear. Beggars can't be choosers."

"Oh, don't talk like that," Judy scolded her as she placed five half gallon jars of milk into the box. "Do you need any butter or eggs? Of course you do." Judy put a pound of butter in the box and a sack of eggs on the table beside the box.

"May the lord always bless you," Mrs. Hardy said, giving Judy a motherly hug.

"How are your children? Have you heard anything from Mr. Hardy?" Judy inquired.

"Oh, they keep me hopping. Earnest, you know, my oldest boy, wants to join the army when he turns eighteen next month. The older three girls are a lot of help around the house, but going through the change from girl to woman has them bickering a lot. The younger three children, the ones I have with me now, require a lot of watching. What one don't think of to get into the other two will."

"And Mr. Hardy? Have you heard from him?"

"Not a word! He wasn't much help around the house anyway. He was more like my eighth and oldest kid," she laughed heartily. "Well, I should get this milk home before it spoils. Thank you again and don't forget the piano."

"Oh, I won't. Thank you, Mrs. Hardy."

Once again, Judy helped Mrs. Hardy to the truck with her things. Panzy and Rover trailed along behind them.

"It's time to finish this canning process and go pick some roasting ears for your daddy's supper tonight," Judy addressed Panzy. "We'll have that and sliced tomatoes, cantaloupe wedges, boiled potatoes, and roast beef. How does that sound?"

"Good!" Panzy replied.

"Come here, Panzy," Judy suddenly stated. "I want you to feel something. Put your hand right here on Mommy's stomach. There, did you feel that?"

Panzy nodded.

"That was your baby brother or sister kicking."

Panzy looked at her questioningly.

"That's right, Panzy. There's a baby in here."

Panzy put her hand back on her mother's stomach, hoping to feel the baby kick again. Eventually, her patience was rewarded. She looked up at Judy, smiled widely, and exclaimed, "Baby!"

Jeff and one of his neighbors who owned a truck were able to move the old upright piano to the Stuart home on Saturday. Judy found that the music teacher at the high school could tune a piano, and soon, Judy and Panzy were spending an hour each day at the piano, singing and playing. Even with her expanding stomach Judy was able to easily reach the keys and pedals. The lessons her mother had taught her had not been totally forgotten, and soon, she was playing quite well. Panzy's fingers were very small, but Judy was able to teach her some two finger drills. Panzy was like a dry sponge, soaking up everything her mother taught her. Judy was so proud of her; she had long ago forgotten that she wasn't her birth child.

As the garden matured, Judy spent a number of hours canning what vegetables she could. She dug the potatoes, onions, carrots, and turnips and put them in the cellar for storage and easy access for winter meals. At every step, Panzy was there, listening to her mother teach. Panzy's questions were testimony to her understanding and retention of the information Judy was conveying to her.

In a large crock, Judy put up some shredded cabbage to ferment and become sauerkraut. She canned many jars of pickled cucumbers and beets. She canned some carrots and peas together and put some small onions in with some of the green beans when she canned them. There were many jars of sweet corn. The empty canning jars from the cellar shelves were eventually all replaced with full ones. The corn that had matured before they could eat it or can it was left in the garden to dry and later used as chicken and cow feed. Judy shelled and sacked the mature dried beans and kept the sack in a cupboard in the kitchen.

One Saturday afternoon in late October, when Judy was more than six months pregnant, she and Jeff and little Panzy gathered the last ears of dry corn and pulled all the pumpkins. They moved the pumpkins behind the shed and dumped the corn ears in a pile near the back porch.

For several hours, Jeff sat on the steps with a bucket between his legs, twisting the kernels off of the cobs. He poured the kernels from the filled buckets into burlap sacks and put them in the shed. The cobs and shucks he scattered over the most barren section of Judy's garden plot. He had no more than just finished this task when it started to rain.

"Perfect timing," Jeff remarked as he came into the house. He picked up the milk bucket and headed out to milk Bossy. Before he left, he put the egg basket on his arm.

"I go gada duh eggs," Panzy said.

"Not this time, honey," he explained. "It's raining pretty hard. You stay in the house and help your mother."

The darkening sky had sent the chickens to roost early, and he had another tussle with old Biddy before retrieving her egg. "I'll ask Judy if you can have some eggs to sit on," he told her as he placed her back in the nest. "Time we had some replacement hens around here anyway." Red, hearing the fuss, had jumped down and was strutting around Jeff's legs in a menacing manner. "You spur me, you old codger, and we'll have stewed rooster for sure," Jeff told him.

He took the eggs to the shed and placed them atop a stack of hay bales. Bossy was restless because of the rain, but he soon calmed her and managed to get a reasonable amount of milk from her. As he milked, he once again let his mind wander.

We got Bossy just after we were married. She calved in August or September, so she has been producing milk for over five years now. She should produce milk for six years total. That means we have to dry her up next year and have her bred again. If she has a bull calf, we'll fatten it up for beef. A nice heifer, and we might have another milk cow.

Suddenly, there was a lightening strike nearby, followed by a loud clap of thunder. Bossy got extremely restless and stopped giving her milk. Jeff stood up and turned her loose. "There you go, old gal," he said. "I got most of it anyway."

At supper, he and Judy ate silently, both tired from the day. Finally, he asked Panzy if she wanted some more milk. She nodded, holding out her glass. As he poured the milk for Panzy, he remarked to Judy, "Bossy only has about another good year of production before we have to turn her dry. Do you want to look for another cow for your milk customers before we have to breed Bossy?"

"We could never find another cow as good as Bossy," Judy replied. "Her milk is so high in cream and butter fat, and it tastes so good! But I know you're right. We can't keep milking her forever."

"Another thing," Jeff went on, just keeping the conversation going. "Biddy didn't want to give up her egg tonight. Do you think it's too cold to let her sit on some?"

"Now, Jeff, you're the one who took agriculture in school."

"I know, spring time, but if you have a warm brooder house, you can hatch chickens anytime of the year. I was just feeling sorry for old Biddy. She's out there, challenging me each time I take her egg, while you're in here carrying your brooder around with you." He patted Judy on her tummy affectionately.

Changing the subject, he remarked, "This rain came just at the right time for your garden. As soon as it dries up enough, I'll get Clifford Dorman to bring his tractor over here and turn under all the vines, stalks, and stubble. In no time, we should be able to get some big fat earthworms out of there for fishing bait. By spring, you'll have fertile soil again."

Judy finished cleaning off the table and went to the back door putting on her shawl.

"Where are you going in this rain?" Jeff asked her.

"I want to get a nice pumpkin so I can make some pies. And maybe one to carve for Halloween."

"I'll do that for you," Jeff cautioned her as he stood up and started toward the backdoor.

"No," Judy said, "I want to pick them out myself."

"Stubborn woman! Don't you hurt yourself!"

Panzy wanted to go with her mother, but Jeff held her back, telling her it was bath time. Judy made two trips in the dark, carrying each pumpkin back to the steps. By the time Jeff got Panzy bathed and into bed, Judy was in the kitchen, admiring the pumpkins. It appeared she was going to clean out one of the pumpkins and cut it up right then.

"Stop that and come to bed," Jeff admonished her.

"I'm not tired. I'll just lie awake."

"Then read, but please don't start making pumpkin pies tonight!"

"Wouldn't you like one for Sunday dinner?"

"Not at the expense of your health." He put his arm around her and coaxed her toward their bedroom. "I wish you wouldn't decide to do all these time-consuming tasks at bedtime."

It was cold enough on Sunday for them to run the heater in the car, but it could hardly hold its own against the cold air leaking into the passenger compartment around the loosely fitting top where it met the windows. Luckily, it was a mere ten-minute drive.

As they moved into the pew, Judy sat next to Mr. Cogswell from the bank. Panzy was between her and Jeff, and Jeff sat on the end of the pew. Before the service started, Mr. Cogswell told them he would really like to talk to them about some important bank business. "Could you come in and see me around nine o'clock tomorrow morning?" he asked.

"I'll be at work," Jeff told him. "Could you talk to Judy? She can let me know all about it."

"Of course, that will be fine. I'll see you at nine o'clock tomorrow morning then," he said, smiling at Judy.

Mrs. Cogswell leaned forward so as to see around her husband and took special notice of Panzy before smiling at all of them.

All during the service, Jeff worried about the important bank business. They had inherited the house from Judy's Aunt Betty. There had been a lien against it for some back taxes, but they had paid all of that. He was sure Judy was current on the taxes. What could it be? He was jarred back to the present when he was called upon to help with the collection baskets. As he stood in front of the pulpit with his head bowed while the minister prayed over the tithes and offerings, he slipped his tithes out of his pocket and dropped them quietly into his collection basket.

On their way home after service, Panzy was seated beside him. As he shifted into high gear, he purposefully let his hand slip off of the knob so he could tickle her on the knees. She giggled delightedly. He put his hand back on the knob and let it slip off again with the same results.

They had done that several times when Judy remarked, "Your daddy used to play that same game with me back when I was in high school."

Jeff put his hand back on the knob and let it slip off again, only this time, he reached across Panzy and tickled Judy's knees. Her knees were very ticklish, and she fought to move his hand away. "Stop, Jeff." She giggled. "Do you want me to wet myself?"

Jeff reluctantly removed his hand. He continued grinning the rest of the way home.

After lunch, Panzy went down for her nap, and Jeff and Judy went to their bed to rest. "I want to get these tight clothes off of me," she complained. She pulled a large loose-fitting gown over her head then undressed completely from beneath it.

"Why are you undressing in a tent?" he asked her.

"It's light in here, and I don't feel very good about my body right now."

"If you'd asked me, I would have closed my eyes."

"Really?"

"Absolutely. I would have closed them—one at a time," he joked.

She settled down on the bed beside him, snuggling as close as she could. "Do you still love me?" she asked.

"Yes, my love."

"Even with my enormous stretched stomach?"

"More than ever before." He kissed her tenderly.

Judy closed her eyes and breathed a big sigh. "I love you too."

It was still very cold on Monday morning, and Jeff would have driven the little Ford Roadster to work in Atherton for the first time, but he knew Judy needed to get to the bank. He waited in the cold at the curve in the highway about ten minutes before the truck arrived. He had told the driver that when it got cold enough, he would start driving himself, and if he wasn't there, he should just go on without him. Thus he was there early so as to not miss his ride.

Judy dressed Panzy warmly yet prettily and made herself presentable before heading off to the bank. She had taken all the papers pertaining to the house out of the cedar chest and was carrying them in one hand while holding tightly to Panzy with the other hand as they entered the bank.

Mr. Cogswell saw her and came to meet her, smiling. He ushered her to a chair near a large desk and helped Panzy into the chair beside Judy.

Judy extended her arm, holding the papers. "Is this what you need?" she asked.

"Oh, no." He smiled. "I wanted to tell you and Mr. Stuart about our banking services."

"This isn't about the house?" Judy asked.

"No, I don't know of any problems there," Mr. Cogswell explained. "This is about your reluctance to put money in our bank."

"My father-in-law lost everything in the crash of '29," Judy explained. "Jeff doesn't trust banks because of that."

Panzy was sitting quietly in the chair beside her mother, watching the large slow-moving ceiling fan far overhead.

"I understand," Mr. Cogswell replied. "A lot of the old-timers feel that same way. But let me explain something. In 1933, the federal government initiated what is called the Federal Deposit Insurance Corporation. Because our bank is a member, each and every deposit in this bank is insured up to $10,000. If anything happens to this bank, you get your deposit back, it's guaranteed by the federal government. Are you with me so far?"

"Yes, sir."

"Okay. A while back, I cashed a check for you. I believe in the amount of $10,000. Was that the correct amount?"

"Yes. It was Panzy's insurance money from her natural father."

"When was that? Six, eight months ago?"

"I think it was either this past March or the first part of April."

"We'll call it six months to make it easy. If you had deposited that $10,000 here in our bank six months ago—guaranteed, mind you, at our 1¾ percent per annum interest rate, compounded semiannually—you would now have on deposit here with us, eh, let me see. Half of $175 is $87.50. You would now have on deposit, $10,087.50. What do you have in your mattress at home? Just the $10,000. What if, heaven forbid, lightning should strike your house, causing a fire, and it should burn to the ground. Then what would you have? Ashes worth nothing. Now if you're wondering why I would want to pay you to keep your money in my bank, let me tell you how it works. A lot of depositors add up to a lot of dollars. I then loan these dollars to a borrower who will pay me 3¼ percent interest on that loan. I make enough to pay you and the other depositors for leaving your money in my bank, and we make a little profit for the bank and its trustees."

"What if we should need the money and you've loaned it to someone else?" Judy asked seriously.

Mr. Cogswell smiled. "That's a very good question. You can always withdraw a portion or all the money with the accrued interest at anytime you need it. We are never going to loan every dollar on deposit at our bank. We keep a large reserve just for emergencies. Now let me tell you about our checking accounts and other bank services."

"Another time maybe," Judy told him, smiling. "Panzy is getting restless, and so is this one," she motioned toward her stomach.

"Of course, please think about what I've told you. Talk it over with Mr. Stuart and come by and visit me here anytime. Please, take these pamphlets. They explain all about our services."

Judy stood up as Mr. Cogswell did. "Thank you for allowing me the time to talk to you this morning. Good day, Mrs. Stuart."

"Good-bye, Mr. Cogswell."

Jeff arrived home as it was getting dark. He was cold, tired, and hungry, not only for nourishment, but also for the sight of his little family. He hugged and kissed Judy who greeted him with her usual, "Supper's ready when you are."

As tired as he was, he got down on the floor and played horsy with Panzy. She climbed on his back, grabbed him around his neck, and giggled while he ran around the living room on his hands and knees. Eventually, he pulled her off of his back, blew on her belly, carried her giggling into the kitchen, and placed her in her high chair.

He washed up at the kitchen sink as usual and sat down to supper. "So what did Mr. Cogswell want? Do we have to move out?" he joked.

"It had nothing to do with the house," Judy told him. "Just listen."

The way Judy explained what Mr. Cogswell had told her didn't take nearly as long. She told him that deposits were now guaranteed by the federal government, and if he wasn't so paranoid about banks, Panzy's money could have earned $87.50 during the past six months for doing nothing.

Jeff, who always submitted to his wife's business sense, asked for her opinion. She thought the bank would be much safer than the cedar chest, now that Mr. Cogswell had explained things, and she thought they should deposit Panzy's money immediately. Jeff then agreed without argument.

"If I'm going to deposit Panzy's insurance money tomorrow morning," Judy told him, "I'll need the car again. I'll deposit the money then get a few things we need from the IGA. That way you can have the car for the remainder of the week."

"That's fine. It's cold on the truck, but Bergstrom stretched a new canvas over the top and sideboards, and if you get up close to the cab, out of the wind, it isn't too bad."

October passed, and the first hard freeze came on the seventeenth of November. With the freeze, the ditch diggers, concrete pouring crews, and masons were soon laid off by Denton & Briggs Construction Company. The remainder of the crew members, who were doing work that could be completed in freezing weather, continued to finish framing and completing as much of each house as possible. They were cut back to sixty hours a week and sometimes didn't get in that many hours due to inclement weather. During any sunny days, when the temperature got above freezing, the roofers worked furiously to complete each roof. Between Thanksgiving and Christmas, the weather was so bad that Jeff and the rest of the construction workers were hard-pressed to get in forty hours in a week. By December 22, the remainder of the hourly wage earners had also been laid off. Jeff was promised he would be rehired as soon as Denton & Briggs resumed work in the early spring.

The Stuarts had spent that Thanksgiving in the traditional American way. Judy, who was now in the beginning of her eighth month, stuffed a small turkey that she bought at the IGA. Panzy was dressed in a newly sewn apron with frills on each side of the shoulder straps and around the bottom. She sat at the table and put walnuts and raisins into the stuffing and into the carrot and apple salad. She also cracked and peeled the boiled eggs, but she wasn't allowed to help with the deviling. Panzy had accompanied Judy to the cellar earlier in the week before Thanksgiving to pick out a pumpkin for the pies. There, she had spotted a jar of pickled beets she wanted. Panzy not only liked the color, she had actually developed a liking for pickled beets as well.

While his ladies were busy in the kitchen, Jeff did all the regular outside chores. In preparation for the coming winter freeze, he cut a large pile of firewood and stacked it near the backdoor. He covered a shallow place over the water pipe coming from the windmill tank where either the chickens had been scratching or the dog had been digging.

By two o'clock that afternoon, the three of them sat down to their Thanksgiving meal. The table was covered in a variety of colorful and deliciously aromatic foods. They bowed their heads, closed their eyes, and held hands while Jeff gave thanks.

"Oh Lord," he began, "today, we give you thanks for the bounty that you have provided. We thank you for our health and strength to do our daily chores. We thank you for our friends and neighbors. I thank you for blessing my life with my beautiful and loving wife, Judy. I thank you for the new little one that is on the way. But mostly, Lord, we want to thank you for the blessing that you sent us in the form of our darling little daughter, Panzy. Amen."

The meal was both delicious and filling. The whole family then went for a walk. Judy wanted to walk at a brisk pace, as recommended by a neighbor who was a midwife, so Jeff put Panzy up on his shoulders. As they walked, their noses and cheeks turned red in the icy cold of the late afternoon wind, and Jeff, aware that the knitted head covering that Panzy was wearing did not protect her face from the wind, pulled her from his shoulders, and carried her in his arms facing toward him and away from the wind.

Hours later, after nighttime chores had been completed and after Panzy had fallen asleep, Jeff and Judy were sitting close together on the settee in their living room, watching a dying fire. Judy got up and went to the kitchen. She soon returned with two pieces of pumpkin pie, each with a large scoop of fresh whipped cream on top, and two steaming cups of coffee. As Jeff took his coffee and pie from Judy's outstretched hand, he remarked, "Two more things to be thankful for!"

"What?" Judy asked him. "Pie and coffee?"

"No," Jeff replied, "I'm thankful that my wife is such a great cook and that she's always so very thoughtful."

PANZY GETS A BABY BROTHER

As Christmas approached, Jeff was remembering the sparse Christmas the year before. There had been nothing under the tree, their only gift being that of the newly arrived Panzy. By Christmas morning of 1946, there was a fresh covering of five inches of new snow on everything. Under the Christmas tree this year were two store-bought gifts for Panzy and a gift for both Judy and Jeff. Panzy was now more than twenty months old and thus old enough to enjoy Christmas morning.

Judy dressed Panzy in a newly sewn dress over long pants with booties sewn into the bottom of the legs to keep her feet warm. Jeff had milked Bossy and had a cozy fire going in the living room fireplace. He had also made a large stack of pancakes while Judy was getting Panzy and herself dressed. They decided to let Panzy see what was under the tree before eating breakfast.

The first thing that caught her eye was the rocking horse with the strands of hemp for the mane and tail. Judy helped her up onto it, and she was soon rocking energetically. When she tired of that, she found the doll. It took her no time at all to notice that the doll's eyes closed when she laid it down and opened when she picked it up. Watching them open and shut kept her occupied while Jeff presented Judy with her gift from him.

"Merry Christmas, my darling," Jeff told her as he handed her the gift.

Inside the box was a fancy comb, brush, and handled mirror set. There were three sizes of combs—a large one with both coarse and fine teeth, a rattail comb, and a small thin tapered comb she could carry in her purse. The brush handle and that of the mirror were similarly turned.

"I love it," Judy told him, giving him a hug and tender kiss.

Judy then gave Jeff his gift. She had ordered it from the Montgomery Ward catalogue, and it had arrived nearly two weeks before. Jeff opened the small box and retrieved the beautiful pocket watch. It was gold in color, and the face was protected under a thin decoratively stamped cover, which he had to open in order to read the time.

"It's beautiful," he told her. "Thank you very much!"

"It's already wound and set, and it's engraved," she told him. "Look on the inside of the cover."

"Jeffrey Stuart," he read.

"Here," she said, taking something from her apron pocket. "I just got this from Olsen's Drugstore yesterday. I intended to wrap it with the watch, but I just couldn't find the time." She handed him a braided leather watch fob.

Jeff attached the watch fob, stood up, and pulled Judy up from her seated position and awkwardly hugged her over her expanding belly. "I love you, my darling" he told her. He checked the time on his new watch then stooped and picked up Panzy. "According to my new watch," he said, "it's time to go have some pancakes."

That evening, as Jeff was getting some cracked corn to put into the feed trough for Bossy, he noticed a small mouse hole in a corner of one of the sacks. As he sat listening to the milk pail fill, he once again let his mind wander. It had been almost a year since he found Fluffy dead in the pasture. She had been such a good mouser that they had never seen any indication of mice while she was alive and on the job. He decided it was past time for them to get another good mouser.

As he carried the milk and eggs into the house a while later, leaving his overshoes just inside the door, he remarked to Judy, "I found a mouse hole in the feed sack."

"Oh, I've been meaning to ask Mrs. Hardy if she wanted to get rid of one of her many cats. She has dozens of them, of all ages."

"With this much snow on the roads, she may not get over here before Sunday. We'll ask her about a cat at church on Sunday. Meanwhile, I'll set some traps in the barn."

For the remainder of December, it snowed several more inches. By New Year's Day, there was an accumulation of sixteen inches, with drifts up to three feet in places. Jeff didn't try to take his family out into the cold blustery days. They stayed comfortable and warm inside the house and waited for warmer weather. They didn't see Mrs. Hardy at all during this time.

God must have been smiling on the Stuart household because on January 14, the weather became unseasonably warm, and temperatures during the day reached into the high thirties for several days in a row. Most of the snow had melted from the streets and roadways around Dexter by January 20, when Judy told Jeff it was time!

Jeff drove his wife to Memorial Hospital in the late afternoon. After she was admitted, he took Panzy to Mrs. Olsen's house. Mrs. Olsen had long ago agreed that when the time came, they could leave little Panzy with her and Mr. Olsen. After he was sure Panzy was secure at the Olsens', he hurried home to see to Bossy and the chickens and feed Rover before returning to the hospital.

On January 21, 1947, just past midnight, a tiny baby boy was born. He had straight brown hair like both Jeff and Judy and appeared to have his mother's pale blue eyes. Jeff, who had stationed himself just outside the delivery room door, was able to get a quick look at his newborn son as a nurse took him from the delivery room to the room where they would clean him up before placing him in the nursery.

He was wrinkled and small with almost burgundy-colored skin. His tiny hands were balled into fists, and his eyes were closed and squinted against the glare of the hallway lights. His tiny feet were sticking out from under the wrap, and Jeff saw that they were perfectly formed with five tiny toes on each foot. Jeff smiled broadly as the nurse disappeared into the room with his newborn son.

Jeff went to wait outside the nursery window until he saw someone place his tiny son in a hospital bassinette. A nurse appeared beside him.

"Mr. Stuart," she addressed him, "your wife is in the mothers' room now. She's ready and asking to see you."

Jeff walked down the hall past the room with the sign over the door labeled Labor Room to the room with the sign over the door labeled New Mothers. There were several beds with screens positioned around them. A nurse approached.

"Mrs. Stuart?" Jeff asked her.

The nurse led him to Judy's bed. She had freshened up and combed her hair, but her eyes looked tired. Jeff bent to kiss her, softly touching her brow.

"Did you see him?" she asked.

"Yes, he's perfect."

"He is, isn't he?" Her smile was radiant. "The nurse will be bringing him for his first feeding in a few minutes."

"After he eats, you both should get some sleep," Jeff advised her. "While you sleep, I'll head on home and do the chores. I might even get a short nap before I come back. Of course, I'll need to check on Panzy too."

The nurse handed the tiny baby to Judy. He was wearing a tiny bracelet made of blue beads. Stamped into each bead was a white letter spelling out the name S-T-U-A-R-T.

After only a few tries, Judy and the baby learned the proper way for him to nurse. Jeff finally got a chance to hold his infant son for a few minutes before a nurse came and took him away. She told Jeff that it was time for Judy to get some restful, healing sleep.

When Judy closed her eyes and drifted off to sleep, Jeff kissed her softly and headed for home. It was 3:30 a.m. when he crawled into bed.

He awoke later than usual. He completed his chores and fixed a small breakfast for himself before heading into town. His first stop was the Olsens'.

Panzy met him at the door and jumped into his outstretched arms. As he lifted her and kissed her cheek, she asked, "Is Mommy heah?"

"Mommy is at the hospital, honey. She and your new baby brother."

"Then it's a boy." Mrs. Olsen pronounced.

"Yes," Jeff replied, smiling from ear to ear, "we now have a boy and a girl. Has Panzy been any trouble?"

"No! Not at all. We love having her here. She's so happy and well-behaved. Mr. Olsen said he wished he'd seen her before you did. We always wanted more children, but after I had our son Neil—you know, the one who was killed at Iwo Jima—I couldn't have any more children, and now with Neil gone, I guess we'll never have grandchildren…" Her voice trailed off

Jeff hugged Panzy proudly. "I'm glad you're keeping her," he told Mrs. Olsen. "Judy won't be coming home until Friday, and if it's okay with you, I'll drop Panzy off with you each time I go to visit her."

"Of course, I'd be hurt if you didn't leave her with me."

"Then I'll keep her with me until just before visiting hours this afternoon. I'll stop off here on my way in to the hospital later. Thank you again."

"It was my pleasure!" Mrs. Olsen smiled.

As Jeff pulled the car into his driveway a few minutes later, with Panzy there beside him, he saw Mrs. Hardy's old truck coming down the rutted dirt road in front of their house. He sat in the warm car to see if she was going to stop out front. Sure enough, she pulled the old truck up behind his car. Jeff picked up

Panzy and carried her to welcome Mrs. Hardy. "Come on in, you and your children. I've banked the fire in the front room, but it won't take me long to get it roaring again."

"Thank you, Mr. Stuart. Where is Mrs. Stuart?"

"She's at the hospital. We have a new baby boy! He was born just after midnight this morning!"

"Well, glory be! Were you all praying for a boy?"

They had all entered the house, and Jeff put Panzy down while he put some more wood on the fire and poked at the embers. "We hadn't discussed the sex of the baby," he said. "I guess we were just praying that both Judy and the baby would be okay."

Mrs. Hardy set the box of empty jars on the kitchen table. "We ran plumb out of milk and just about everything else during that long spell of bad weather. Couldn't get out of my own driveway!"

"I know what you mean," Jeff told her. "Mrs. Hardy, we've been wanting to ask you about a cat. We haven't had a good mouser here in months, and I've been seeing mouse track in my barn and shed. You wouldn't have an extra cat at your place that you'd like to sell, would you?"

"Lordy, yes! I got cats coming out of my ears! How many can you take?"

"We just want one good mouser. Maybe about a year or so old. Lean and hungry so he'll do a good job. How much would you charge me for just one?"

"Sure you don't want a dozen?"

"No, but it would also need to be docile so Panzy could handle it without fear of getting scratched."

"I think I have just the one for you. She's about eighteen months old and very friendly. Mind you, she ain't pretty. She has different colored spots all over. Half her head is white, the other half, two-tone brown. The kids call her Patches. I'll send Earnest over with her as soon as I can get back home."

"You still haven't told me how much you want for her."

"I should be paying you for taking her off of my hands."

"I may be at the hospital visiting Mrs. Stuart when Earnest comes by. Would you just tell him to put her in the shed. I'll put out a pan of milk and some meat scraps for her before I go. Now, how much milk can you take off of our hands? You weren't the only one who didn't come by during the cold, and we are over loaded."

"Whatever you think is right," she said.

"Well, it looks like we can only get six half gallon jars in this box. Judy keeps more boxes in the cellar. Let me get you another one." Jeff put four more jars in the second box with two pounds of butter and told Mrs. Hardy to help herself to the egg bin. "The chickens have slowed down some because of the bad weather, but we still have a pile of them."

Jeff helped Mrs. Hardy to her truck with her supplies. "Judy will be home with the new baby on Friday. You will come by and see her and the new baby then, won't you?"

"Wild dogs couldn't keep me away! Now you give that little mother my love, Mr. Stuart."

"Thank you, Mrs. Hardy. I will."

After Mrs. Hardy and her children had gone, Jeff spent a happy rest of the morning playing with Panzy. She rode her rocking horse for only a short time before wanting to ride her daddy's back. After Jeff's knees could take it no longer, he put her on his shoulders and trotted around the living room. Then she helped him fix their lunches. After they ate, he and Panzy lay down on his and Judy's bed, where she soon fell asleep. While she napped, he fixed the pan of milk and scraps for the new cat. He was about to take it outside when he noticed that Earnest was driving up out front. Jeff went to meet him. Earnest had his sister, Paula, with him. She was holding the cat on her lap.

"I thought since she was a barn cat, you'd have to catch her up in a burlap sack," Jeff remarked.

"No sir," Ernest told him, "all of our cats are very tame. My sisters play with all of them all of the time."

"This is Patches," the little girl told him. "Take good care of her."

"I will, and you can come visit her anytime you like. Is that okay, sweetheart?" Jeff asked.

"That really isn't necessary," she said. "We have twenty-one more of them."

Jeff took the cat from the little girl and held it gently in one arm. It immediately started to purr. "Tell your mother thank you," he called after the truck as it began to move away. He took the cat and the cat feeder into the barn. As he sat the feeder down, Patches jumped down from his arm and immediately began to drink the milk.

"Eat up," Jeff told her. "That's the last complimentary meal you'll get till you rid this barn and shed of the pesky mice."

Jeff checked his pocket watch and realized he would have to get Panzy up and ready to leave if he was to make it to the hospital by visiting time.

At the hospital, he was able to persuade the nurses to allow Mrs. Olsen and Panzy to visit Judy for a short period of time. Judy was as happy to see Panzy as Panzy was to see her mommy. Panzy climbed up on the bed and hugged her mommy before Jeff took her away. He led her to the nursery window. A nurse seeing them there, held up baby Stuart for them to see. Mrs. Olsen oohed and aahed and brushed away a tear at the sight of the tiny baby.

"That's your baby brother," Jeff explained to Panzy.

"Baby," Panzy said, pointing at the baby and smiling up at her daddy.

Soon, Mrs. Olsen took Panzy by the hand and led her toward the exit.

"I'll drive you back to your house," Jeff stated. "Then I'll come back and visit Judy."

Jeff returned to find Judy feeding the baby. She smiled lovingly up at Jeff as he entered the room. "He eats all of the time!" she told him. "He kept me up most of the night."

"How are you feeling?" Jeff asked her.

"I'm fine. Just a little tired. I don't know why they are keeping me here until Friday. We want to go home now!"

"Now, Judy, you and I both know that you would be up trying to do all of your chores and taking care of me and Panzy and caring for the baby too. You might want to take full advantage of your time here to rest—when he isn't eating. You'll be back home doing all those things soon enough."

"I miss you and Panzy. I'm homesick."

"We miss you too." He bent to kiss both her and his tiny son. He pulled the chair closer to the bed so he could sit and softly touch the back of the baby's head as he nursed. "He's so tiny," he observed.

A nurse came in to take the baby back to the nursery. Judy turned and looked at Jeff, a warm smile on her face. "I still have trouble believing it's true," she told him. "You and me, we really made a baby."

"A beautiful baby boy," Jeff replied, holding her tenderly. They just looked at each other, smiling for a little while. "I put Panzy's bassinette in our room for him to sleep in when he gets home. When did you repaint it?"

"One of those long days when you were working in Atherton. I made a new ticking for it too. I made it with the new sewing machine that my husband gave me." She smiled up at him. "Panzy helped me stuff it."

"I got a mouser from Mrs. Hardy today."

"Really? What did Panzy say?" she asked.

"She was napping when Earnest and Paula brought the cat to the house. She hasn't seen it yet. I'm sure they'll get acquainted very soon."

"You make sure he doesn't scratch her."

"She's a little female, Judy." he told her. "Her name is Patches. According to Earnest Hardy, she is very tame."

"Tame cats scratch too! You make sure Panzy doesn't get hurt!"

"You boss me around even from your hospital bed." He grinned. "Don't worry, I'll keep an eye on her and teach her how to hold and carry a cat. I wish I could take you and the baby home with me right now."

"I wish you could too," she told him. "I've been thinking we should have Panzy dedicated at the same time we have the new baby dedicated."

"That's a good idea," Jeff said seriously. "We don't know if she was ever baptized into any church. Should we use O'Toole or Stuart at the ceremony?"

"Her birth certificate has her name as Panzy O'Toole. I think we have to use that name."

"O'Toole or Stuart, she's still our daughter!" Jeff stated emphatically, "and I'll fight any man who says otherwise!"

"I know how strongly you feel about this and how much you adore her, but you don't have to yell at me."

"Sorry, darling," Jeff apologized as he kissed her softly. "You're already thinking about a dedication, and we don't even have a name for the baby. Do you want to name him after your father? Woodrow is a powerful name. Woodrow Stuart, I like it."

"I will not have my son going through life with the name Woodrow!" Judy stated emphatically. "I've had time to think about this, and I want him to be named Jeffrey Wayne Junior. I want him to have your name."

Jeff looked at his wife lovingly. "If that will make you happy."

Soon, Jeff was able to take his wife and baby son home from the hospital. After many nights of interrupted sleep, baby Jeffrey finally began to sleep through the night, and things became routine, although not exactly normal.

During the remainder of January and all of February, it was too cold for Jeff to work construction. They were living off of the canned foods that Judy had put up and the savings from the cracker tin. As spring began, Jeff was finally able to go back to work in Atherton.

In late March, the county graded the road in front of their house. Judy detected a strange smell and, looking out her front door, saw a county truck spreading hot oil. She soon saw other trucks spreading gravel behind the oil truck. Panzy was bundled up in a new coat Judy had made for her to protect her from the brisk March wind. She watched from the porch as the man on the big machine with two big rollers drove slowly up and down the road, pressing the gravel into the oiled surface. When they were finished, the county workers had oiled and graveled the four and a half miles from the curve in the highway a mile and a half west of the Stuart place to the river bridge three miles east of them.

On April 18, Panzy had her second birthday. Judy dressed her up in a beautifully handmade dress with frills and lace. She was waiting on the front porch when Jeff came driving in from work that evening. As he climbed out of the car, she ran to meet him. Jeff picked her up in his arms and received her kiss, returning it with vigor. "Happy Birthday, sweetheart!" he said.

"Happy Buffday," she replied.

Jeff laughed. "It's your birthday, honey, not mine," he explained.

Judy was waiting just inside the door with Jeffrey in her arms. Jeff shifted Panzy to his left arm, hugged and kissed Judy, and accepted Jeffrey into his right arm, cradling his head in his right hand.

"I wish I had a picture of that," Judy told him. "Jeff Stuart, family man. And to think not so long ago, we thought we were always going to be a childless couple. Now you have your arms full."

"I just wish I had another arm to hold you with," he said while smiling happily. He placed Panzy in her highchair and rocked Jeffrey in his arms for a few minutes before returning him to Judy.

Judy accepted the three-month-old Jeffrey and recited her now old but familiar refrain, "Supper is ready when you are."

After supper, Judy brought out a small cake. This year, the cake had two real store-bought candles for Panzy to blow out. Soon after the cake was served, Judy had to go take care of the baby, and Jeff and Panzy were left alone at the table. Panzy had been taught by Judy to be very tidy at eating, and there was only a few crumbs of cake on her bib and a little bit of icing around her mouth.

"You are such a grown-up," Jeff remarked while giving her a hug. "Do you want to help me clear the dishes?"

"Uh-huh." Panzy nodded.

Later that night, when Judy was finally able to come to bed, Jeff remarked on how much help the little two-year-old Panzy had been. "You've taught her well," Jeff told Judy, holding her tenderly against him. "She was a big help in the kitchen tonight."

"She loves to help me with Jeffrey too. But she is still just a baby, Jeff. Let's not grow her up too fast. She already tries to do everything I do. Yesterday, I saw her holding her doll and trying to nurse it. She opened the top of her dress and everything. It was so cute."

"I wish I had been here to see that," Jeff told her while holding her close to him. "I love you, Judy. Good night."

WHAT IS "POSSIBLE?"

On April 27, old Mr. Clayton Barfield died, leaving the two sections of land just south of the Stuart place to his heirs. They immediately sold the land to a developer for $50 per acre. The developer then divided the land into one-acre lots, which he was selling for $125, $150, and $200 per acre, depending on its location in the development.

After streets and alleys were laid out, there were 44 one-acre homesites along the two-mile stretch just across the pavement from the Stuart place. The land developer had listed the homesites on the paved road for $200 per homesite. Another 44 one-acre homesites on the section line road, an improved caliche road one mile south of them, was listed for $150 per homesite. The remaining 1,032 one-acre homesites on the internal graded streets were listed at $125 per homesite.

Jeff saw this as an opportunity to change his lot in life. He discussed it with Judy over several evening meals.

"We have almost completed all of the homesites in Atherton. I'm sure I'll be laid off in two or three more weeks. I want to borrow some of Panzy's money and buy up some of the lots just across the road and hire me a crew and build a single-family house on each lot. I know how to build now, and I have plans in my head that I know I can put down on paper. We can make a profit off of every house we sell, and I'll soon be able to put all of Panzy's money back into her account."

"No!" Judy said emphatically. "We will not touch Panzy's money. It's in the bank, drawing interest for her. If you are so sure of yourself, go talk to Mr. Cogswell and ask him for a loan.

Don't forget that besides the money you'll need to buy the land, you'll also need some working capital. By that, I mean money for materials and payroll."

"Come with me, Judy. You can talk Mr. Cogswell into loaning us the money. You'll be my bookkeeper and write all the checks. Wouldn't you love it if I was working just across the street?"

"If you borrowed enough to buy up all forty-four lots along the pavement and enough to build a house on each lot, there is no guarantee that you could sell any or all forty-four of them. Meanwhile, you would still be obligated to pay the bank each month regardless. Are you ready for that much responsibility?"

"We can do this, Judy! I won't try to build on all of the lots at once. We'll build one house, sell it, and use the profit to start another. The oil fields southwest of Atherton are bringing in a lot of young families that need homes. I want to do this now, before some other construction company gets in here ahead of us."

With much persistence, Jeff was eventually able to persuade Judy to support his dream of being his own boss. She accompanied him to the bank where she did most of the talking as she slowly convinced Mr. Cogswell and his bank to back their adventure into entrepreneurship.

They were able to get a large enough loan to cover the cost of the twenty lots, starting just across the pavement from their house and continuing east to the section line. The loan also included what Judy considered enough to cover building supplies and labor costs for two houses. The land, the equity in their house, and the fact that they had more than $10,000 in Panzy's account on deposit in his bank was enough collateral to secure Mr. Cogswell's favor. He was also impressed with the blueprints of the two different floor plans Jeff provided him.

Jeff put together a crew of workmen that, among others, included John Wilbanks, Jack Morley, Ernest Hardy and his dad, Mr. Stanley Hardy, who had recently returned to the Hardy farm broke, very skinny, very hungry, and ready to work.

❧

While Jeff worked across the street, things in the Stuart home continued to be very simple, with only slightly noticeable changes.

One day, Panzy came into the house carrying a multicolored baby kitten in each hand. They neither one had their eyes open and were frantically mewing for their mother.

"Where did you get those kittens?" Judy asked her.

"Kitty," Panzy said, holding them up for Judy to inspect.

"Don't squeeze him. You'll hurt him. Hold him like this. Now show me where you found them," Judy instructed her, taking one of the kittens from her. She followed Panzy as she headed for the barn.

Panzy went to a hay pile where a bale had fallen apart and pointed at a hollowed out place behind it. There was Patches with three other multicolored kittens, all three mewing and trying to nurse.

"Here, Panzy, give Patches back her babies," Judy told her. "She's trying to feed them."

Panzy put the kittens down with the others and observed for a few minutes. "Ik you do Jeffy?"

"Yes, that right. Little babies of all kinds need their mothers to feed them. These little babies don't even have their eyes open yet. If you take them away from their mommy, they might get lost and never find their way back to her. You wouldn't want them to be lost and hungry and sad, would you?"

"No, Mommy," Panzy agreed, shaking her head.

"You can come out here and check on them every day. Now, let's go get Patches some cream to help her make milk for her babies."

At 5:30 p.m., Jeff came in from the building site across the road.

"You're early tonight," Judy told him. "Is everything okay at work?"

"I took off early. There's a city council meeting tonight at eight, and I want us to attend. Do you think Mrs. Olsen can watch the children for a couple of hours?"

"Why do you want us to attend?"

"I think if we can sell the city on the positive things about having these new homes out here, maybe we can convince them to annex the area. Then they will be obligated to run city services to each homesite. That will save us the cost of drilling a well for each home. And we won't need to dig a septic tank for each home either. It should make the houses easier to sell. You can put these things into words much better than I can."

When Jeff asked to address the council later that night, he was brief and to the point. The council listened politely but looked unconcerned. Jeff then introduced Judy. "Mayor, members of the council, may I present my wife, Judy Stuart."

"Welcome, Mrs. Stuart," the mayor said. "You may address the council. Please keep your remarks to fifteen minutes or less."

"Thank you, Mr. Mayor. Gentlemen," she began, "my husband and I own twenty homesites just outside the city limits, so of course, you can readily see how his proposal will benefit us. I would like to try to explain how this could also benefit the city of Dexter.

"Jeff—that is, Mr. Stuart—is in the final stages of completing the first home on one of those sites and has already started a second. In a few short months, there will be at least twenty new families living just outside your taxing jurisdiction. They will, however, be paying county taxes. While the county is banking all of those tax dollars, the city will be collecting nothing from these home buyers. Very soon, there will be more students in our schools, more shoppers for your businesses needing groceries, furniture, clothing, and automobiles, new neighbors worshiping in our churches, and yes, even some new voters.

"Now, it is true that if you were to annex this property, the city would be committed to providing city services such as water, sewer, police and fire protection. But not only will these new home owners be shopping in our city, they could be paying fees for city services as well. They could also be paying property taxes, hospital taxes, and school taxes. I think the city council should seriously consider my husband's proposal to annex the property we call the Barfield Addition. Thank you."

"Thank you, Mrs. Stuart, and thank you, Mr. Stuart. The council will take your recommendation under consideration, and we will have a vote at our next meeting one month from today."

On the steps just outside the Dexter City Hall, Jeff pulled Judy to him and kissed her excitedly. "You were superb in there. I knew you would be. You're a natural born saleswoman."

Two days later, Mayor Rothstein drove up at the site where Jeff was putting the finishing touches on the first house. He had with him three other city council members, one of which was Mr. Cogswell, their banker. The mayor asked Jeff for a tour of the almost completed home for himself and the council members and also asked to look around the developed land site. Jeff was excited to show them all the modern conveniences he had built into the new home and showed them several of the still undeveloped lots.

It had, in fact, been Judy's speech to the city council that caused them to vote unanimously to annex the Barfield Addition at their next regularly scheduled meeting. Their only stipulation was that the land developer dedicate at least two acres to a children's playground and park.

Soon afterward, city workers began putting in waterlines and water meters in the alley behind each homesite. Another crew started installing a sewer line with connection stops behind each homesite. Not far from the waterline, they installed natural gas lines and meters. The city had recently invested in a natural gas plant located northwest of the city, and they were purchasing natural gas from the nearby gas and oil fields southwest of Atherton.

Also running down the two miles of alley were many electrical and telephone poles.

As each house was completed, it was Judy who found the buyers and negotiated the sales. Her connection with Mr. Cogswell at the bank helped make many of the home loans possible. Jeff remodeled their own home to include two more bedrooms. He enlarged the living room and built Judy a combination sewing room and office. He even had a telephone installed in their home with an extension at her desk. To help in her realtor duties, Jeff bought Judy a fireproof three-drawer locking file cabinet. Judy put a realtor sign out front on the chestnut tree and placed placards in the windows of the new houses with her name and telephone number.

In July, when Jeffrey was six months old and Panzy was two years and three months, Jeff and Judy took them to church where they were both dedicated at a special church service just for the two of them. Jeff stood proudly with his arm around Judy while she dabbed at her eyes and the minister pronounced the names, Jeffrey Wayne Stuart Jr. and Panzy Mae Stuart. The shiny strawberry-blonde curls and bright blue-green eyes of little Panzy stood out in stark contrast to the other Stuart family members. Others at the service may have noticed, but the Stuarts never made an issue of their children's blood or differences in appearances. After the dedication service, there was a dinner on the ground service where all their friends and neighbors came out to partake of God's bounty. Little Panzy was one star attraction while some of the ladies took turns passing tiny Jeffrey around. Although she had been christened Panzy Mae Stuart and her christening certificate had that name on it, the Stuarts were painfully aware that she was not their legally adopted daughter.

One of the first houses Judy sold was the one almost directly across the road from where the Stuarts lived. The family of six consisted of the father and mother—Pablo and Maria Bando—five-year-old Julio, three-year-old Yolanda, and one-year-old baby Juanita. Pablo's brother Enrique, also known as Henry, occupied one of the bedrooms of his brother's house.

They were able to secure the $6,600 loan to purchase the new house because of Pablo's job with Jeff. Pablo, known as Paul to Jeff and his coworkers, was a first-class mason. Henry mixed the mud and was his hod carrier. Together, they could lay more foundation blocks and more brick than any other two men known to Jeff. If they were not busy laying brick, Jeff often used them to help install and finish Sheetrock.

It wasn't long before the Bando children, Julio and Yolanda, came across the street to meet the cute and precocious Panzy. They played on her tire swing and were treated to a lunchtime snack provided by Judy.

Panzy was intrigued by Julio's black hair and eyes. She tried to hold his head still so she could get a closer look, but he shook her hands off and raced around the yard while she chased him.

As Jeff and his crew completed each house and Judy found a buyer for it, a number of things began to happen. The Stuarts were able to pay off the loan at the bank. Their bank account, which had replaced the cracker tin when Jeff and Judy started their new business, began to grow rapidly.

The large number of children arriving to live in Barfield Addition gave Panzy an ever-growing circle of friends. She became very social, and soon, the pretty little girl with the strawberry-blonde hair was a favorite visitor in many of the homes up and down the road across from the Stuarts.

By the time she was five and starting kindergarten, Panzy was already considered a leader by the kindergarten set. As the name recorded on her birth certificate was Panzy O'Toole, she was enrolled under that name. Beautiful and precocious and tall for her age, she soon became the teacher's pet as she helped the teacher with the children who were less ready to start school—the ones who were not really ready to be away from their mothers. Not only did her bright curls and neat appearance stand out, but due to Judy's constant teachings, her academic endeavors were also outstanding. By the middle of the year, she was allowed to advance to first grade. Although a year younger than most, she quickly caught up to the rest of the students in her class and was soon considered a natural leader there also.

The school bus stopped at the section line road just one-half mile west of the Stuart home. Every morning, a large group of students caught the bus there, and every afternoon, one could see a line of them—sometimes in twos or threes and sometimes in single file—stretched out along the street going to their respective homes.

There was always a group of children around Panzy, who seemed to draw people to her like red flowers draw humming birds. One could hear her strong but pleasant voice as she held counsel on the day's lessons or recited some other interesting thing. Those in her closest circle of friends, which included Julio and Yolanda Bando and Guy Barnett and his younger sister, Barbara, would often stop at her house for a refreshing drink before continuing home.

Panzy's nickname for Julio was Leo, and she called Yolanda Yolie. Due to Panzy's skipping part of kindergarten, she and Yolie were now in the same grade while Leo was two grades ahead of them and Guy one grade ahead. Barbara was still in kindergarten. Still, the five of them were almost always together when not in school.

As she placed a glass of lemonade in front of each child, Judy asked the group, "How was school today?"

Panzy, who was tending to Jeffrey, replied by handing her mother her papers from the day. Others mumbled things like "Okay" or "Fine."

Judy looked over Panzy's papers and watched until her friends had finished their lemonade then invited them to hurry home to their parents so she and Panzy could practice piano.

As they started to go to the piano, Judy suddenly slipped on a wet spot on the kitchen linoleum where one of their visitors had inadvertently spilled some of their drink earlier. She fell, her legs twisting under her. She landed hard on her butt and right elbow, wrenching her right shoulder and upper back.

Later that evening, after supper was ready and they were waiting for Jeff to get home from work, Judy decided to take a quick bath, hoping to soak out some of the soreness from the fall. She was in the bathtub, unable to use her bruised and throbbing arm to reach her back properly. She called out to Panzy.

"Would you come wash my back for me, honey?" she asked her.

As Panzy was sponging her mother's back, she asked Judy, "Is that all right, Mama?"

"No, honey," she told her. "Wash as far down as possible." Then in a rare moment of jocularity, Judy continued, "I'll wash possible."

Panzy giggled as if they had a secret, and Judy laughed too, giving Panzy a hug and getting her dress wet in the process. Later, Panzy helped Judy by buttoning her dress for her and helping her tie a sling for her arm. Then Panzy set the table.

As usual, Jeff came in just before dark, tired and dirty. Panzy and Jeffrey met him on the porch with a kiss and a hug. He picked up Jeffrey to play with him for a little while. As he did, he saw Judy standing in the kitchen door with the sling on her arm. He quickly put Jeffrey back down and rushed to Judy. She explained that the sling was nothing but a precaution. She told him she had fallen, but the fall had caused nothing more than bruises and sprains. He quickly washed up and was about to help Panzy put supper on the table when he discovered she had already done it all.

"You did all of this by yourself?" he asked.

"Mama cooked everything. I just put it on the table."

"She's been a godsend," Judy stated. "She even helped me with my bath."

Judy and Panzy looked at each other, smiling and nodding.

"What am I missing?" Jeff asked.

Judy smiled at her husband. "It's a little something between a mother and her daughter. Maybe I'll tell you someday."

"Well, I'm very proud of you, Panzy. You are very grown-up."

They ate in silence for a while. Jeff kept looking at Judy to ascertain if she was in great pain and just not telling him. Finally, unable to determine the extent of her suffering, he turned his attention to his children. "Guess what, Jeffy?" he said. "I heard the circus is coming to town this weekend. We are only going to work a half day this Saturday so all the men can take their families and go. Would you like to go to the circus, Jeffy?"

Jeffrey was looking at his father with an inquisitive expression on his face.

"He doesn't know what a circus is," Panzy explained to her father.

"Oh? And you do?"

"Yes, of course. I read about one in a book at school!"

Jeff glanced at Judy with a wink and a grin. "Then why don't you tell Jeffy all about it."

"Okay," Panzy replied. Then turning to her little brother, Panzy explained about the wild animals, the trained dogs and horses that did tricks, the clowns and trapeze artists, cotton candy, and peanuts in the shell.

Jeff was very impressed with all the knowledge that Panzy seemed to retain from any book she read. He reached across the table and patted her on the shoulder. "You are so much like your mother," he told her. "Judy was a whiz in school too."

Panzy and Judy looked at each other, smiling.

While Jeff and Panzy cleared the supper dishes and cleaned the kitchen, they talked about other things she had learned in school that day. She told her father she would make her own lunch in the morning before going to the bus stop. As he listened to this tiny girl, barely six years old yet talking like such a grown-up, his heart swelled with pride. He looked at her—her beautiful hair, her pretty little face now with a sprinkling of freckles on the upper part of her cheeks and across her nose. As she wiped the last dish and put it in the cupboard, he suddenly picked her up in his arms and kissed her lovingly.

Judy, with the use of only one arm, was still able to get Jeffrey into bed. She was waiting for Jeff to help her get undressed and into her night clothes when he finally came into the bedroom.

"What hurts?" he asked.

"Everything. I slipped on some spilled lemonade. I did the splits and pulled some legs muscles. I hit hard on my rump and bruised it, somehow twisted my back so it hurts, and landed so hard on my elbow I'm not sure I didn't crack a bone. I took a couple of aspirin. I'm just waiting for them to take effect."

"Do you want me to rub some liniment on your sore muscles?" Jeff asked as he unbuttoned her dress.

"Not tonight. Maybe tomorrow. We'll just have to wait and see."

"Do you think you'll feel well enough to go to the circus Saturday?"

"I'll go!" she vowed. "If it's the last thing I ever do."

Jeff took the sling off of her arm and helped her out of her clothes. Then gently threading her wounded arm through the sleeve in her gown, he maneuvered the gown up and over her head while she put her other arm into the other sleeve. Then he let it fall down around her.

"Thank you," she said then cautiously climbed into bed.

When Jeff returned from the bathroom a few minutes later, she was sleeping quietly. He bent and kissed her softly before easing into bed.

PANZY TRIES CONSTRUCTION WORK

Since Jeff still drove the 1936 Ford Roadster to work each day, with the rumble seat filled with his tools, he and Judy had decided to purchase a family automobile. It was a 1950 Chevrolet that they bought just before the 1951 models appeared on the show-room floor. They were able to save $139 off of the original cost of $1,390 when the dealer discounted all of last year's models, hoping for a quick sale to make room for the new models. Judy had imposed a low dollar threshold for their checking account which she would never allow to be crossed, so part of the $1,251 had to be financed. Consequently, the Stuart family arrived at the circus that Saturday afternoon in the new family car.

They marveled at the size of the huge canvas shelter. It was held high in the air by two very tall wooden poles. Below, on the dirt floor, were three large rings standing about one foot high. Temporary bleachers had been erected all around the inside of the tent. Panzy sat on the edge of her seat, taking it all in.

A scantily dressed lady was riding on the neck of a huge elephant which reared up and walked on his hind legs. As he returned to a standing position, she slid down from her perch, and he caught her with his trunk. He then began to swing her around. Next, he held her high in the air as she lay on her back on his trunk. Then the huge pachyderm gently placed her on the ground just in front of him. After they both took a bow, the elephant lifted her gently into the air once again with his trunk so she could slide back into her position behind his ears before they quickly exited.

On one end of the tent, a woman in tights clamped her mouth shut over a device on the end of a rope which was dangling from somewhere high above her. Then holding to the rope with only her teeth, she was slowly raised into the air. Suspended there, she began to rotate her body in slow circles, gradually spinning faster and faster.

In the center ring, they had stretched a net from one tent pole to the other. High above this net, a man in leotards was standing on a platform, holding a bar swing in his hands. Across from him, on another tiny platform, was a man and woman also wearing leotards. The woman was also holding a bar of a swing.

Suddenly, the first man began to swing swiftly back and forth, still holding the bar swing by his hands. As it swung back and forth, he raised himself up and started swinging while hanging by his knees from the bar. On his signal, the woman on the other platform started swinging back and forth on her bar. Suddenly, she released her grip on her swing, did a summersault in the air, and was caught by her wrists by the man on the other swing. When she released her swing, it was caught by the man still standing on the platform that she had started from. Now the man swinging by his knees was holding her by her wrists as they swung back and forth. Suddenly, the second man let go of her swing, and the man holding her wrists let go of her. She turned quickly in the air, caught her swing, and swung up and onto her platform.

They repeated this act three different times. The second time, the woman did one and a half summersaults before the man caught her by the ankles. The third time, she did three summersaults before being caught by the wrists. Each time, the crowd would hold its breath in unison until the man had caught her. Next, each of them did several summersaults from their respective perches onto the net far beneath them, took a bow, and ran out of the tent.

Then in one of the rings, a large cage containing several lions was uncovered. A man with a whip and a chair went into the cage with them. Then, snapping his whip, he had them climbing on top of barrels, growling menacingly, and batting the air with their huge paws.

Next, a small red car entered the tent and drove around and around the perimeter just outside of the circles, honking a funny sounding horn. Suddenly, it stopped, and clown after clown climbed out. There was even a very small dog in a clown outfit that came out of the tiny car. He began running around on his hind legs, chasing one of the clowns.

There was a bear on roller skates, tumblers, jugglers, and a girl who rode two horses at the same time, standing with a foot on the back of each. There were dogs doing tricks, a man shot from a cannon on one end of the tent, landing in a net on the opposite end of the tent, and several more acts of skill and daring.

Jeff should have been enjoying the show, but he was too interested in watching and enjoying Jeffrey and Panzy's reactions to it all. Panzy's sparkling big blue-green eyes were wide with wonderment. When the concessionaires came by with cotton candy, peanuts, and balloons, he bought everyone one of each. Jeffrey was seated on his knee, Panzy on his right, between him and Judy. He reached across behind Panzy and placed his arm around Judy's shoulders. She turned to look at him, a smile of enjoyment on her face. Jeff smiled back at her. Nothing was more important to Jeff than having his family with him and seeing their happiness.

That night, as Judy prepared for bed, she was still favoring her right arm and walking somewhat stiffly. "I thought you looked uncomfortable toward the end of the show this afternoon. Were the wooden bleachers too hard for your bruises?"

"A little," she admitted, smiling at him.

"I love the way you never complain, but it keeps me from knowing just how much you are really suffering. Please let me know the next time."

"And have you usher everyone out in the middle of something the children were enjoying so much? What little pain I endured was more than worth the happy expression on their faces."

Jeff pulled her tenderly to him, and they caressed. "I love you so much!" he whispered. Soon, they were asleep in each other's arms.

At school, the following Monday, Panzy gave a short report to the class on her visit to the circus. Some of her classmates had been to the circus, but the ones who hadn't seen it were kept spellbound by her colorful and realistic description. Her teacher, Mrs. Barnett, sent a special note of acclamation home with her that afternoon. Jeff and Judy were so proud of her that they could hardly contain their enthusiasm and praise. They tried to temper their pride with acknowledgment and encouragement while still leaving room for improvement.

As the house Jeff and his crew were working on was about to be completed, he took Panzy with him to the homesite one Saturday afternoon. He tied a nail apron around her tiny waist and told her he needed her to help him pick up all the nails she could find in and around the house. As she found different sizes and kinds of nail, Jeff told her what each was and what it was used for.

"Put the larger ones in the right pocket and the smaller ones in the left pocket," he instructed her. "When we have them all picked up, I'll let you sort them for me. That's an eight penny common nail. That's a sixteen penny box nail. That's a roofing nails. The ones with the double heads are used for forming."

"What's this kind used for, Daddy?"

"That an eight penny finishing nail. It's used for finishing work. The tiny smooth head allows us to countersink it. That means drive it into the wood far enough that the head is below the surface of the wood. Here, let me show you. See this trim board on the door frame. Do you see that small hole? That's where we drove a finishing nail. All of the holes will be filled with putty before we paint the trim. I think we've found about all the nails. Now, I need you to pick up any small blocks of wood you can find and put them behind the house. There's a wheelbarrow back there to put them in. Then we need to gather all of my tools before we can head back home."

"What is putty, Daddy?"

"It's a lot like the molding clay you have at school, only it's oil-based. You know how when the clay gets thick and hard to use, the teacher has you mix some water into it to soften it up? Well, putty is sort of like that, only it has linseed oil mixed into it to keep it soft."

As she picked up the wood scraps, Panzy noticed the piles of concrete blocks, bricks, and lumber on the site next to the empty house where they were working. "What is all that for?" she asked. "Is that for the next house you're going to build?"

"Yes, you are exactly right! Come along, and I'll tell you more about it. These are called cinder blocks. We use them for the foundation. That's what we build the house on. This is called reinforcement steel. We use these steel rods to strengthen the cement in the footings under the cinder blocks. The bricks will be used in the construction of the chimney and for a veneer across the front of the house. These boards are called two by fours because they are almost two inches thick and four inches wide. They come in many different lengths. These are two by sixes, these are two by eights, these are two by tens, and these are two by twelves. The thinner boards over there, although no thicker than three quarters of an inch, are called one bys. One by four, one by six, and so on. Now let's go gather the tools and straighten out my toolbox."

Jeff explained what a chalk box was and what it was used for. He showed her a plumb bob, a level, the difference between an eight-point saw and a twelve-point. He explained the uses of the trisquare and framing square, showing her the markings that allowed him to lay out the framing for his studs and joists sixteen inches on center. He even showed her how he used the framing square to help him cut the correct pitch on the rafters. He showed her rasps and chisels and his brace and bits and even explained the peen and claws on his hammer.

The thing that was most interesting to Panzy was the surveyor's level. It was brass and shiny and had a polished glass piece in two different places. It had its own small bubble levels, leveling screws, dials and markings, and a tripod to put it on. The target pole also had markings that intrigued her.

Panzy was taking everything in nodding and asking questions. She seemed so grown up that Jeff almost forgot he was talking to a child. He put the toolbox and tools into the rumble seat and helped Panzy into the passenger side.

"When I grow up, I'm going to be a builder just like you!" Panzy stated happily.

Jeff smiled proudly at her. "Honey, you can be anything you want to be! I promise you that your mother and I will be there backing you no matter what you choose to be. Now today, was your first day in construction. You put in a little more than an hour picking up nails and those small wood pieces. The pay for that is 75¢ per hour. Here's four quarters for your piggy bank."

As Panzy accepted her pay, she smiled sweetly up at Jeff. "Thank you, Daddy," she said.

Jeff's heart swelled with love as he smiled back at the lovely little daughter that God had blessed him with. She was so bright and so beautiful.

As they entered the house a few minutes later, Panzy explained to her mother that she had been learning the construction business from her daddy and wanted to be a builder just like him. "I've already earned a dollar!" she told her excitedly.

Judy hugged her adoringly before Panzy skipped away to put her quarters into her piggy bank. Judy turned to Jeff, and they hugged and kissed. "What have you been filling her head with?" she asked, smiling.

"I just explained a few things about tools and materials. She's the one who decided she wanted to follow in my footsteps. She's a bit small now, but I believe she will be able to do anything she puts her mind to. You know how smart and ambitious she is! Where's Jeffy? We need to get started on the chores."

They were now milking a young Guernsey heifer they called Daisy. She had only recently had her first calf. Daisy produced slightly less milk than Bossy had, but still too much for the Stuart family, so Judy still had her milk sales business.

Bossy had been sold to the Hardys while she was dry and awaiting her third calf. Stanley Hardy's job with Jeff made it possible for the Hardys to purchase Bossy, who could easily produce enough milk each day for their large family. Bossy had given birth to a little bull calf which was now being fattened up for beef by Mr. Hardy.

Jeffrey came running as Jeff picked up the basket and milk pail. As they left through the back doorway, Jeff noticed that Panzy had washed up and was now helping Judy in the kitchen.

"I'll gather the eggs!" five-year-old Jeffrey exclaimed, taking the egg basket from Jeff.

Jeff watched as his son reached under each hen and collected an egg. "Take them into the house and give them to your mother. Then join me in the barn," he told him.

Jeff poured a measure of feed into the trough, let Daisy into the stall, locked her head into position, and began to wash her teats just as Jeffrey returned.

"Can I milk her tonight?" Jeffrey asked.

"Sure, let me get her started then you can finish."

Jeffrey's small hands could barely fit around Daisy's teats, but he was able to get some milk into the pail. Jeff was more patient with him than Daisy was, and soon, he had to take over and complete the milking chore.

As they entered the house a while later, Jeffrey proudly announced, "I milked Daisy!"

Judy stooped to hug him and brag on him.

Panzy also complimented him, but she finished by saying, "I used to milk Bossy when I was your age."

Jeff and Judy exchanged a knowing smile.

Jeff was busy straining the milk when he heard Panzy say, "Supper is ready when you are." Once again, he looked at Judy and smiled.

"Looks like we are about to be replaced," he remarked. "Jeffy taking over the milking and Panzy taking over supper."

Panzy was a year younger than the other students in her class, so she was still only seven years old when she came home one day, quieter than usual. Judy inquired as to her state of mind.

"Mama," Panzy started, a serious look on her face, "Martha Burns told me something today that is very scary. She said there is something boys do to girls that makes them bleed down there. Is that true, Mama?"

Judy had been aware that someday she would have to explain to Panzy about sexual things, yet even as precocious as Panzy was, she hadn't thought it would be this soon. She made sure Jeffrey was busy outside and then took Panzy into her room.

"Martha has her facts all wrong," she told her. "She's talking about two different things. First, let me explain about the bleeding."

Panzy was wide-eyed but excited to learn that it was all a part of growing into a woman. Judy explained thoroughly, even showing Panzy one of her own Kotex pads.

"Now the thing about what boys do to girls," she explained. "That's something that should only be done when you love the boy and you are married to him."

She went on to explain in detail so Panzy could understand. She let her ask as many questions as she wanted and tried to explain so a seven-year-old could understand. Panzy was well-aware of the differences in boys and girls because she had helped her mother with the changing and bathing of Jeffy when he was a baby. Now she more fully understood the reason for the differences.

"I knew Jeffy came out of your stomach," Panzy said, "but I didn't know how he got in there. Did it hurt when Daddy planted his seed in you?"

"No, it's a joyous thing! You'll see someday, when you're all grown up and married."

"I want to marry someone just like Daddy!"

Judy smiled. "I want you to marry someone as special as your daddy too."

PANZY LEARNS THE TRUTH

It was when Panzy was ten years old that she discovered the truth about her biological parents. Panzy had stayed home from school on Friday due to an upset stomach and a slight fever. Judy thought she might have something that was contagious and insisted she not go to school that day. Panzy was restless and wanted something to do. She had finished the book report on the novel she had just completed and began pestering her mother.

"You can help me straighten up my files," Judy told her. "Here, separate these letters. Put all of the letters from each client together with the earliest date on the bottom and each subsequent date on top of it." She handed Panzy a stack of papers from the bottom drawer.

Panzy was quietly sorting papers when she suddenly said, "This paper has my name on it!"

Absentmindedly, Judy asked, "What does it say?"

"Certificate of live birth."

Judy stopped what she was doing and turned quickly in her chair. "Yes, that's your birth certificate. Here, let me have it. It shouldn't have been in the papers I gave you."

Panzy was still holding it and reading it. "It has Myrtle McFarland in the space for mother's name and Sean O'Toole in the space for father's name."

Judy's shoulders slouched as she sat back in her chair. "I had hoped you would be older when you discovered this. And I wanted your daddy to be here at the time we told you. You see, Panzy, when you were very little—just a baby, in fact—the parents you were born to, Myrtle and Sean O'Toole, went to live with God. That's when your daddy and I brought you home to live with us. Since that day, we have loved you and raised you as our very own."

"Then it's true what Martha Burns has been saying, that you aren't my real parents. I always wondered why I don't look like you or Daddy and Jeffy does. Why haven't you told me this before?"

"No, honey. We are your parents! It's true I didn't give birth to you, but you are as much my daughter as if I had."

"There are some other papers here with it. One is titled Certificate of Guardianship, and this one says Certificate of Death."

"I'll take them too," Judy said.

Panzy handed Judy the certificate of guardianship and the death certificate. "May I keep this birth certificate? I want to learn all I can about my real parents."

"Yes, you may, but please, honey, take very good care of it. Keep it some place safe." Judy studied Panzy's face for signs of angst. "I think your daddy can tell you some things about your natural mother. He met her before she died. There may be some information on your natural father in the newspaper archives in the public library down town. He was a war hero. You look flushed. Has your fever returned? Come over here and let me check."

Judy touched the inside of her wrist to Panzy's brow. "Yes, you feel warm again. Let's get something cold to drink, and I think enough time has elapsed since you took the last aspirin so that you can safely take some more."

Judy gave Panzy some more aspirin and fixed them each a glass of cold lemonade, and they sat at the kitchen table to drink it. Panzy was looking first at the birth certificate and then at Judy. Judy was sure she was formulating several questions in her mind, and she was apprehensive about having to answer them, but at the same time, she was anxious to ease any pain Panzy might be feeling.

"I'm feeling cooler now," Panzy informed Judy after a few minutes. "I'll put this on my dresser and help you finish with the file cabinet."

"Thank you, honey."

There was nothing more said about the birth certificate until Jeff and Judy were in bed that night. Jeff had tried to be affectionate but found Judy preoccupied. "You seem distant tonight, my love," he said as he kissed her tenderly. "Is there something troubling you? Something I should know about?"

"Yes," she answered, "Panzy stumbled onto her birth certificate today. I think she has a million questions but just doesn't know where to start. It's all rather sudden and confusing to her. She thought we were her natural parents and now..."

"What did you tell her?" Jeff asked.

"I told her that her parents had gone to be with the Lord when she was a baby and that we brought her home to live with us as our little girl," Judy replied.

"How did she react to that?" Jeff asked.

"I believe she was a little shocked at first, but then she withdrew into herself and got very quiet," Judy responded.

"I'll get the crew started in the morning, then while you take care of Jeffy, I'll take her out to where her mother is buried and try to answer as many questions as I can," Jeff stated with authority.

"Why don't we all go, Jeff? Jeffy is eight now, and I think he should find this out from us before he hears it from Martha Burns or some other uninformed source."

"As usual, you're right," Jeff told her. "Panzy is going to tell him anyway. They never keep anything from each other. She sometimes acts like they are the same age. We'll make it a family outing. Can you help Panzy fix a bouquet of flowers for the grave?"

"Of course," Judy promised.

"Well, we knew this day was coming," Jeff said, "but I must admit, I haven't thought about it in years. In my mind, she's always been yours and mine. I love that girl with all my heart. I hope this doesn't hurt her emotionally. I pray we can find the right words to say. I know you are much better with words than I am, but I also feel I should take the lead on this. What do you think?"

"I think you are right," Judy told him, "but I also know Panzy. She'll sort it all out in her brilliant little mind and make something positive from it and end up smiling. She can't possibly overlook your unconditional love for her."

"Nor yours, Mama Stuart." He hugged her tightly. "I love you, and I think I can sleep now."

She nestled against him. "You always know just what to say to ease my mind."

"You do the same for me," Jeff said sleepily. "We make a great team."

On Saturday morning, a few minutes before 10:00 a.m., the Stuart family drove out of their driveway, heading east toward the river. The Dexter cemetery was located on a hill about half a mile past the river bridge and just south of the road. It took Jeff only a few minutes to find the stone of Myrtle O'Toole. Panzy stood looking at the stone and reading the engravings as she laid her bouquet of flowers on it—Myrtle McFarland O'Toole, 1922 to 1945.

"Where is my father's stone?" Panzy asked.

"He was lost at sea," Jeff told her in a quiet and solemn tone. "I don't think his body was ever recovered."

As they stood there by Myrtle O'Toole's headstone, Jeff, with his arm around his daughter, told her about meeting Myrtle O'Toole at Olsen's Drugstore when he worked there as a soda jerk many years ago. He described how beautiful Myrtle was with long, strawberry-blonde hair just like Panzy's. He told her that it was obvious Myrtle loved her very much and was constantly attending to her needs. He told her about the day she was left in his care so her mother could apply for a job across the street at the library. He described the inclement weather of that late October day and how her mother was struck down by a careless driver in a terrible accident. He explained that Myrtle had been in a coma for days before she was finally released from her pain. He told her how he and Judy had immediately become emotionally attached to the tiny baby that had been entrusted to them and how they swore to forever love and protect her.

"I hope you believe your mother chose the right people to raise you. Both Judy and I love you very much," Jeff told her.

Panzy stood silent for a while, taking it all in. Finally, she asked Jeff to take a picture of her by the side of her mother's stone.

While all this was taking place, Judy was explaining to Jeffrey just what they were doing.

"You mean Panzy isn't my real sister?"

"She doesn't have the same blood as you, but she is still your sister," Judy told him. "Hasn't she always looked after you and loved you? Nothing has changed today except that you now have some new knowledge. Panzy just came to us in a different manner than you did. We are still the Stuart family, and we all stick together."

It was lunchtime by the time they got back to the house. Panzy went into her room and got her birth certificate and handed it to Judy before she helped her fix lunch.

"Will you keep it in a safe place for me?" she asked Judy.

"I'll put it in the file cabinet. You can look at it anytime you wish," Judy promised.

As they were sitting around the table, Panzy asked Jeff if she could ride her bicycle to the library after lunch to see what she could find out about her birth father.

"If it's all right with Judy and if you have completed all of your chores," Jeff answered.

"I'll help with the dishes," Jeffrey said. "That way, Panzy can go right after we eat."

"Are you sure you don't want to go with her?" Judy asked.

"It's all right, Mommy," Jeffery replied. "Panzy says I always make too much noise at the library."

"It's true." Panzy laughed. "He just won't get a book and sit down. He wants to look at every picture book."

"A chip off of the old block," Jeff told him, patting him on the head. "I was the same way at your age. Who needs words when you can look at pictures?"

Judy and Panzy were looking at each other. "Men!" they said in unison.

Panzy's research into her father's short but heroic past took her several weeks. There was a short item in the Dexter paper from August 2, 1945. It was about a local farm boy from the small community of Lowry by the name of Sean O'Toole. He was missing at sea after his ship, the USS *Indiananpolis* (CA-35), a heavy cruiser, had been sunk by the Japanese just off the Philippine Islands. She did some further research in other books on sea battles of World War II and was able to get even more information. One book described how the USS *Indianapolis* had been torpedoed by a Japanese submarine on July 30, 1945, while it was steaming in the waters of the Philippine Sea. Of the 1,197 crew members aboard, only 317 survived. Some went down with the ship; others died of exposure and from the lack of drinking water or other nourishment during the many days of floating in salt water. Some drank the sea water and died, others were eaten by sharks, and some just gave up and slipped off their life jackets and sank to their deaths in the sea. A direct quote from one source stated, "After almost five days of constant shark attacks, starvation, terrible thirst, suffering from exposure and their wounds, 317 of the 900 that made it into the water were rescued from the sea."

Panzy didn't know which fatal category her father fell into.

While she was compiling the information on her father, Jeff suggested they get a plaque honoring Sean O'Toole's sacrifice and place it near Myrtle's stone in the Dexter cemetery. Panzy happily agreed.

Panzy was able to find leads from back newspaper stories that led her to elderly people who knew her mother's history, at least as far back as the McFarlands. She found the name of the orphans' home where Myrtle had once been housed until adopted at age thirteen by Mr. and Mrs. McFarland, but that was as far as she was able to go at that time.

By the time Panzy got all her research, including a bibliography, completed and written up, almost four weeks had passed. She submitted the final document to her sixth grade English teacher. She received an A plus and was asked to read it at the end of school, during the sixth grade graduation assembly.

On the day of the assembly, all the Stuarts had been invited. Panzy was dressed in a new grass-green rayon dress Judy had made just for the occasion. The dress set off her bright, blue-green eyes in a spectacular manner. Her glossy strawberry-blonde curls fell adoringly on either side of her head—some curls in front of her shoulder, others behind. Jeff, Judy, and Jeffrey were seated in the front row; Jeff's smile was so wide that it should have hurt.

Mr. Matlin, the grade school principal, gave Panzy a glowing introduction. "Ladies and Gentlemen, distinguished guests, members of the graduating class, today, we have in our midst the youngest person to ever graduate sixth grade at this school. She also has the highest grades in her class or in any class in recent memory. Ladies and Gentlemen, may I present to you Miss Panzy O'Toole Stuart!"

Panzy took her place at the podium with grace and poise. She spoke in a loud clear tone so everyone could hear. The name of her piece was, "Sean O'Toole and Myrtle McFarland O'Toole, My Biological Parents." Her story wasn't very long, consisting mostly of the information she had gleaned in her research, but she tied it all to her existence, and at the end, she told the audience how special she felt because she, in contrast to all the other children that she was acquainted with, had two sets of parents who had loved and nurtured her—the ones who had given her life and the ones who later chose her to be their daughter. There was sustained applause. Jeff and Judy looked at each other smiling, then gazed at Panzy with great pride.

There was a reception and banquet in the gym after the assembly to be attended by the families and guests of the graduates. Panzy O'Toole was the center of attention. Many of her classmates wanted to have their pictures taken with her. One person who was often present in her company and in some of the pictures was Guy Barnett. He had just completed seventh grade and was there with his parents and his younger sister, Barbara, who had just completed fifth grade.

Once back at home that night, the celebrated Panzy removed the green rayon dress and hung it carefully in her closet. She put on her everyday clothes and went to help out with the chores. She felt proud and happy to be part of this family unit. Later, as they all sat around the piano, Panzy played and sang several of the current songs. The family joined in harmony on the chorus of any they recognized. Judy then took her seat at the piano and for the next hour, the refrains of many old hymns could be heard. The folks there in the Stuart home were as happy as they had ever been.

PANZY'S FIRST KISS

Panzy's time in junior high school went by rapidly. She carried a heavy academic load, but she excelled in everything. In math, English, history, science, language, music, and art, she almost always received an A. She was also active in extracurricular activities and in sports. Tall and slender, she excelled in track, tennis, softball, and basketball.

By the time she was thirteen and entering the tenth grade in high school, she was already five feet seven inches tall. She was slender and beautiful and just beginning to fill out. She had her fourteenth birthday just six weeks before school was out that spring.

That was the year that Guy Barnett turned sixteen and got his driver's license. He began begging Panzy to go out with him. Both Jeff and Judy were firm in their resolve that Panzy would not be allowed to go on an unchaperoned date before her sixteenth birthday. Not to be deterred, Guy began to spend more and more time in her presence at church, at school, and after school, spending many hours in the Stuart home. Often, he brought his younger sister, Barbara, to give the appearance that it was no more than a gathering of young people. With Jeffrey, they had four for board games such as Monopoly and Wahoo. Yet it was always Guy and Panzy who sat closest together on a pew or on the couch.

This did not go unnoticed by Judy, who took Panzy into her room for another mother-to-daughter talk one evening immediately after the Barnett children had gone home.

"Guy is very attracted to you. Are you aware of that?" Judy asked.

"Of course, Mama. He tells me so all of the time."

"Do you feel the same way about him?" Judy asked.

"Sometimes, when we're sitting close together and he presses his leg against mine, it excites me, so I press back. At other times, when he looks at me a certain way, I feel all flushed and excited."

"That's no more than your teenage hormones reacting. God made us to be attracted to members of the opposite sex. As you change from girl to woman, the chemical changes in your body will make you feel many different ways."

"I know all that, Mama. I've read all of the books. But I don't feel that way when I'm around Leo Bando or Melvin Fergesson. I just feel strange when I'm near Guy Barnett. There is just something about his blue, blue eyes and his wavy black hair, and that smile!"

"Yes, I agree. He is very attractive, and maybe he is the one, but don't lead him on. You both have a lot of growing up to do. Although I must admit, you are physically and mentally advanced for your age, I don't believe you are anywhere near that advanced emotionally. Take your time, sweetheart. True love will find you, or you'll find it. It will be worth the wait."

"How long did you have to wait before you found Daddy?"

"Oh, honey, that's a long story. I'll tell it to you another time. I will say this much, I knew him for many years before we finally married. I first met him when I was fourteen. He asked me out the first time when I was sixteen. I was twenty-one when he asked me to marry him. But this was supposed to be about you."

"I hope I can find someone to make me as happy as Daddy makes you."

"You will, sweetheart," Judy vowed as she hugged Panzy. "Now promise me we will always talk like this to each other."

"We will, Mama."

It was that same spring, shortly after Panzy's birthday, that they got a very wet, unseasonably late snowstorm. More than fourteen inches piled up on the roof and in the yard.

Old Rover, who was now in his last years, was waiting by the door, needing to go out, when Jeff got up that morning and saw the snow.

"Hurry back, old boy," Jeff told him as he opened the back door for him.

Rover hesitated, sniffing the cold air. He turned and looked back at Jeff with his sad-looking hound dog eyes then hobbled down the steps.

Jeff got the milk bucket and went to milk Daisy. When he returned with the full pail a short time later, Judy and Panzy were in the kitchen fixing breakfast. It wasn't until they were cleaning the table and scraping the plates into Rover's dish that they remembered him.

"I let him out about an hour ago," Jeff said. "He hasn't come back yet? His eyesight isn't so good these days, and his sense of smell is gone too. I better go look for him."

"Can I go with you, Daddy?" Jeffrey asked.

"I guess so. Why don't you look around the barn and shed, and I'll look out front. We should be able to follow his tracks easily in this snow."

Jeff found no prints in the front of the house and was just rounding the corner at the back of the house when Jeffrey came running out of the barn. He was crying and calling, "Daddy! Daddy! Rover is dead!"

Jeff caught Jeffrey in his arms, held him for a few minutes until he temporarily gained his composure, then asked him, "Where is he?"

Jeffrey led him to the barn door that had been left partially ajar. There, inside the barn, on a small pile of hay, lay the body of faithful old Rover. He was lying on his side, legs stretched out, his eyes closed as if he were sleeping. His mouth was slightly open and his tongue was, as usual, sticking out of his mouth.

"Here, let's cover him with some burlap bags," Jeff instructed Jeffrey. "When the snow melts, we'll bury him behind the shed. Now let's go tell your mother and Panzy."

Jeffrey was crying again when he entered the house. Judy immediately went to him asking what was wrong. Panzy was just as concerned.

"It's Rover," Jeffrey cried. "He's dead."

Judy held her son and smoothed his hair and talked to him in low soothing tones until he could get control of his emotions. She was unaware that Panzy had gone to her room to cry softly into her pillow. Judy herself was feeling a terrible sense of loss. Rover had been a part of the family for almost sixteen years. Her children had not known a day without Rover being there to guard over them. It was a sad, somber day at the Stuarts'.

Two days later, the snows had disappeared. Jeff and Jeffrey dug a grave behind the shed, and the whole family watched as the body of Rover, wrapped warmly in burlap, was placed lovingly to rest. Jeff had fabricated a cross of wood; Panzy had lettered it while Judy and Jeffrey had found some early spring flowers to place on top of the mound of wet earth.

It was just two months later, on June 14. Judy was having a very important birthday. It was to be her fortieth. She begged Jeff not to get her anything that might remind her of how old she was becoming.

"You are still the most beautiful and desirable woman I've ever known. You just keep getting more and more attractive to me," Jeff told her as they prepared for bed the night just before her birthday.

"And you just keep getting more and more full of flattering nonsense. You'll say anything to get what you want."

Jeff smiled. "You can read me like a well worn-book, Judy, but I mean it. You are more desirable today than you were on the day we married, and as you might remember, I was extremely excited on that day. You will always be my one and only love."

That night, like so many before, they slept in each others arms.

The next morning, Jeff was up early and fixed Judy a birthday breakfast. He helped Panzy and Jeffrey clean up the kitchen while Judy, at his insistence, relaxed with a cup of her favorite hot chocolate in her living room chair. Shortly after, he was off to work. The children were in their rooms and Judy was still relaxing with a last cup of hot chocolate when she saw Jeff drive back into the yard. He got out of his car carrying a large cardboard box. He carried it into the living room and set it in front of her chair.

"Happy Birthday, darling," Jeff told her, grinning from ear to ear.

Judy was about to scold him when the box suddenly popped open by itself, and a small buff-colored golden retriever pup stuck its head out. It was too small to get out of the box on its own. Judy was across the floor and on her knees beside the box in seconds. As she lifted the pup from the box and caressed it, Panzy and Jeffrey suddenly arrived on the scene.

"Can I hold him, Mama?" they asked in unison.

Jeff, seeing he had accomplished what he had come back home for, started to leave. Judy passed the pup to Jeffrey and grabbed Jeff's hand.

"You couldn't have given me a better gift, Jeff. Thank you, honey." She kissed him enthusiastically. Jeff smiled, returned her kiss, and headed back to work.

The puppy was soon named Rover II at Jeffrey's insistence, although she looked nothing at all like Rover the first, who was a male redbone coonhound. Judy and the children took on the task of housebreaking and training the good-natured puppy, and soon, she was a loved and accepted member of the family.

When Panzy entered her junior year in high school in August of 1959, she was fourteen years old. Guy, who was now seventeen, was in his senior year. He wasn't the only boy interested in the swiftly maturing and voluptuous yet untouchable Panzy O'Toole. Many boys and girls from fourteen to eighteen years of age were in her entourage as she moved about the school. Her self-assured demeanor, her height, and her physical development added to her popularity. It seemed everyone wanted to be counted among her friends.

Besides carrying a straight-A average, she was also editor of the school newspaper, captain of the girls' basketball team, vice-president of the student council, and easily voted most popular girl. She had time for all these things and her chores at home because she was, according to her parents, still much too young to date. This eventually began to erode her otherwise sparkling personality, and in early October, she finally brought it up with Jeff one beautiful Saturday night as he was relaxing on the porch.

"Daddy," she began as she sat down beside him, "I know all of your arguments against it, but I feel that I'm mature enough, intelligent enough, and old enough to go out on a date with Guy. I know better than to use the argument that all of my friends are dating, but they are. I'm probably the only girl in the junior class who isn't out somewhere with her boyfriend tonight."

"Have you ever had a boy try to kiss you? I know about teen-age boys. He's going to want to put his arms around you and try to put his hands where they don't belong! Do you really think you are ready for all of that?"

"Guy isn't like that! He wouldn't try anything like that with me. We're just very good friends who enjoy each other's company."

"Then you can enjoy his company at church or here in the house with your mother or me."

"Why do you always have to be so difficult?"

"Believe me, honey. I would love to say yes. It's not because I don't trust you that I'm being so 'difficult' as you put it. I'm really just trying to be a responsible parent. I believe someday, you'll understand my position."

Just then, Judy joined them on the porch. Panzy fell silent. "I heard you two talking. Is this a secret conversation?"

Panzy got up, said good night to her parents, and moodily went back inside the house.

"I almost weakened," Jeff told Judy as she eased in beside him on the porch swing. "I love her so much, and I always want to please her. Do you think she's mature enough to date? She is right, you know. Everyone else in her class is dating."

"Jeff, darling, I hate to join the opposition, but she is more mature than most of her older classmates. And remember, she has never done anything but bring us pride. Maybe we should give this some more thought."

Jeff was silent for a long while, keeping the swing moving slowly back and forth. He had his arm around Judy, holding her possessively. He was shaking his head, nodding his head, and shaking it again as he turned things over in his mind. Finally, he drew in a deep breath and let it out in a sigh. "Okay," he pronounced, "I'll rescind my rule, but I'm going to give her some new rules. Rules for dating!"

Judy took his hand. "Let's go talk to her."

Jeff knocked softly on Panzy's door. "Your Mother and I would like to talk to you. Are you decent?"

Panzy opened her door. It was obvious by the open book under her desk light that she had been reading. Judy sat down on the edge of Panzy's bed. "Here, honey, sit down beside me," she said to Panzy.

Jeff stood leaning against the door, his arms folded across his chest. "Your Mother and I have been talking. We are both very proud of you. I don't have the words to express just how pleased I am with you. So I'm going to let your mother talk now."

Judy put her arm around Panzy and hugged her before placing her hands in her own lap and turning toward her. "As your father said, honey, we have been talking. We have decided that you have now reached the age and maturity where we should let you go on the occasional date. We believe, however, that we should not let you take such a major step without arming you with as much knowledge as possible and giving you another set of ground rules."

Panzy smiled. "And the rules would be your idea, right, Daddy?"

Jeff grinned. "Of course! But I thought you would be jumping for joy as soon as you heard your mother say we had changed our minds about you dating."

"Please, I'm not that immature!" Panzy replied, grinning back at him. "Okay, now what are your rules? I promise I'll abide by all of them, and I won't disappoint you, Daddy."

Jeff went first, setting a curfew and telling her the boy had to come into the house, ask for his permission, and pass his inspection. She could not date on school nights unless it was a special function, and no more than one date per week. "I may have a few more rules as we go along."

"You can leave us now," Judy told him, "I want to talk to Panzy alone."

Jeff had retired to bed before Judy finally came out of Panzy's bedroom. "What were you two females hatching up in there?"

"I was just talking to my daughter. I think you made a wise decision tonight. The man who wins her heart will be the luckiest man in the world."

"Second luckiest," Jeff said, pulling Judy down on top of him. "No one is as lucky as I am. I have the love of both of you."

Later, Jeff lay awake, torn by his decision. Had he let his love for his daughter's happiness cloud his judgment? Would he rue this day? He liked Guy, and his parents were sound respectable members of their church and the community, but both Guy and Panzy were so young and naïve. He finally consoled himself by thinking about how proud Panzy had always made them. *She'll keep her head no matter what the situation,* he thought. *I'll just have to trust her.*

It wasn't that long before Jeff got a chance to test his resolve. Guy and Panzy sat together at church the next day, and the family had hardly arrived back at the Stuart home before Guy's old 1941 Ford pulled up behind their car. He followed them into the house, holding his hat in his hand. As Judy began to prepare the noon meal, Guy addressed Jeff.

"Mr. Stuart," he began, "I would like your permission to take Panzy to the movies tonight. I'll bring her home immediately after the show. You have my word on that."

Jeff looked at the sincere young man. "Do you plan to treat her like a lady?"

"Yes, sir!"

"What's the name of this movie?"

"Eh, I don't know, sir. If you want, I can find out for you."

Jeff grinned. "No, it doesn't really matter. I suppose it would be okay for her to go. She can go to the movie with you, but then you bring her straight back home. What time will you be calling for her?"

"The movie starts at eight. Would seven thirty be okay? We'll need time to get some popcorn and find our seats."

"We'll see you at seven thirty then."

Guy stepped forward and offered his hand. As they shook hands, Guy said, "Thank you, sir. May I speak to Panzy now? I need to ask her if she'll go with me."

Panzy, who had been observing from her bedroom doorway down the hall, suddenly appeared in the living room. "Of course I'll go with you, Guy!" she exclaimed. "Can you stay for lunch? Is it all right if Guy stays for lunch, Mama?"

"Yes, of course, honey."

"Thank you very much, Mrs. Stuart, but I can't. I need to get home right now," Guy stated while looking at Panzy admiringly.

"I'll pick you up at seven thirty, Panzy." He turned and almost missed the doorway as he hurried out.

Panzy hardly ate anything at lunch. "May I be excused?" she asked.

"Yes, of course" Judy told her.

"I'll help with the dishes as soon as everyone is finished," she promised.

Jeffrey was soon finished with his meal and hurried outside to fly a kite for an hour or so before it was time to do chores.

"I thought Guy was very brave confronting you that way," Judy teased.

"When you have it as bad as that boy, you'll walk through fire for the girl you love. I was easy on him. I didn't even quiz him on his driving skills or threaten his life if he hurt her or tried anything with her."

"You are all bluster! You know you like that boy."

"Yes, I like him, but at the same time, I hate him. He wants to take my little girl away from me."

"Jeff, it's only a first date!"

Judy started clearing the table. Jeff was scraping his plate into the dog bowl when Panzy entered the room. She went over to Jeff, hugged him around the neck, and kissed him on the cheek. "Thank you, Daddy," she said. "You have nothing to worry about. Let me have that plate. Mama, go into the living room with Daddy. I'll finish up in here."

"Thank you, honey. I will."

The evening chores were over, and a light cold October rain was falling. Jeff and Jeffrey were enjoying a game of Wahoo. Judy had fixed Panzy's hair, and now Panzy was scurrying around almost in a panic, trying to find just the right dress to wear.

"Calm down," Jeff called. "What does it matter? The theater will be dark anyway!"

"Hush now, Jeff," Judy admonished him. "This is out of your sphere of expertise."

Eventually, Judy was able to help Panzy choose exactly the right dress. Judy then left Panzy alone to do some last-minute primping and went to join Jeff and Jeffrey in the living room. A short time later, they heard a knock on the door.

"That can't be Guy already," Jeff said, only half believing his own pronouncement. "It's only ten minutes after seven."

Judy answered the door. Guy was dressed in new Levi's, a bright new western shirt, and polished boots. There was a small Band-Aid on his chin, testimony to the fact he had recently tried to shave. His wavy black hair was slicked down with hair oil. "Please come in, Guy," she told him.

Guy, who had been in and out of their home since he was a small boy, suddenly became shy. He was holding his hat nervously and hopefully looking down the hallway toward Panzy's room.

Jeff offered his hand. "You're a bit early, aren't you, Guy?"

"Uh…yes, sir."

"Come in and have a seat," Judy said invitingly. "Would you like something to drink?"

"No, ma'am. Um…that reminds me. Panzy told me I should confess. I'm the one who spilled the lemonade that time when you slipped and fell. I'm very sorry that you hurt yourself."

"Oh, that was so long ago, Guy. I hope you haven't been staying awake at night and worrying about it."

"Well, it has bothered me at times. I just wanted to say I'm sorry."

Judy walked over to where Guy was seated rigidly on the edge of a chair and gave him a motherly hug. "Let's just forget all about it so you can go enjoy yourself tonight. I'll go see if Panzy is ready." Judy went and knocked softly on Panzy's door. "Guy is here," she called.

"One minute, Mama," Panzy called.

A second later, Panzy appeared in the hallway. Guy stood up and watched her approach. "Hi, Guy," she said cheerfully. "You look very nice!"

"You look...v-very pretty," Guy replied hesitantly. "It's raining. Do you have something to keep your hair and that pretty dress from getting wet?"

"How thoughtful, Guy," Panzy flattered him. "How are you going to stay dry?"

"Here, stop all this nonsense and take this umbrella," Jeff said. "Now you kids go and have a good time!"

As soon as the two young people were out of the house, Jeff addressed Judy. "Those two kids have been playing together for years. You throw the word *date* into the mix, and suddenly, they act like they were just meeting each other for the first time!"

Guy was a gentleman the entire night with two exceptions— he held her hand in the movie and asked for a kiss at the door. Panzy had been tempted, but she remembered her promise to her father. They were back home a few minutes before 10:00 p.m.

Panzy's bedtime on school nights was 9:30 p.m., so she merely told her parents good night and hurried off to her room.

Panzy lay in bed that night, going over and over the occurrences of her first date in her mind. She recalled the thrill she felt when Guy held her hand. She remembered how he had leaned against her and how she had laid her head on his shoulder in the darkened theater. She had sat close beside him on the ride home, clutching his hand when he wasn't using it for driving. At the door, when he asked her for a kiss, she had wanted so badly to kiss him, but her father's image kept her from doing it. She was so happy and excited that she could hardly sleep. Eventually, she fell asleep while thinking how she would tell everything to her mother after school tomorrow.

The movie they saw—*Young at Heart* with Doris Day and Frank Sinatra—had a lasting affect on Panzy. Two days later, she took money from her piggy bank savings and used it to buy the sheet music to the title song. With very little effort, she was soon playing and singing it. Panzy had a natural talent for all things musical.

On Monday evening, Panzy and Judy were in the kitchen preparing supper. Jeffrey was finishing the outdoor chores, and Jeff had not yet returned from work.

"Mama," Panzy began, "what's it like to kiss a boy?"

"I thought you were going to tell me." Judy smiled.

"We didn't kiss, but I sure wanted to."

"With the right man, it's very nice, very exciting, but it can often lead to other things. You should never give your kisses away frivolously. You should save them for that special someone."

Panzy's voice was soft as she answered, "I think Guy *is* someone special."

"I'm sure you do. If you weren't kissing, what did you do at the movies?"

"He held my hand, and I laid my head on his shoulder. It was dreamy. It felt so nice. But I was afraid that Daddy would show up at anytime and pull us apart."

"Your daddy just wants you to be happy. He's worried that you might make a choice that could carry with it some lifelong consequences—things like we talked about Saturday night. Look, here's your father now."

Jeff entered through the front doorway and accepted a kiss from his wife and a hug from Panzy. He held her when she tried to get away and kissed her on her cheek. "Too old to kiss your daddy hello?"

Panzy returned his kiss by brushing his cheek softly with her lips.

"Someone is stealing my kisses," he said, loud enough for the whole house to hear.

Panzy bristled. She had only thought about kissing Guy, and her daddy was already accusing her. The mere thought of it caused her to blush.

Jeff noticed her reddening face and hugged her again. "I'm only teasing you, honey. You better get used to it. It comes with being old enough to date." As Panzy hurried away, he turned and asked Judy, "Where's Jeffy?"

"He hasn't come in from milking Daisy."

Jeff winked at Judy and went out to help Jeffrey with the chores. At twelve, Jeffrey was very capable and was just turning Daisy into the lot when Jeff arrived.

"We're getting low on chicken feed," he told his daddy. "We probably have enough for two more days. I'm sorry. I should have noticed it last week so we could have gotten some Saturday when we were in town."

"That's okay, son. I'll get some during my lunch break tomorrow. Here, let me carry the milk."

"Panzy has been acting weird all day. She seemed to be dreaming or something. I asked her if she wanted me to help her carry her books to the bus stop, and she didn't even answer me."

"Panzy is going through a change right now. Just try to be tolerant with her. She'll be herself soon enough." They entered the house. "Go wash up for supper while I strain the milk."

When supper was over and Panzy and Judy were finished in the kitchen, Panzy went over to Jeff and took his hand and tugged on it. "Daddy, can I talk with you outside for a minute?" she asked him.

"We'll need a jacket out there tonight. That cold front that brought the rain yesterday brought a lot of cold air with it. Can we just talk in your room?"

"Okay."

Panzy moved her desk chair out so Jeff could sit on it then took a seat on the edge of her bed. She looked seriously at her father while gathering her courage. "Daddy," she began, "Guy wants to start driving me to school each day and bringing me home after school. Is that okay with you?"

Jeff hated disappointing his daughter so he stalled. "Remember my first rule of dating? The boy comes and asks me."

"He's already asked you. Does he have to ask you every time?"

Check! Jeff thought. *She is better at this than I am.* "Eh, no, not every time, just every boy. Look, you're changing the subject. As I told you, I don't think you and Guy should have more than one date per week. A Saturday night or Sunday night movie, something like that."

"But he wants to tell everyone at school that I'm his girlfriend. He drives past our house every morning and every evening. It would be easier for him to pick me up here than me walking to the corner and riding the school bus. Besides, he always has Barbara with him. We can take Jeffy with us if it will make you feel more comfortable."

Checkmate! Jeff thought. *I'm going to need some time to study my next move.* "Let me think about it and talk to your mother about it. I'll let you know in the morning before you leave for school."

"Thank you, Daddy," Panzy said, standing and giving him a hug and a kiss.

"There's my kiss," Jeff said, smiling at his beautiful daughter. "Whatever my decision, I want you to always remember this, Panzy—I love you very much."

In bed that night, after Judy and Jeff had exhausted their physical love for one another, Jeff told her about Panzy's request.

"I think they are moving way too fast. She's had one date with him. She's fourteen. She is still my baby girl!"

"Now, Jeff, we decided that the age thing was not going to be a factor. What harm could there be if she rides to school and back in his company. They used to sit together on the school bus, and you had no objections to that. And she told you that Jeffy and Barbara will be there too. Don't worry so much."

"I wasn't on the bus to observe their behavior. Jeffy and Barbara? So I guess now we could call that a double date," Jeff replied.

"How old was I the first time Jeffrey Stuart took me home after school? Remember that?" Judy asked him. "I missed my bus, and you and some of the other senior boys were tossing a football around. You came over and offered to drive me home. I was fourteen, the same age that Panzy is now."

"You were pathetic. I thought you were going to cry. And I certainly didn't know you lived that far from town, or I might not have offered you that ride. But then again, you were awfully cute."

"Well, that day was the day I first set my cap for you. It took me two years to finally get you to ask me out. So do you really think a ride to school or back can lead to anything negative?"

"That's a pretty weak argument," Jeff teased. "Look what happened to you, but I'll let you have it on points. Point being I can't think of any other arguments against it. You and Panzy win. I guess Guy wins too. I'm going to sleep now. I love you."

At breakfast the next morning, Panzy looked at her father. He was busy reading the paper and munching some toasted and buttered homemade bread. "Daddy," she asked softly, "did you come to a decision?"

"Um-hmm," he said without looking up.

"Well? What is it? Can I tell Guy yes?"

Jeff raised his head slowly and looked at her, trying to look as stern as he could. "Well," he said, drawing out his words, "taking everything into consideration…weighing the pros and cons… considering the positives and negatives—"

"Oh, stop teasing her, Jeff!" Judy said indignantly. "Yes, honey, your father said yes!"

Jeff watched as Panzy suddenly jumped up and ran out of the room. He expected she would tell Guy at school that day, but she was on the phone with him before Jeff could finish another bite. He looked at Judy with a confused look on his face. "When did I lose control? She used to ask permission to leave the table, she used to be quiet and respectful. I want my Panzy back," he whined.

Just then, Panzy rushed up behind him, hugged him, kissed him on the cheek, and said, "Thanks, Dad. I have to go get ready now." She rushed to her room.

"'Thanks, Dad'?" he said to Judy. "I used to be 'Daddy!' I used to get some respect. What have I done?" he said dolefully.

Judy just smiled at him lovingly. "Just think," she said, "the teenage years are just beginning for her, and Jeffy will be entering them in less than three months."

"I can't wait," Jeff said dejectedly. He got up from the table and declared, "I'm going to go pound some nails!"

Jeff was just backing out of the driveway when he saw Guy's maroon 1941 Ford stop in the street just in front of their house. He waved Guy into the spot beside him and rolled down his window. "Drive carefully, Guy. I'm holding you responsible for the safety of my children."

"I will. I'll be careful, Mr. Stuart. Thank you for letting Panzy ride with me."

Jeff waved and backed out and headed to the latest building site.

Panzy and Guy occupied the front seat, Barbara Barnett and Jeffrey Stuart the backseat, as they headed off to school. As soon as Guy let Barbara and Jeffrey off at junior high school, Panzy slid across the seat and sat as close to Guy as she could without interfering with his driving. When he had pulled into student parking and shut off the engine, he put his arm around her and tried once again for a kiss.

Panzy pushed him away and climbed out. "If my dad had seen that, I wouldn't be able to ride with you again. You have to promise me you won't try anything like that again."

"I only promise that I'll ask first."

"And if I say no? Will you respect my wishes?"

"Yes, *if* you say no."

They walked the remainder of the way to their classes in silence. Panzy wouldn't even let him carry her books.

At supper on Thursday evening, Jeff was feeling the results of a long day of bending and driving nails into subflooring boards and was a bit out of sorts. Judy could read his mood and was extra-attentive to his needs. Panzy, on the other hand, was still in awe of her newfound teenage dating status and was pushing the boundaries.

"Daddy," Panzy asked, "does the Friday night football game count as the weekly date if Guy picks me up here before the game and drops me off after the game? I'll be in the stands with the band, and he'll be on the field. It won't feel much like a date."

"You know what, Panzy? Why don't you keep score? I'm beginning to feel like your warden. You take the responsibility of deciding what a date does or does not consist of."

"Are you angry with me, Daddy?" Panzy asked, trying to slide onto his lap.

"No, honey, I'm just tired and feeling a little out of sorts. Mark this down, everyone. Friday night football games—in fact, any varsity night games—do not count as an official weekly teenage date!"

Judy looked at him. "You are awfully certain. Have you ever watched what goes on in the stands at a basketball game?"

"That wasn't my little girl in the stands!" Jeff stated with authority.

On Saturday morning, after Jeff had gone off to work and Jeffrey was in his room reading, Judy and Panzy were alone in the kitchen. "Mama, I have to tell you something. I let Guy kiss me last night when he brought me home after the game."

Judy was silent, just looking at Panzy, who was looking at her for approval.

"It was just like you told me, Mama," Panzy continued, "very nice and very exciting. I wanted to stay for more, but he sort of rushed me out of the car after that and walked me to the door. I think he was afraid Daddy would catch him, so he didn't try to kiss me at the door. I don't think I would have cared if Daddy had caught us. I just wanted him to kiss me again."

"You must slow down, Panzy. I also told you what kissing can often lead to. You're still only fourteen. You have a lot of years ahead to do the kissing. Save some of them for your true love. For your future husband. You are much too young to be thinking about doing all of that."

"Are you going to tell Daddy?"

"Not unless you want me to. I think you should tell him. If you don't think you can talk to your father about something, then you must feel as if what you have done is wrong."

"I understand, Mama. I'll think about it."

The phone rang, and when Judy answered it, she was talking to Guy. "No, Panzy is still doing her chores. I'll have her call you when she's free. That's okay. Good-bye, Guy."

"You can call him when you have finished everything," Judy said. "I'm sure he wants to ask you out again tonight."

"He already asked me last night. I can go, can't I?"

"I believe, under the circumstances, you should talk to your father about that."

"You want me to tell him about the kiss, don't you?"

"No, I want you to keep your father fully involved in your life. Let him feel like he still has a little say in what you do and where you go. Remember how he reacted Thursday evening when you asked him to exempt football games? I think he's feeling a little bit like he's losing you."

Panzy called Guy as soon as she was able to. "I haven't asked them yet...My mama wants me to ask my daddy...He's never going to let me stay out that late...Do you want to ask him?...On Saturdays, he usually gets home around five...Okay, I'll tell them you're coming for supper...Be here when he gets home...Bye."

"You asked Guy to supper?"

"Yes, there's a double feature at the movies tonight, and it doesn't get out till after eleven. I told Guy he should ask Daddy. I thought if we all had supper together it would lighten the mood. Daddy with a full stomach is easier to talk to."

"You like to play your father like you would a Steinway piano," Judy scolded.

"When he's in tune, he's about as much fun as I imagine playing a Steinway would be."

Supper at the Stuarts was cordial with some light banter. Panzy was the server, seeing to it that everyone had all they wanted and that their glasses were always full of their beverage of choice; she even got to eat a few bites herself. After the meal, she insisted that Jeff and Guy were situated in the perfect arrangement for comfortable conversation. Guy looked at his watch before addressing Jeff.

"Mr. Stuart," he began, "I would like to take Panzy to a double feature at the Center Theater tonight. *Pillow Talk* with Doris Day and Rock Hudson and *Operation Petticoat* with Cary Grant and Tony Curtis—"

"Get to the point, Guy. I don't need the credits."

"Yes, sir. Well, it starts in just a few minutes—seven o'clock to be exact—but the second feature doesn't end until fifteen minutes after eleven. I wondered if you would let Panzy stay out that late."

"Please, Daddy," Panzy begged.

Jeff looked at Judy, who was standing in the kitchen doorway, drying her hands on her apron. Her face showed concern, but he couldn't tell if it was for Panzy's sake or because she was in sympathy for his having to make such a difficult decision. He took a deep breath, smiled, and said, "Panzy has a 10 p.m. curfew as part of her privileges to date once a week. Why don't you kids hurry along and catch the first movie? When it's over around nine o'clock, come on back and have some cake and punch with Judy and me. I'm sure they'll be showing the other movie again sometime very soon."

Panzy rushed to get her purse and jacket, kissed Judy and Jeff good-bye, and hurried out of the door on Guy's arm.

Judy eased onto the couch opposite Jeff. "Why don't we take Jeffy and go see that *Pillow Talk* movie too?"

"I'd love to, but please, not tonight. I need a shower and about eight hours' rest. We finished all the wall framing and put up most of the rafters today." He paused and looked at Judy seriously. "Before I go shower today off of me, do you think I did the right thing with Guy and Panzy? It hurts me to disappoint her."

"I know it does, but remember how readily Panzy agreed that she would keep all the dating rules? I think you did exactly the right thing. It's the rules she accepted."

"Thank you, sweetheart. I need your support. Well, I'm off to the showers."

"I'll get Jeffy settled and join you," Judy promised.

"Will you soap my back and massage my tired aching back muscles?" he asked.

"Yes, of course. Get the water nice and warm, and I'll be right there."

Panzy was sitting very close to Guy as they drove to the movies. He put his arm around her. "Your dad's mind can't be easily changed, can it?"

"Not the way you went about it. I could have changed it, but we were running out of time. We're barely going to make the first show as it is."

As they stopped at the stop sign at the highway intersection, Guy pulled her closer. "Why don't we skip the show?" he asked. "We can drive over by the park and do something else for the next two hours."

"Like what?" she asked innocently.

"Like this," Guy said, trying to kiss her.

"No," she said brusquely, pushing him away and sliding over in the seat. "You told my parents you were taking me to the movies, and that is exactly where you will take me, Guy Barnett!"

"Don't get so excited. All I did was try to kiss you."

"I thought you liked being with me because I was fun. I thought you liked sharing movies and popcorn with me. I thought you liked me! Is that all you want to do? Just kiss and fool around? What about what I like to do?"

"Oh, you are such a baby!"

Panzy began to seethe. "Turn this car around and take me home this instant."

"I will not. You promised to go out with me, and you are going with me. You'll go wherever I say and do whatever I tell you to!"

Panzy had now taken up a position against the passenger door. Her teeth were gritted, her jaw was set, and her eyes were slightly squinted. Her hand was on the door handle. As soon as Guy had to stop for a downtown traffic light, she opened the car door and jumped out. She marched up the street to Olsen's Drugstore. She got some change from the clerk behind the soda fountain counter and called home. Jeffrey answered the phone.

"Hi, Jeffy. Can I please talk to Daddy?"

"Just a minute." He returned a few seconds later. "Mommy and Daddy are both in the shower. Do you want me to get them out?"

"Oh great. That's a mental picture I could have lived without right now. No, just tell Daddy when he gets out that I'm at Olsen's Drugstore, and I need a ride home."

Panzy bought a cherry-lime soda and waited and watched out the window for Jeff. She ducked out of sight each time she saw the lights of Guy's car as he drove up and down the street looking for her. "What a total jock!" she told herself. "Only two things on his mind—scoring touchdowns or scoring with girls. I can't say I wasn't warned. Mama talked to me for over an hour about boys like that."

In a few minutes, she saw her father pull into a parking spot on the street in front of Olsen's Drugstore. She returned her empty glass to the counter and hurried out to the car. Jeff drove home in silence, with his arm around his daughter's shoulders. He didn't ask her for an explanation. He could see the hurt in her pretty blue-green eyes. He removed his arm only when he needed to use both hands to maneuver into the yard. As soon as he stopped, she got out.

"Thank you, Daddy," Panzy said as she hurried off and into the house. As she passed Judy in the hall, she said to her with tears in her voice, "You were right, Mama." She went into her room and closed the door quietly behind her.

Judy immediately went and knocked on her door. "Are you all right, honey? Do you want to talk to me about it?"

"In the morning, okay, Mama?"

Jeff and Judy were no longer interested in making love to one another. They lay close together, discussing what might have gone wrong and how much it could have hurt Panzy.

"I wish she would talk to me tonight," Judy said, "I'll not sleep till I know how much hurt she is feeling and for what reason."

"Do you want me to go to her? She had all the time it took to drive her home, and she didn't say a word to me. I let her know that I love her, but that wasn't enough. If he hurt her physically, I'm not sure what I might do to him."

"No, let's just let her tell us when she's ready. You'll just go in there and bluster around and make threats you can't keep, and that won't help remove the hurt she must be feeling."

"I can't imagine what could have taken place to change the happy little girl who left here into the sad little girl I picked up just thirty minutes later. Well, yes, I can imagine, and that's what worries me."

"Mama," Panzy's voice called softly from their bedroom door, "can I come in and lay down with you for a few minutes?"

"Sure, come here," Judy said, her arms outstretched.

Jeff moved over so Panzy could crawl onto the bed between them. He pulled her to him and kissed her forehead. "It's just like when we first got you," he told her lovingly, "Judy, you, and me all in the same bed."

"What is it, honey?" Judy asked sympathetically.

"I don't think I want to date anymore. At least not until I'm sixteen," she said. "I'm not ready for it. I don't like the emotional roller coaster."

Jeff lay silent, listening to Panzy and her mother talk.

"I should warn you, honey. Being sixteen isn't going to change that. Dating, loving, marriage, having and rearing children, and life itself, they arc all a scrics of emotional roller coasters. We just have to strive to cope with them. Having someone who loves you to talk to can be a great help."

"Thank you, Mama. I feel better now." She sat up and started crawling off of the bed. "I just wish I hadn't let Guy Barnett kiss me after the game last night!"

She was gone from their room before Jeff had a chance to respond.

THE GRANDPARENTS

With the trials of a dating teenager temporarily behind her, Panzy concentrated on her many courses and extracurricular activities for the remainder of the school year.

Within days of the incident with Guy and dating, Panzy had shown an eagerness to learn how to drive. Jeff first taught her to drive his 1936 Ford and, later, the family automobile. In mere days, she had mastered the skill. She was allowed to drive in the countryside but told she could not drive into town before her sixteenth birthday when she could obtain a driving permit.

On April 18, 1960, the lovely Panzy had her fifteenth birthday. A number of young men asked her to the prom, but she steadfastly refused their invitations. She had made a vow to herself and to her parents to wait until she was sixteen before trying the dating scene again.

Guy Barnett tried several times to make amends for his behavior that night in October, but Panzy made it abundantly clear that they could never be anything but friends.

When Guy graduated on May 29, Panzy and her family were in attendance, but it was not solely for Guy's benefit, but for that of her many other friends in the graduating senior class.

Just four months after her fifteenth birthday, Panzy started her senior year in high school. Once again, she excelled in almost everything. Now president of the student body council and captain of most sports teams she was involved with, she had no time to think of dating. She completed and mailed applications to several universities.

As she continued to mature both mentally and physically, she was a vision of enticing beauty and challenging intelligence. Her superior intellect and vow to remain dateless and chaste, however, caused her to appear aloof. Many would-be suitors didn't even make the attempt to be friendly. Thus, by the middle of the year, the once-celebrated Panzy found her circle of friends dwindling. She was still a favorite of all her instructors, but she had fewer friends of her own age.

Judy became aware of this and was concerned for her. She talked to Jeff about it. "I'm so worried about Panzy," she told him. "She seems to be by herself an awful lot these days. She spends entirely too much time in her room studying. Other girls her age spend most of their time on the telephone talking about boys."

"You are always worrying about something. If she was on the phone all the time, talking with her friends about boys, you'd worry she wasn't studying enough. Give yourself a break. Don't worry so much. Panzy will be just fine."

"But she is just fifteen, Jeff. She should be having crushes on older boys, wearing sloppy clothes, listening to rock and roll music, painting her toenails, talking for hours on the telephone and just...well, being a scatterbrained teenager. She's missing so much by being so...intelligent."

"I know what you're talking about, Judy, honey, but we can't change things by worrying. We can only continue to love her unconditionally and be ready to help her if she happens to fall. We knew almost from the day we got her she was special—walking and talking months ahead of schedule, potty training herself long before most children do. Panzy is just special!"

"She is, I know that, but I also hurt for her when I see how much she is missing. She already has her life mapped out. When most kids are wondering what's for supper, she wants to know if Juilliard will accept her."

Jeff caressed his wife lovingly. She melded into his arms, allowing the strength of his big strong arms to assure her everything would turn out okay. She had used this method of reassurance all through the lean years when they had so little. Their love for one another had always been strong. After a sufficient time, he relaxed his arms, kissed her tenderly, and released her.

At breakfast one Saturday morning, Panzy asked if she could use the car to drive over to the community of Lowry. She told her parents that she had learned that there might be relatives of her natural father still living in the area.

"Can I go with you?" Jeffrey asked.

"Not this time, Jeffy. I'm taking my camera and notebook and doing some research. I might be gone for hours. You'll just get bored and want to come back home before I'm ready."

"No, I won't. I promise."

"Now, Jeffy," Jeff interjected, "I believe your sister wants to be alone. I think you should stay home with your mother. Maybe she'll let you visit the building site later today. I'll let you earn some money gathering and stacking some scrap lumber."

Panzy was gone for about four hours before she came home all excited. She had discovered the O'Toole family plot in the cemetery behind the Lowry community church. She found her birth father's military marker there. No grave, just a plaque inside the family plot.

She had talked to several people in the community who had stories about Sean and his family. She had been given the names of Sean's parents, Shamus and Mary O'Toole, and had been told they were living somewhere back east. Someone thought they might be in Philadelphia, Pennsylvania; another thought it might be Camden, New Jersey.

She had visited the farm where her natural parents had once lived. She found the house she thought she had been born in. It was rundown and deserted. There were no more O'Tooles living in the community. She had determined the approximate location of the family farm and wanted Judy to take her to the courthouse in Jackson. She wished to find the name of the recorded owner.

"I have to pick up Jeffy at Daddy's job site," her mother explained. "I'll see if your father wants to take some time off and go with us. Would you like me to do that, Panzy?"

"Sure, Mama, whatever you think. I want to type up my notes and put them in my journal. I'll start that while you're gone."

At the job site, Jeff was annoyed at the tardiness of the FHA inspector. He had just received word that he would not be out until the following Monday. He gave everyone the rest of the day off to some grumbling about short hours and told Judy he would be home shortly to go to Jackson with them.

Judy and Jeffrey returned to the house where Panzy was still typing.

"Your father will be home shortly," Judy told Panzy. "I think he needs a break from his work anyway. He doesn't seem to be as happy building as he once was. He loves the work, seeing the progress of each day and the finished project. He just doesn't like the tedium and stress of the logistics and responsibility for it all."

Jeff came in very shortly. He cleaned up, and the whole family piled into the car and headed for Jackson. While Panzy and Jeff were in the courthouse in the records section, Judy planned to take Jeffrey with her to do some window shopping.

"We'll all meet in front of the courthouse in one hour," Jeff told them as he parked on a side street beside the courthouse.

Jeff was familiar with the records section and plat maps, and with Panzy's description and directions from the Lowry community church, they were quickly able to find the farm she described. It was an eighty-acre plot, two miles north and four miles west of the Lowry community church. It had last been transferred in June 1942 from a Shamus O'Toole to a Sean O'Toole for the sum of $80. It was still registered in his name.

Panzy jotted down the plot location and legal description. They found that the property had a lien against it for $237.68

for back taxes and penalties owed. Armed with that knowledge, the help of a local attorney, and funds from her insurance money, Panzy laid claim to the O'Toole farm. Also with the attorney's help, she was able to locate her grandparents in the Camden, New Jersey suburb of Cherry Hill.

She carefully and meticulously crafted a letter to them explaining her existence and waited impatiently for an answer.

The answer came on a Tuesday just before Thanksgiving. Mary O'Toole had answered her letter. Her words seemed tentative and questioning. She was unaware of a marriage between Sean and Myrtle McFarland and definitely didn't know anything about a child. They had heard rumors, when they had been in Lowry in 1946, for a ceremony to honor Sean, but they had no more information other than that.

Jeff and Panzy went back to the courthouse in Jackson a few days after Thanksgiving to ask for a copy of the marriage license of Sean O'Toole and Myrtle McFarland. She also asked them to make a photostatic copy of both Panzy's birth certificate and Myrtle's death certificate. Armed with these three documents, Panzy again wrote to her grandparents and enclosed the copies she had obtained. She also enclosed a recent photograph of herself.

The answer that she received was more to her liking. Her grandmother, Mary, was delighted to know Sean had a daughter and that she had another granddaughter. She remarked on how beautiful Panzy was and how she thought she had Sean's eyes and chin. Enclosed was a one-page letter from her grandfather Shamus, scribbled in barely legible handwriting. It told her how happy he was to know about her and that he wanted her to visit them at their home in Cherry Hill, New Jersey.

PANZY FINDS TRUE LOVE

In January 1961, Jeffrey Stuart turned fourteen. In April that same year, Panzy had her sixteenth birthday, had a sweet sixteen birthday party, and got her driver's license.

Six weeks later, Panzy graduated as valedictorian of the high school senior class. In June of that same year, she started classes at the university. She was able to pay room and board and tuition with money from the life insurance Sean O'Toole had left her. Her majors were in art and music. She was also taking some education courses as her minor. She was able to excel in all aspects because of her exceptional IQ, her work ethic, and study habits.

Panzy had now grown into a more mature woman. She stood five feet nine inches tall and weighed one hundred and twenty pounds. Tall and thin, yet perfectly proportioned, she had a face and figure that could be the envy of many a movie star. Men often took a double take, but Panzy seemed unaware of her exceptional beauty.

Panzy spent so much time on her academic pursuits and her desire to be perfect in everything she attempted that she had no time for social events. At the university, just as in high school, she was able to excel in each endeavor. Still, she knew instinctively that something major was missing from her life. She just didn't ever let it invade her thoughts.

One morning in March 1965, near the end of her senior year at the university, Panzy was sitting at an outdoor table at the bistro she often visited. She was sipping a cup of coffee and working on her theme paper when a sudden gust of wind blew several of her completed papers away. As she rushed to retrieve them, she was aided by a tall well-dressed young man. Together, they were able to save all of her work.

"These are a part of my thesis," she told him. "I could have lost a lot of work and research time. I want to thank you. May I buy you a cup of coffee to repay you for your efforts?"

He looked at his watch. "I guess I could sit down for a couple of minutes," he said as he followed the pretty strawberry-blonde woman to her table. "By the way, my name is Ben."

"Hi, Ben," Panzy said, extending her hand. "My name is Panzy."

Ben accepted her hand and kissed the back of her fingers. He smiled down at her from his height of six feet four inches. Panzy noticed he was dark-complexioned, with light brown eyes and wavy black hair.

"Pansy? Like the flower?" he asked.

"No, Panzy with a zee," she told him.

"Pan zee," he said, grinning. "I assume, from your papers, that you are a student at the university?"

"Yes, I am, and you?"

"I'm an attorney with Bakker and Steinmann. My office is in the Finlay building. I have to tell you, I go by here every day on my way to and from work, and I've noticed you and your beautiful head of hair many times. It's rewarding to finally meet the pretty face that goes with it."

Panzy blushed charmingly and smiled at him. "Thank you," she said, her blue-green eyes sparkling adoringly.

They ordered, and while they waited to be served, they continued their conversation. "I see you out here studying all of the time. Have you settled on a major? You are a freshman, I presume."

"You presume wrongly. My dual major is in art and music with a minor in education. I'm working on my senior thesis."

"You are teasing me, aren't you?" Ben asked. "You can't be more than eighteen."

"You're very close. I'm nineteen actually." Panzy said proudly.

"Okay, what's the joke?" Ben asked. "That would mean you started your freshman year when you were…what? Sixteen?"

"That's right," Panzy assured him.

Ben was looking at her intently as their coffee arrived, trying to decide if she was being ingenuous. Her face was so pretty yet innocent-looking, with a sprinkle of freckles across her cheeks and nose. She was so adorable; he felt himself drawn to possess her like one would pick a dainty flower. He studied her face for some time while she smiled at him sweetly. Eventually, he forgot about everything except the enchantress seated across from him.

"Would you have dinner with me sometime?" he finally asked.

"Maybe, when do you think you would have the time?" Panzy asked sweetly.

"Tonight? Seven o'clock, maybe? Do you live near here?" Ben asked, still not sure if she was being completely truthful with him.

"I live on campus in the women's dorm," she explained. "Yes, I can be ready by seven. Should I dress in casual or formal attire?"

"Just casual dress," Ben told her. "After we eat, I want to take you to a place where formal attire may be out of place."

"And where might that be?" Panzy inquired.

"It will be a surprise, but I'm sure you'll love it," Ben told her. "You don't suffer from acrophobia, do you?"

"Oh, you own your own plane?" Panzy asked innocently.

"No, I do have a pilot's license but no plane at the present time. Stop guessing. You'll ruin my surprise.

They continued talking for almost half an hour. He told her his name was Benjamin Silverman. "Ben to my friends." He was from the northeast section of the country. Both his father and mother were attorneys, and studying law had been expected of him. He had only been practicing for two years. His field of expertise was in corporate law, but someday, he wished to have his own practice, where he could delve into all aspects of the law.

Panzy informed him of her last name and that she was from a downstate farming community. She had been raised on a farm, yet she had learned many other skills from school and her talented parents. She told him she had one brother, Jeffrey, who was now seventeen.

Ben suddenly looked at his watch. "Please forgive me," he said as he arose from his seat. "I'm already late for an appointment!" He kissed her hand again softly, excused himself, and began to walk hurriedly away.

"Wait!" Panzy called, walking swiftly beside him to keep up. "I'll meet you in front of the woman's dormitory tonight at seven o'clock."

He turned toward her, walking sideways hurriedly. "I'll be there," he promised. He then turned and began jogging away from her and toward the Finlay building.

Panzy couldn't explain it, but she had felt an immediate attraction to this tall, dark, handsome man. She watched him as he hurried away, his unbuttoned topcoat flapping in the breeze, his briefcase swinging rapidly back and forth at the end of one of his long arms. It was difficult for her to return to her books and her thesis.

At 7:00 p.m., Panzy was waiting just inside the main entrance to the women's dormitory. She was dressed casually yet appropriately. Her naturally curly strawberry-blonde hair framed her pretty face and was hanging loosely down over her shoulders. She saw Ben approaching and went out to meet him.

Ben handed her a single red rose, kissed her fingers, took her arm, and escorted her to a waiting taxi.

"Did you make it to your appointment on time?" she asked.

"Just barely," he replied. "Did you complete your thesis?"

"Almost, I need to read through it one last lime before I type it up for submission. Let's not talk about that tonight."

"Okay, I won't quiz you about school if you won't quiz me about work."

Just then, the taxi stopped under a large portico. Ben climbed out and aided Panzy as she exited the cab. They dined on the mezzanine floor of the Triumph Tower. After an expensive meal and several glasses of wine, Ben escorted her to the sky room on the top of the building. There, they danced far above the street. A partially enclosed walkway and observation deck made almost entirely of glass allowed them to look straight down to the street some twenty-five stories below.

Panzy wasn't sure if it was the height or the wine, but she suddenly had a feeling of vertigo as she was leaning out and watching the movement of the vehicles so far below. She turned and almost fell into Ben's arms. He caressed her, and she felt safe in his strong muscular arms. They looked into each other's eyes; there was an unspoken assent. Ben tenderly kissed her, and she responded in kind.

Panzy immediately felt a strong urge to love this man completely and unabashedly, as her long-repressed sexual desires came to the fore. Instead, however, she took control of her emotions and merely smiled sweetly up at him.

"I think the wine has gone to my head," she said apologetically.

"Let's go get some fresh air," Ben suggested. "How about a walk in the park?"

"I would like that," she answered sweetly.

They walked and talked for hours. They found a park bench where they continued to talk far into the night. It was well past two in the morning when Ben kissed her good night at the entry of the women's dorm.

Panzy was sure she was in love, though her logical mind told her it was impossible to fall in love that quickly. She could think of nothing else during the remainder of the night and during classes the next day. When she went for her noontime snack at the bistro, she found Ben was already there at the table they had shared only yesterday. Her heart suddenly beat faster, the mere sight of him caused stirrings inside of her that she was not familiar with. When he stood to take her hand, she didn't hesitate. She stood on her tiptoes and kissed him passionately on the lips. Ben held her tightly for a few seconds before releasing her and holding her chair for her.

"You are beautiful this morning, as usual!" He said, smiling broadly, his dimples showing.

Panzy was almost breathless with her newfound emotions. "You are too!" she all but whispered.

"Where are your books this morning?" he asked, taking her hand and holding it gently.

A tingle went through Panzy's body as he touched her hand. "I'm taking a break from studying," she answered him.

They ordered their coffee and talked while he sipped on his. Panzy was so intently looking at him and letting him hold and gently caress her hand that she let her coffee get cold without ever touching it.

They made plans to go out again that evening. When Ben finally told her he had to go, they stood close together and embraced for a long minute. Panzy closed her eyes and pressed hard against him as she kissed him long and passionately. She felt her passion rising to a level she had never felt before. Slowly, he released her from his embrace, kissed her fingertips and hurried off toward his office.

As she watched him go, she picked up her cold coffee and downed it in one big gulp. Panzy realized she had never had such intense feelings. She had not wanted to let Ben leave just now. She had made many male friends during her life and had even shared a kiss with some of them, but nothing she had ever experienced had caused the strange physical things that happened to her body while Ben caressed her. She watched him disappear before turning to leave. She felt as if she were floating as she walked back to her dorm.

For weeks, Panzy and Ben saw each other every spare minute of every day and night. On her birthday, Jeff and Judy called her early in the day to catch her in her room.

"Happy Birthday, darling," Jeff announced. "Has it really been twenty years since we first saw you?"

"Happy Birthday, honey," Judy said from the extension phone in her office. "How is everything?"

"Mom, Dad, first of all thank you for the birthday wishes, but there is something I've been dying to tell you. I've met the most wonderful man. His name is Ben, and I'm madly in love with him!"

"Oh, that's just wonderful, honey," Judy replied, a smile in her voice.

"Hold on just a second, Panzy," Jeff spoke with fatherly authority. "I want to know more about this man who has stolen your love."

"His name is Benjamin Silverman. He's an attorney at Bakker and Steinmann. He's tall, taller than you Daddy, and very handsome. He's twenty-five years old, and I just love him so much!"

"We can't wait to meet him, honey," Judy said. "Will you be bringing him with you when you come home in June?"

"I may not come home right after graduation. I'm in negotiations with the university about an assistant professorship. I have an opportunity to teach and take some post graduate courses. I'm going to work towards my doctorate in both art and music. Maybe we can go for a visit sometime later this summer. I'll let you know."

"Happy Birthday, sweetheart," Jeff reiterated. "I love you and miss you something awful." He hung up his phone.

Panzy and Judy talked for several minutes more before she hung up the phone. When she found Jeff a few minutes later, Judy spoke to him with a sigh and a hint of sadness in her voice, "Panzy sounded so grown-up, Jeff. I don't think she needs us anymore."

Jeff placed an arm around her shoulders. "She hasn't really needed us for a long time now, except for those late night phone calls between you and her. Oh, yes, I know about them. How long have you known about this Ben person?"

"Just a few weeks now, but I insisted that she be the one to tell you about him. To hear her tell it, he can walk on water."

"Just the way you used to look at me," Jeff teased.

"Not entirely," Judy grinned at him. "Although with your big feet, you would have a better chance than most at pulling it off."

"I just hope he loves her as much as I love her and as much as I love you, Judy Stuart. If he does, then nothing can hurt her."

Judy reached up, put her arms around his neck, and kissed him tenderly. She was forty-five and Jeff forty-eight, but he could still light a fire of desire in her. Judy was confident that she could also ignite his fire.

In June, when Panzy graduated, she had to vacate her room in the dorm. After an exhaustive search for an apartment, she eventually let Ben talk her into moving in with him. They were still living together when they went to the Stuart farm for the Thanksgiving holidays later that year.

Jeff and Judy were delighted to have Panzy at home and to see her so happy. Although unaware of Panzy's and Ben's living arrangements, they were pleasantly impressed by her choice of a male companion.

Jeff and Ben had a heated discussion about the anti-Vietnam war demonstrators at the White House. Although they were on opposite sides of the debate, they each respected the other one's point of view.

Jeffrey, in order to avoid being drafted into the US Army, had only recently volunteered for service in the navy and was still in boot camp in San Diego, California. Thus Jeff had more at stake in his arguments to support President Johnson. Ben, living in a city with a university, was more in tune with the radical leftist elements protesting America's involvement in the war.

Each stated his position emphatically. Ben, used to arguing case law, was more smooth and refined in the delivery of his arguments. To compensate for Ben's confidence, Jeff occasionally raised his voice and waved his arms when trying to emphasize his points. When Judy and Panzy called them to the Thanksgiving table, it was like calling a truce.

After the relaxing meal and cleanup was finished, the men went into the living room to watch some football and resume their verbal sparring. Ben was a Washington Redskins fan, and Jeff was rooting for the Dallas Cowboys. The arguments and exaggerated statements continued most of the day.

Judy and Panzy went to fix a bed for Ben in Jeffrey's room and put clean sheets on Panzy's old bed. "It's not necessary, Mom. Ben and I have been sleeping together for months now."

"You know your father and I do not condone such behavior. You'll sleep in separate bedrooms while you are staying with us. Please respect our wishes."

Panzy hugged Judy. "Okay, Mom."

After the game, Jeff saw an opportunity to get Panzy alone. "Let's you and me go for a walk," Jeff said, handing Panzy her jacket. "I haven't had a chance to talk to my daughter alone in ages!"

They walked arm in arm around the yard, around the old barn and cow shed, and past Rover's grave. Jeff expressed his pride in her and all her accomplishments. He told her he was very fond of Ben and complimented her on her choice of men friends. He reiterated his love for her and told her he had been observing Ben and was happy in his belief that Ben showed a genuine fondness for her.

"Are you two really in love?" Jeff questioned her.

"Yes, Daddy," Panzy said, squeezing his hand. "I love him very much. And Ben has told me many times that he loves me. He always treats me like I'm very special."

"Well, you are! I'm happy for you, sweetheart."

The couple stayed one more night before leaving midday Saturday. Ben had to be back in his office on Monday and wanted

Sunday to do some case preparation work. Jeff asked Panzy if they would be coming back for Christmas, assuring them both that he and Judy would love to have them visit again soon.

"We've already promised Ben's folks we're going to visit them for Hanukkah this year. We promise we'll spend next Christmas with you. Won't we, Ben?"

"That's a long way off," Ben said. Then he looked at the frown on Panzy's face and continued, "Of course we will. Anything you want, Zee."

Jeff and Judy hugged Panzy and kissed her good-bye.

As Jeff shook hands with Ben, he smiled. "Take good care of my girl. She's very special to me!"

"I will, sir. She's special to me also."

Panzy and Ben continued to live together in love for the next several months. Panzy completed her postgraduate work and was soon given a full professorship. Ben made partner in early 1967. They soon moved from his apartment into a nice large home in the more affluent section of town. It seemed they had everything.

The wildcatter who had developed the oil field near Atherton was looking for a place to drill a test well in the area around Lowry and contacted many of the land owners in the area. When Panzy got her letter, she and Ben talked it over. Ben had some environmental issues with it, but the strong-willed Panzy saw it as a way to possibly insure her future. She met with the prospector on her farm near Lowry one weekend. After securing written promises that the ground water would not be contaminated and the land would be returned to its current condition, she signed a lease agreement.

State law regulated the drilling of oil wells to be no more than one well per forty acres. The wildcatter hit oil and gas on his first try and was sure of a hit on his second try. With two wells on her land, Panzy soon began to bank royalties for both oil and natural gas.

Meanwhile, Jeffrey had graduated boot camp, spent several months in a specialty training school, and been assigned to an ammunition ship operating in the war zone. Like many young sailors away from home the first time, he was remiss in his letter writing. Judy patiently watched for his letters and worried about his safety.

On Panzy's twenty-third birthday, Judy as usual called her. "Happy Birthday, sweetheart. How are you? How is Ben?"

"We're just fine. I've been thinking a lot about you and Daddy lately."

"We think about you all of the time too. I saw some kittens in the barn just yesterday and remembered when you found your first nest of kittens. Do you remember that?"

"Yes I do, Mama. They were so cute and yet so homely." She laughed. "They were colored as if someone had spilled several cans of paint when they got their markings."

Panzy paused for just a second before continuing, "Mama," she said excitedly, "guess what? We're pregnant! That's right. Ben and I are expecting a little bundle of joy sometime around Halloween!"

"Oh, I'm so happy for you! Then I assume you and Ben finally got married?"

"No, Mama, marriage and a marriage license doesn't mean anything. They're just a ritual and a piece of paper."

"It's more than just a document, Panzy. And the ceremony is to show the whole world that you and Benjamin swear before God to pledge your life and love to one another. And it makes everything legal."

"A document won't change the way I feel about Ben. Look, Mama, you and Daddy loved me and raised me, yet you never officially adopted me. You never made it legal. Did we need a paper to prove your commitment, your love for me, or my love for you? No!"

"Oh, Panzy, your arguments have always been so logical, but why must you make your father happy and sad at the same time? How am I going to tell him he's going to be a grandfather but his grandchild is going to be a—"

"Don't say it, Mom! Daddy will support me. He always does."

"Of course he will. He loves you dearly, but it won't change the fact that it will hurt him. Jeff has loved you unconditionally since the day we brought you home. I wish you would think of him once in a while."

"You may not believe this, Mama, but I think about you and him all of the time. You're both on my mind a lot. But Ben has a stake in this also. I have to consider his wishes."

"Is he happy about the baby?"

"Yes, very much so."

"Then he or she will be loved, I'm sure. That is the most important thing."

"It's your turn to put up with us for Christmas this year. The baby will be here by then. Do you think Ben and I can share the same room this year?"

"I'll have to think about that. Now, Panzy, take very good care of yourself. Do all the right things so you can have a healthy baby. Are you having any morning sickness?"

"Not yet. I have my fingers crossed. I have to go now, Mama. I love you."

"I love you too, Panzy dear. Give my love to Benjamin."

Panzy's pregnancy took her out of the classroom for a few months, and she concentrated on writing an opus that she would dedicate to their baby. This occupied some of the lonely hours, but Panzy was so used to doing so many things at the same time that she sometimes became bored. She painted and decorated the nursery then painted all the other rooms. She began an oil painting of the Stuart family farm as she remembered it.

The three projects kept her busy enough that she was no longer bored. Ben walked around the remnants of her projects with caution, always marveling at her energy, always complimenting her on her work. By the time she was ready to deliver, she had completed her house painting and the canvas and was just needing an ending for her opus.

She took the canvas with her completed painting of the Stuart family farm to a frame maker and ordered a beautiful ornate frame to be fabricated to fit it. When it was completed, she put it in the back of her closet facing the wall.

On Sunday night, October 27, Panzy began to feel that the baby would soon be there. Ben packed her small bag according to her instructions and helped her to the car. She was exactly right, no sooner had they entered the hospital corridor than her water broke.

Three hours later, just past midnight, a tiny baby girl was pushed into the world; she had such strong lungs that her cries could be heard down the hall. Ben was present at the birth and was the second to get to hold his baby daughter. After Panzy had examined her, she passed her to Ben for only a few minutes before she was carried away to be cleaned up and prepped for viewing by the rest of the world.

The birth certificate recorded this: Miriam Lilah Silverman, female, 12:23 a.m., October 28, 1968. Two tiny footprints adorned the back of the certificate.

Two days before Christmas, Panzy, Ben and seven-week-old baby Miriam arrived bearing gifts. It had just begun to snow when they arrived. Judy took Miriam into her arms while Jeff hugged Panzy and greeted Ben.

Miriam had beautiful hazel-brown eyes with just a hint of green. Her curly dark brown hair, hardly a half an inch in length, reflected reddish highlights when the sunlight fell on it just right; she was just about perfect.

"She is so perfectly lovely, Panzy. Her face and eyes are shaped exactly like I remember yours being," Judy remarked.

"Let me in on some of that!" Jeff begged.

Judy reluctantly gave the baby to Jeff.

As Jeff loved on her and saw her beautiful little smile, he looked at Ben and teased, "You couldn't have had anything to do with this. She is much too beautiful and too perfect."

"Jeff, that wasn't very nice," Judy scolded him.

Ben grinned. "No offense taken. I'm glad she looks so much like her mother."

While Jeff was playing with his granddaughter and Ben was unloading the car, Judy and Panzy were discussing the sleeping arrangements.

"I've arranged for you three to share the guest bedroom. The beds in the other two rooms are too small. I got Jeffy's crib—it's also the one you used—out of the shed and cleaned it up. It's in the guest room too. Jeff and I decided that the sleeping arrangements won't change anything."

Panzy hugged her mother. "There's something I want to show you. I wasn't sure just how or when to tell you," she said, holding up her left hand so Judy could see her fingers.

Judy observed a small gold wedding band. "Oh, Panzy, darling, I'm just thrilled. Your father will be excited also. When did that happen?"

"After I talked to you on my birthday, I realized that my beliefs were more like yours and Daddy's. Ben and I talked about it. I remember he said something like, 'Anything that will make you happy, Zee.' So we went to a minister and had a quiet ceremony on May 1st. A couple, Jane and Freddy Novak, friends of ours, were the only other people there. I'm sorry, Mama, but a big ceremony didn't seem right, considering everything."

"Let me be the one to tell your father if he doesn't discover your ring before I have a chance to tell him."

Just then, Jeff came looking for Panzy. Miriam was fussing, and he was unable to get her to stop. He handed Miriam to Panzy.

"She is unhappy with her grandpa!" he told her.

"It's time for her to eat," Panzy informed him. She sat down on the edge of the bed and started unbuttoning her blouse. "Please excuse us."

Jeff and Judy joined Benjamin in the living room.

"What do you hear from your son, Jeffrey?" Ben asked.

"The last we heard, his ship was headed to a dangerous area just off the coast of Vietnam. We haven't heard from him in weeks. We're very concerned. Things are so dangerous and uncertain over there right now."

"Yes," Judy added. "Sometimes, I think he must have broken the fingers on his writing hand. They get free postage, you know!"

"He's probably just too busy defending our freedoms," Ben offered.

On Christmas Eve, they opened their gifts. Jeff and Judy were excited and pleased to receive the painting. It was painted from the prospective of the artist floating above the farm while painting it.

"A bird's-eye view," Ben described it. "Zee spent hours on it. Then, of course, she had to find just the right frame."

"We love it," Judy exclaimed.

"I must find the perfect place to hang it!" Jeff said, setting it on the fireplace mantel.

"You just did," Panzy told him. "You just need to put it up a little higher."

That night, they got another two inches of fresh snow on top of what they had received on the twenty-third.

The next morning, Christmas day, they had enjoyed a leisurely late morning breakfast. Everyone was in a cheery mood. Judy and Jeff were in the living room, engaged in a brief embrace.

"I love you, Grandma," Jeff said happily.

"I love you too, Gramps. Only one thing could make me happier—if Jeffy were here to enjoy Christmas with us."

Jeff went over and picked up Miriam from Panzy's lap. "Here," he told Judy as he handed Miriam to her, "stop worrying about Jeffrey and enjoy your granddaughter."

Panzy, with her hands now empty, had started back into the kitchen for another cup of warm cider. As she passed close to the front door, the doorbell rang. "I'll get it," she said, using a tone to reflect the obvious. She opened the door.

"Hi, Sis!" Jeffrey said. "Merry Christmas!"

CANDICE AND PAUL

HERBERT DURBIN

CHAPTER 1

The pretty red haired woman sat quietly on the park bench just off of the bicycle path and pedestrian walkway. She was holding a book in her hands and staring straight ahead. She was concentrating on the sounds of the many birds singing in the trees surrounding her and enjoying the cool breeze of this midmorning spring day. She was not often so bold as to come to the park alone, but today, she had her best friend Bo with her. Bo was a three-year-old golden Labrador retriever. She was so interested in identifying the birds by their sounds that she didn't hear the cyclist pedaling down the bicycle path which ran directly in front of her bench.

Suddenly, she stood and took a step forward directly in front of the bicycle. The young man on the bicycle swerved to avoid hitting her. As he did, he inadvertently knocked the book from her hands as he wobbled and crashed onto the grass just off of the bicycle path.

"Are you hurt?" she asked, still staring straight ahead. Bo had leaped to his feet and was now standing by her right side.

"I'm okay," he answered, "no thanks to you!"

"I'm very sorry. I didn't know you were there," she said softly.

"What? Are you blind?" he asked indignantly.

"Yes, as a matter of fact I am," she answered.

It was then he noticed her dark glasses and the harness on the dog. "Now I'm really embarrassed," he said, picking up her book. "I'm sorry I snapped at you. What are you reading?"

"*The Rainmaker*," she answered.

He flipped through the pages, noticing it was in Braille, then placed the book in her outstretched hand.

"I'm Candice," she said, extending her hand again, "and this is Bo."

"Hi, I'm clumsy Paul," he said, taking her hand. "Did I hurt you?"

"No, you didn't. It was really my fault," Candice said. "I was listening so intently to an oriole that I didn't hear you coming." Then smiling prettily, she added, "I'm very pleased to meet you, Clumsy Paul."

Paul patted Bo softly on the head. "I wasn't exactly paying attention either," Paul said. "If I had been, I'm sure I would have noticed a pretty woman like you, sitting here. Were you about to leave?"

She felt the watch on her wrist. "Yes, I was. It's nearly eleven, and I must catch a taxi to my hairdresser's. It was nice meeting you, Paul." She picked up the handle on Bo's harness.

"May I walk with you to the taxi stand?" Paul asked.

"If you'd like."

They walked along side by side, talking casually. Bo was leading the way. Paul was pushing his bicycle. Candice was holding firmly to Bo's harness. At the cab stand, Paul held the door for her and Bo as they got into a taxi. Just before he shut the door, he called out to her, "It was very nice meeting you, Candice."

Paul stood there for a few minutes, watching as the taxi disappeared. It had been such a poignant meeting, and he somehow felt drawn to this woman. He wondered if what he was feeling for her was merely pity. She certainly didn't need it; she seemed very self-assured. Paul realized that he wanted to get to know her better, and he didn't have any information about her other than her first name and the name of her dog. He continued to muse over the accidental meeting as he rode the remainder of the trail around the park and back to his automobile. *Some detective*, he thought. *You didn't even get her last name.*

Paul strapped the bicycle unto its carrier on the top of his car and drove back to his apartment. As he entered the apartment a few minutes later, he checked his messages. "Hi, it's me." He recognized the voice of Helen. "Give me a call when you can. It's about tonight."

Paul and Helen had been dating regularly for a number of months, whenever he was able to get a break from his heavy schedule at the precinct. Their romance had been on-again, off-again for a long time. Helen would pressure him for a deeper commitment at times then give up on him and date other guys, but soon, she was calling him to start things up again. They were in one of their on-again phases.

He dialed her number on his cell phone as he removed his sweats and got ready to enter the shower. He got her voice mail. Instead of leaving a message, he pressed the off button and tossed his cell phone onto the bed. After a quick shower, he dressed, put his service revolver into its shoulder holster, pocketed his badge, and looked into the refrigerator for something to eat. "Leftover pizza or bologna," he said. "I choose neither." He slipped into his jacket, picked up the cell phone, and dropped it into the side pocket. A few minutes later, he was pulling into his designated parking spot at the third precinct.

"Hey, O'Keefe," the sergeant at the desk hollered as Paul entered the room, "the captain wants to see you!"

"Thanks, Brownie," Paul answered as he walked to his desk. He made a quick scan of all the files lying on top of his desk, picked one at random, and carried it in his hand as he went to the office of Captain Bower.

"Get in here, O'Keefe!" Captain Bower ordered. "Where's Stewart, and where are you two bozos on this Hernandez case?"

"Hal's running down a lead right this very moment!" Paul lied, waving the file in the air. "We should have a break in the case at any moment."

"Good! I don't have to tell you that the commissioner is on me night and day about this case. If we don't see some results soon, I'm going to have to demote a couple of dicks and give the case to someone who can solve it! Now get out of my office and go do some detective work!"

"Yes sir, Captain. Thank you, Captain." Paul turned and walked back to his desk. He was just getting settled when Hal Stewart walked up behind him and slapped him on the shoulder.

"Morning, partner," Hal said to Paul, setting a hot beverage container on Paul's desk, "Here's some real coffee from down the street. You know, that Marisa gets cuter every day."

"Hal, you do know that Marisa is married, don't you?"

"So what? I was too at one time. Didn't keep me from looking!"

"You got anything new on this Hernandez case? Did you check out that plate number?"

"Yeah, dead end."

"Well, the Captain just read me the riot act," Paul explained. "We better find something fast, or he's going to blow a gasket."

"He's always up tight. I think he needs a good laxative! We still have five more prospective witnesses to interview. What do you say we get out of here and get started?"

"You drive. I need to call Helen. Have you eaten lunch yet?"

"No. I'll hit Smitty's Bar-B-Q and get us a couple of sandwiches while you call Helen."

"Thanks."

While Hal ran inside Smitty's, Paul remained in the unmarked unit and made his call to Helen. She wanted to argue with him about his not being able to be with her at her parents' home. "If you miss tonight, Paul, I will never forgive you!"

"Look, Helen, you know I'm on duty till midnight. I've been telling you that for days now."

"And I've been telling you for days that it's my parents' thirtieth wedding anniversary!"

"Well, give them my best. I'll try to call you tomorrow."

"Don't you dare hang up on me, Paul O'Keefe!"

"Bye now." Paul pressed the Off button. Helen was starting her pushy stuff again, and Paul thought it was time for another of their off-again phases.

Helen was pretty, very bright, very independent, and fun to be with most of the time, but it seemed she always wanted something just a little more than he was capable of giving. It seemed she always wanted him to do something that he was not in favor of doing.

They were, in most cases, exact opposites. He assumed the attraction they felt for each other was nothing more than physical. Helen had long blonde hair; his was black and wavy. Her eyes were blue; his were brown. She had a college degree; he only had two years of college and a diploma from the police academy. She came from a very well-to-do German family; his Scotch-Irish family had always been dirt-poor. Yet they did, from time to time, have some fun and, at other times, some very memorable romantic encounters.

As Hal climbed back into the unit, he handed him a sandwich. "What's our first address?"

"Six-two-zero-three-five Ryman. It's the house across the street from where they found the old man's body. This guy never seems to be home when we call on him. Tell you what, let me out in back then you go around to the front and bang on the front door. I'll grab him as he runs out the back."

"Ten-four!"

"What the hell is that?"

"TV jargon!"

"Well, talk English!"

Paul waited just outside the back door, and sure enough, as soon as Hal banged on the front door and called out, "Police," the backdoor flew open, and a young man ran right into his grasp.

"It was an accident," he blurted. "We didn't mean to kill him!"

"Hold on now," Paul said as he cuffed the young man. "I need to give you your Miranda."

Paul led the young man to the unit, did a first-class pat down, pulled out his Miranda card, and read it verbatim to his suspect. "You understand all of that?" he asked.

"Yes, sir."

"What's your name, son?"

"Juan Moreno."

"Well, Juan, I'm Detective O'Keefe. We're going to take you to the station for a little talk. You can tell me all about it there."

Hal soon returned to the unit, and they drove back to the station where they all three went into an interrogation room. Juan told them that he and his pal, Luis Reyna, were sure *viejo* Hernandez had lots of money hidden in the house because he was always hiring people to do things. He had his groceries and other items delivered to the house. When he left, he always had money for a taxi ride.

On that day, he and Luis were sitting on the front stoop smoking a couple of joints when they saw *viejo* Hernandez ride away in a taxi. They talked it over for a while before deciding to go over, break in, and see if they could find the place where he hid all his money. They were still in the house searching for the money or other valuables when the old man suddenly returned.

He told them Luis hit the old man first, but he wouldn't go down, so he had picked up a wooden stool and hit him with it. As the *viejo* fell, he hit his head on the kitchen sink. They thought he was just knocked unconscious until they saw the body being carried out the next day.

"Did you guys take anything out of Mr. Hernandez's home?" Hal asked.

"No," Juan said.

"Where can we find your pal Luis?" Paul asked.

"He usually stays with his grandparents, up in Fernando Heights."

"Do you know their name or address?"

"His *abuelo*'s name is Gilberto Gonzales. I don't know the address."

Hal left the room to put out a pickup notice for Luis Reyna. He stuck his head into Captain Bower's office. "We have a suspect in the Hernandez case. Got a confession. Looks good!"

"About damn time!" Captain Bower shouted. "Bring me something I can show to the commissioner!"

Hal closed the office door. "Show him your vacation pictures," he said just loud enough so the captain couldn't hear.

CHAPTER 2

The taxi let Candice out just in front of the elite high-rise, Truxton Tower Apartments. The doorman held the door for her and Bo and commented on her new Dorothy Hamill– style hairdo. "Your hair looks very nice, Miss MacFarlane."

"Thank you, Herman. Are all of the elevators working today?"

"Yes ma'am. That one has been repaired. Would you like me to get one for you?"

"No, thank you. We'll manage."

Herman watched while Bo led her to the elevators. He saw her press the Up button. Bo stood quietly without moving until a set of doors opened. He then led her inside. Candice deftly felt of the elevator buttons, which were also marked in Braille, and soon, they were exiting on the eighth floor. Bo took her down the hall to her apartment.

Candice worked as an at-home translator in her apartment. Her employer supplied her with either cassette tapes or CDs of recent best sellers. While she listened to them, she translated them using her Braille typewriter. She was paid very well for each completed work. Candice loved to read, so her work wasn't really work at all. Her work hours were totally of her own doing. If she was really enjoying a book, she often worked many hours, losing track of whether it was day or night. For that reason, she had a clock that announced the time every hour.

Since she loved to listen to the sounds of nature, she tried to keep track of the mornings so she could go to the near by park, find an empty park bench, and listen to the birds sing, the squirrels bark, or the sounds of happy children at play.

She had lived alone since she completed college and moved away from her parents' home. Now, at age twenty-seven, she was self-sufficient and totally comfortable with her life. She had never experienced the romance she often read about and listened to while translating. At times, she had felt stirrings of a physical nature when listening to or reading about some of the romantic liaisons. Sometimes, she would find herself longing for such a romance in her own life. In her present circumstances, however, she did not have sufficient social life to meet many persons of the opposite sex.

Candice arose from a restful night's sleep. She thought about the man she had met yesterday. He had told her his name was Paul. He had crashed his bicycle because of her. He had then walked her to her taxi. He had a very pleasant voice and seemed to be very nice. He didn't seem to be put off by her blindness like so many others. She did her morning hygiene procedure, thirty minutes of exercise, then showered and slipped into shorts and a short-sleeved pullover blouse.

Candice placed a CD of the latest best selling romance novel into her CD deck, put on her headphones, and placed her hands on the keys of her Braille typewriter. She placed her foot on the remote control switch and pushed play. For the next several hours, she continued to transcribe the first chapters of the novel. She was feeling the pangs of hunger when the male-sounding voice of the clock announced, "Nine a.m."

Candice pushed the stop on the remote control under her foot, removed the headphones, and stood up. Expertly, she turned and walked directly into her kitchen. She opened a can of dog food and emptied it into Bo's dish. While he was eating, she opened a container of yogurt for herself. After eating, she changed into a nice dress and dressy but comfortable walking shoes. Shortly, she and Bo were entering a taxi in front of the Truxton Tower Apartments. "Midtown Park please," she told the driver.

Bo led her up the path to the park bench she had used the day before. "Is this bench taken?" she asked. When no one answered, she took her book, wrapped in a cloth, from her book bag. She felt for the bench with her telescopic cane, located it, wiped off the bench seat with the cloth and sat down. She listened to the birds for a while before opening her book to begin reading.

"I was hoping I would see you here today," she heard a male voice say.

"Is that you, Paul?"

"Yes. It's a beautiful day, Candice. Do you mind if I sit down beside you?"

"Not at all. I can hear that you are still able to ride your bicycle."

"Oh, the bicycle wasn't hurt. The only thing bruised yesterday was my pride. I guess you could say, I really fell for you."

She smiled; Paul thought she had a beautiful smile. "Your hair is different this morning."

"Yes, do you like it? It's shorter than I usually wear it, but I think it has a nice feel."

"I think it suits you very well. I must confess, I've always been attracted to ladies with red hair."

"I've been told I have red hair, but I don't think that red hair feels any different than blonde hair. Some black hair feels thicker and coarser."

They talked casually for several minutes. Paul explained he usually rode there in the park every morning for about an hour, between ten and eleven, before having to go in to work.

"I also like to come here in the mornings. Maybe we'll meet again," she suggested.

"I would like that," Paul told her. "I would like that a lot. Tell me about *The Rainmaker*."

"You haven't read it? Well, it's about a young lawyer and his first case. That's all I'm going to tell you. I don't want to spoil it for you."

"Is that all you do? Just read?"

"No, sometimes, I stand in the way of bicycles. What else do you do besides riding around, trying to run over people?"

"That takes up a lot of my time. However, when I need to make a few bucks, I do a little detective work."

"You're a private detective?"

"No, I work for the police department."

"How interesting. Working on any big cases right now?"

"I got a big case of Pabst Blue Ribbon in my apartment right now, been working on that."

"And you're an amateur comedian! Emphasis on amateur."

"Oh, that hurt. I had convinced myself you were a nice lady."

They continued the light banter, flirting with each other, until Paul finally told her he had to get back to his apartment. "I have my car here at the park. Can I give you a lift somewhere?" he asked.

"If it's not out of your way, I live in the Truxton Tower Apartments."

"I know where they are. Won't be out of my way at all. By the way, Candice, I'm a terrible detective. I don't even know your last name."

"MacFarlane," she said, "Candice MacFarlane. And you?"

"Paul O'Keefe," he said, "amateur sleuth, amateur comedian."

Paul took her arm as they walked to where his car was parked. He helped her into the front seat and coaxed Bo into the rear seat. "I'll just be a few minutes," he told her. "I have to strap my bicycle onto the roof."

As he pulled up in front of the Truxton Tower Apartments a few minutes later, Paul stated, "I could pick you up here in the morning on my way to the park if you'd like. Say about nine-thirty?"

"Yes, that would be very nice of you."

As Herman opened the car door and held it for her, Paul was letting Bo out of the back. Bo positioned himself to her right, and she reached for the handle on his harness. Paul took her left hand and squeezed it gently. "Till tomorrow then," he said. Paul quickly drove away and headed back to his apartment.

"Your friend seems quite nice, Miss MacFarlane," Herman said.

"Yes, he does seem nice," she said. "Tell me, Herman, what does he look like?"

"I'd say he's about six feet two or three inches, well-built, fairly good-looking with wavy black hair. I didn't get a look at his eye color. He was wearing bicycle shorts and a sweat shirt."

"Thank you, Herman. Have a nice afternoon." She followed Bo to the elevators.

CHAPTER 3

Paul checked his messages as he entered his apartment. "Paul, Hal here. We need to find that Reyna kid. Uniform said his grandpa doesn't know where he is. See you at the station."

"Paul, this is your mother! Are you coming home this weekend? You better call me!"

"Paul, darling, it's me, I forgive you for hanging up on me. I even forgive you for last night. Mom and Dad were very disappointed you couldn't make it. I explained about your work. Please call me back as soon as you get this. Love ya."

Paul pulled off his clothes and stepped into the shower. He pushed the messages out of his mind and thought about the pretty Candice. That had been fun today, verbally sparing with her. *She has a quick wit and a disarming smile,* he thought. *I wonder what kind of flowers she likes. Something pungent? Something mild and sweet? I'll try a sweet-smelling rose first.* He toweled off, dressed, and headed for the station.

"O'Keefe," the sergeant began.

"I know, Brownie, the captain wants to see me."

"He wants both you and Stewart in his office ASAP."

Paul walked over to Hal's desk. Hal looked up from his coffee and handed Paul a cup. "Captain wants—"

"I know!" Paul stated emphatically, "I know! Let's go."

"Do you two bozos ever do anything right?" the captain wanted to know. "That Moreno kid has lawyered up. He's recanted his confession, and they posted bail not more than an hour ago. I told you to get me something I can take to the DA and the commissioner, and this is what you bring me?"

"We fingerprinted him and sent his prints to the lab to be compared with the ones we lifted at the scene," Paul told him. "We have his confession on videotape. We have a signed written statement. If we can tie his prints to the prints on the stool, we can use his confession against him, even if he does want to change his story now. Hal and I are just on our way to pick up his accomplice."

"Yeah," Hal bragged, "we'll get you a second confession before the night is over."

"You'd better!" Captain Bower barked. "Or I'm going to gather me a couple of pieces of tin! Now get out of here!"

Paul and Hal climbed into the unmarked unit, Paul behind the wheel. "Captain seemed to be in a very good mood today," Hal said.

"Yeah, I noticed that too. What's the grandpa's address out in Fernando Heights?"

Gilberto Gonzales was sitting on his front porch in an old rocking chair with wide flat arms. He held a beverage glass in his hand, resting it on one of the arms. On a TV tray to his right sat a half bottle of tequila gold, a bowl of lime halves, and a salt shaker.

The two men approached. "I'm Detective O'Keefe, and this is my partner Detective Stewart. We'd like to ask you a few questions."

"Luis, no aqui!" the old man stated.

"Can you tell us where he might be?" Hal asked.

"No lo se!"

"You have any objections to our looking inside for ourselves?" Paul asked.

"No."

The two detectives entered cautiously. After thoroughly checking every room and every potential hiding place and after they were certain that Luis was not there, they once again asked

Mr. Gonzales if he knew his whereabouts. "It will be a lot better for him if he turns himself in," Hal explained.

As they drove away from the Gonzales home, Paul suggested they drive back to the Moreno home and talk to Juan again. "He had enough grass in his pockets when we pulled him in the last time to get him some jail time. Maybe we can find him with something on him today. He might trade a few nights in jail for some info on Reyna."

They were about two blocks from the Moreno home when they spotted Juan Moreno and another man walking toward them. As Paul stopped the unit and started to get out, the second man suddenly turned and darted into a nearby alley. Hal jumped out and sprinted after him, easily overtaking and collaring the overweight man.

Paul approached Juan. "So that's Luis Reyna," Paul stated knowingly. "Why did he run?"

"I don't know!" Juan told him. "Why don't you ask him?"

"Put your hands on top of the unit and spread 'em! What's this, Moreno? A concealed weapon. Whoa! Pearl-handled service .45. Looks just like the one missing from the Hernandez home! Two bags of hash, Juan? I think that's enough to get you a charge of intent to distribute." Paul put the cuffs on him and put him in the rear seat of the unit.

Meanwhile, Hal had completed his pat down of the other man up against an alleyway brick wall and was now walking the handcuffed man back to the unit. "Let me introduce you to Luis Jesus Reyna," Hal said to Paul. "He was in possession of both illegal drugs and a concealed weapon, to wit, a switchblade knife. Throw in resisting arrest, and we got ourselves a three-time loser."

They were going through the booking procedure at the precinct a few minutes later. After getting statements from both suspects and completing the paperwork for the evidence locker, Paul declared his hunger to Hal. "I haven't eaten since breakfast. Let's go fill the void."

"Shouldn't we give the captain something?" Hal asked.

"Nah, let him stew. He's never satisfied anyway."

They were sitting in Smitty's Bar-B-Q a short time later. "Reyna's statement corroborates what we got from Moreno," Hal opined. "I think we got enough to get a conviction without the fingerprint evidence. Still, it would be good if we got a couple of matches to the one we took from the Hernandez scene."

"Great barbecue!" Paul said, taking another big bite. "You gonna eat or talk?"

Hal turned his attention to his sandwich, chewed a few bites, then grinning at Paul, he remarked, "I talked to Marisa again today!" Paul opened his mouth to say something, but Hal held up his hand and continued, "Wait, she said her and her old man have split up again. She thinks it's for good this time."

"Separated not divorced," Paul sermonized. "I've told you over and over again that screwing around with another man's wife can only get you killed! Hey, but you do what you have to do. Maybe it's time I broke in another partner anyway!"

Hal smiled. "I love you too, partner," he said.

Paul excused himself and placed a call to Helen. She was sweet and conciliatory until he told her he could not see her tonight. "All right, Paul," she said. "It's plain you don't care for me. Just don't call me anymore! I'm through playing second fiddle to your career!" The line went dead.

"That went well," Paul mused aloud.

Back at the precinct a few minutes later, Paul completed all his paperwork, made out a report for the captain, and finding him gone for the day, dropped it on his desk before signing out for the day. At his apartment, he realized he was exhausted and soon fell asleep.

CHAPTER 4

Paul awoke to the sound of the radio alarm by his bed. He stretched, yawned, and wiped the sleep from his eyes. Slowly, he climbed out of bed, got out of yesterday's clothes, and climbed into the shower. As the cold water brought reality back into his mind, he began to think about the beautiful red-haired Candice. He had promised to pick her up at her apartment at nine-thirty this morning. He dressed in street clothes and hurried to a nearby flower shop.

"Which rose is the most aromatic?" he asked the florist.

"This deep purple one. Notice the thickness of the petals. Here, I'll bruise a petal so you can smell."

Paul held the petal close to his nose. "Yes, that is just perfect!" he told the florist. "What a beautiful perfume! I'll take one."

"One dozen, sir?"

"No, just one, but if it has the effect I'm hoping for, I'll be back every day for another. Let me have one of your freshest."

The florist striped the thorns from the long stem of a beautiful fresh deep purple rose, wrapped it in waxed paper, and handed it to Paul. "Remember, sir, for the best perfume, just lightly bruise one of the petals."

"Thank you, Paul said, paying the florist. "I'll see you tomorrow."

At nine twenty-five, he was pulling into the loading zone in front of the Truxton Tower Apartments. Herman recognized his car because of the bicycle on the top and saluted him. Paul climbed out and approached him.

"Miss MacFarlane is on her way down, sir," Herman said. "Would you like to meet her at the elevators?"

"Yes, thank you," Paul said, walking past the door being held open for him by Herman.

Paul waited impatiently by the elevator doors until he finally saw them open. She was beautiful in a colorful spring dress with matching shoes and scarf. Bo started to lead her past him, but he addressed her. "Good morning Candice."

Candice gave Bo the signal to stop as she smiled toward his voice and said, "Good morning to you, Paul. I expected to meet you out front, if indeed, I met you at all today. I'm so happy you came."

"My car is in the loading zone. Can I take you to breakfast before we go to the park?"

"That would be very nice. They have menus in Braille at La Dolce Vita."

"You won't need a Braille menu this morning. I'll read the menu to you. I know where there's a place with the best home cooking in the whole city. I'm sure you'll love the food there."

They had reached his car, and he helped her into the front seat and coaxed Bo into the rear. A short time later, they were seated in Mamacita's, a cozy little out-of-the-way, family diner. Bo was lying at her feet. Paul waited until he had ordered for both her and himself before laying the rose on the table in front of her. He had purposefully pushed his thumbnail through one of the outer petals.

"Tell me about Mamacita's Paul. Tell me what you see. What is that perfume? Wait, I smell roses. Are we sitting near an open window or a vase of roses?

Paul reached across the table. "Let me have your hand," he said.

Candice raised her hand above the table about five inches and extended it carefully toward him. Paul took her hand, turned it palm upward, and placed the rose in it. Candice slowly and carefully examined the rose from one end to the other with her hands before raising the bloom to her face. "You brought me a rose?" she asked. "How thoughtful. It has a very heavy perfume. Will you describe it to me?"

"Have you ever seen colors, Candice?"

"Yes, when I was quite young. I didn't completely lose my sight until I was about three or four."

"Well, this rose is deep purple. The tips of the petals are a lighter purple fading into a pink."

"Yes, I can almost see it. Thank you."

Their meals came, and they continued to converse while they ate. He wanted to know how her clothes and shoes could always be so perfectly coordinated as to color and style. She explained she had help when purchasing them and always kept them separated in her closet and drawers and when sending them out to be cleaned. It had become so routine that she no longer had to think about it.

By the time their meal was over and they were able to leave, Paul explained he had only about half an hour before he had to be going back to his apartment to get ready for work. "I'll take you to the park so you can read, and I'll say good-bye there."

"No, don't leave yet. I can miss a day of reading since you're missing your cycling. Can we just walk in the park for a few minutes? It's such a lovely day."

They walked along the path, Bo to the right of her and Paul to the left. She was carrying the rose in her right hand and not holding on to Bo. Her left hand was resting on Paul's arm. "Tell me what you see, Paul. I hear a mockingbird overhead. She seems to be upset about something."

"I think it's us. She must have a nest nearby, and we are probably too close. She's following us, flying from tree to tree."

She checked her watch. "I think you need to take me back to my apartment now if you're going to get to work on time."

They turned about and started walking back to his car. "Can we do this again tomorrow morning?" Paul asked.

"We'll see. You have brown eyes, don't you, Paul?"

"Yes, how did you know?"

"I've been imagining how you look. From little things you do, I get hints." She smiled teasingly. "Actually, Herman told me you had black hair. The odds were in favor of brown eyes."

"May I call you sometime?"

"Yes, of course." She smiled prettily. "Just call the Truxton Apartments' main switchboard and ask for me by name. I intend to get a voice-activated cell phone soon—if they ever get to a price that I can afford."

At her apartment building, he walked her to the elevators and waited until she was about to enter. "Thank you for a wonderful morning and this beautiful rose," she told him, softly touching his hand.

"Thank you!" Paul replied, squeezing her hand tenderly. "The pleasure was all mine."

CHAPTER 5

Paul returned to his apartment for a quick shower and a change of clothes. He didn't take the time to check his messages and was soon back at his desk at the precinct.

"O'Keefe, you and Stewart get in here!" Captain Bowers called from his office door. "Now this is more like it!" he said as they entered. "The DA thinks we have enough on this Hernandez case to go to trial. I think this will make the commissioner happy."

"We did it all for you, Captain!" Paul remarked.

"You and your ulcer," Hal told him.

The captain handed Paul a folder. "Here's your next case. I hope it doesn't interfere too much in your socializing. Do you two think you can spare enough time away from the coffee pot to look into it?"

"We'll sure try," Paul said, giving Hal a raised eyebrow and a knowing look. "Come on, partner. We better hit the bricks!"

Back at their desks, Hal and Paul caught up on each other's lives before opening the new case file.

"I took Marisa out last night after we got off," Hal said. "Had a great time. I haven't been to sleep yet."

"To which funeral home would you like me to send your body?" Paul asked. "Megan Reed just made detective. I'll ask for her to replace you when you're dead. God knows she smells better than you do!"

Hal grinned. "Jealous because you can't find the time to spark Helen?"

Paul ignored him and opened the folder. "Really?" he said, "A missing person case? Here, you look at it. I need some coffee. You want a cup?"

"Not that mud! I'll get mine from Marisa." He grinned.

Leaving word with dispatch that he could be reached on his cell phone, Paul left in the middle of the workday with the excuse that he had to run down a lead. He stopped off at a bicycle shop, where he purchased a girl's twenty-six inch single-speed bicycle with coaster brake. He then strapped it on top of his car next to his bicycle. Next, he called the Truxton Tower and asked for Miss MacFarlane.

"Do you own a pair of jeans?" Paul asked her.

"Yes, why do you ask?"

"Go put them on and meet me at the elevators in the lobby in half an hour. Give Bo the day off. I'm going to take you somewhere where the jeans will come in handy."

Shortly, he arrived at her apartment building. Candice was waiting out front with Herman. She was dressed in formfitting jeans and a short-sleeved button-down plum-colored blouse.

"You're beautiful this afternoon, as always!" Paul told her.

"Thank you." She smiled.

Within the hour, they were entering the gate of the closed WWII air force base just west of the city. Paul drove to one end of the old runway before he parked.

"Have you ever ridden a bicycle?" he asked.

"No," she said hesitantly.

"Want to learn?"

"I don't know."

"Come on," Paul said, helping her out of the car. "Wait here while I get the bicycles off of the car top. Now feel the seat. Is it too high? Too low? Here, sit on it." Paul adjusted the seat to fit her. "Now these are the handlebars. This is how you steer the bicycle. Put your right foot on this pedal, now your left foot on this pedal. Don't worry, I won't let you fall. You pedal forward like this to make it go. If you want it to stop, you push the pedals backward like this. To coast, just stop pedaling. I'll be right beside you all of the time. Now start pedaling. That's right. If you feel you are falling to the left, turn the front wheel gradually to the left until you feel the bicycle has righted itself. It's the same for the right. That's great! You're doing great. Okay, I want you to make a turn. Turn the front wheel to the left and lean towards the left just a little. Feel that? Perfect. Now go straight ahead. You're doing fine. Okay, another turn around, great! Now when I say stop, I want you to try a stop. When you push the pedals backward and the bicycle stops, it will fall over to one side or the other, so be prepared to put you feet down as soon as you stop. Okay, now stop."

As she stopped, she was late putting her feet down, and the bicycle fell from under her. Paul quickly caught her in his arms, holding her gently to him, enjoying the moment immensely.

"I'm okay. You can turn me loose now." Candice smiled. "Oh, this was so much fun! Can we go again?"

"Sure," Paul said, picking up the bicycle.

Candice positioned herself as he had previously instructed her and started pedaling. Paul just ran along beside her, occasionally giving hints to improve her riding. She was making large ovals on the runway. She was such a quick study that very soon, Paul was standing in the center of the oval and merely telling her when to turn around. When she was able to make the turns without prompt, he climbed onto his bicycle and rode along beside her. They rode that way for many minutes, making the ovals longer and longer.

"It's getting dark out, and I think we should start back. Aren't you getting a little tired or hungry?" Paul asked.

"No, I'm not tired at all. This has been so much fun, Paul. I can never express to you how much this has meant to me."

"It has been a pleasure," Paul said, a smile in his voice. "And we can do this again and again. Now can we go eat? I'm famished!"

With his instructions, she rode her bicycle right up to the car, dismounted, and even put the kickstand down.

As Paul headed the car to a restaurant later, she was still bubbling on about being able to ride a bicycle. She was slightly bouncing in her seat, turning her head from side to side in a happy manner.

"I was extremely proud of you today, the way you mastered the bicycle," Paul said. "Is there anything that you can't do?"

"Yes, plenty of things." She laughed. "For instance, I can't drive!"

They ate a late meal and sat talking until near midnight. Later, Paul took her to her apartment building and walked her to the elevators. "You have to come up and say hi to Bo," she insisted.

"All right," Paul said, "just for a minute."

On the eighth floor, as they got off of the elevator, she took his arm. "Twenty-seven steps," she told him.

He walked silently beside her so she wouldn't lose count. At her apartment door, she felt for the keypad, entered a code, and opened the door. Bo greeted them. "Does Bo need to go out?" Paul asked.

"No, Herman walks him for me."

"That means he knows the combination to your apartment. Is that safe?"

"Sometimes, you have to trust people, Paul, like I trusted you today." She led him around her dark but neatly arranged apartment. "This is my workstation and living room, my kitchen, my bedroom and bathroom."

"Do you mind if I turn on a light?" he asked. "I really haven't seen anything you've shown me."

"Oh, I'm so sorry, Paul. I think there is a light switch near the door."

He found it and switched on the light. "That's better," he said. "We sighted people are at a disadvantage in the dark. Yes, I like the arrangement of your home very much. I can see how you would be comfortable here."

"Can I offer you something to drink? Cola, wine, coffee? I'm afraid I don't have any Pabst Blue Ribbon."

"No, thank you. I really should be going. I'll try to call you tomorrow."

"Paul, wait." She stepped close to him and took his hand. "Thank you for a most joyous day," she said softly, "one I shall never forget."

"You're very welcome," Paul said. He turned out the light and closed the door as he left her apartment.

Paul entered his apartment and checked his messages—one from Hal, another from his mother, and three from Helen. "I thought she said she never wanted to see me again," he said aloud. He checked the time. His mother would be in bed, and he didn't want to talk to Hal. He didn't really want to talk to Helen, but he called her anyway.

"What do you need, Helen?"

"I need to hear your voice. I miss you, Paul. When can I see you?"

"Helen, honey, it's just not working, me and you. You know my work schedule, yet you still put demands on me. You will never be satisfied with someone you can't order around. Why don't we agree to leave it alone? We can still be friends."

"I'm here at Federico's, all alone. Can't you come by for at least one drink?"

"I don't know. I just got in. I'm not dressed for Federico's."

"Please, Paul! Please don't leave me here all alone!"

"All right, one drink, but just one!"

A few minutes later, he slid into the seat across from her. Helen was, as usual, perfectly dressed and coiffured. Her beautiful blue eyes twinkled smilingly as she greeted him. "You are especially beautiful tonight!" Paul told her.

"You've been missing me!" she exclaimed.

"Bourbon and water," Paul told the waiter, "and another vodka martini for the lady."

"Very well, sir."

"How many have you had?" Paul inquired.

"Not enough."

"That means too many. Okay, after this one, I'm taking you home. How did you get here?"

"Well, if you're going to take me home, let's go now before our drinks come."

"How did you get here?" Paul repeated.

"I drove myself!"

"Give me your keys!"

"No!"

Paul stood up, grabbed her purse, and while she pounded on his back with her half-closed fists, he removed her keys and gave her purse back to her. "You are not driving in this condition!"

She sat back in her chair and smiled sweetly. "You do care about me."

"Of course I do."

Paul pulled a large denomination bill from his wallet and placed on the table. He took Helen by the hands and pulled her to her feet. They met the waiter about two steps away from their table. "Never mind about the drinks," Paul told him. "Emergency at home."

He drove her to the home she shared with her parents. She had her own separate entrance so her parents were not disturbed as he led her inside. He showed her that he was putting her keys back into her purse. "You can take a cab to Federico's in the morning and pick up your car. Have you eaten anything today?"

"Not since breakfast."

"That was yesterday. Get into your night clothes, and I'll be right back."

Paul went into her kitchenette and fixed her a grilled cheese sandwich, saturated with butter. When he returned, Helen was seated on the side of the bed, wearing only a lacy pajama top.

"Here, eat this!" he ordered, handing her the sandwich and a napkin, "It has medicinal properties."

"Then will you make love to me?" Helen asked in her sexiest tone.

"I like to know that I'm pleasing a woman, and you're too drunk to know! Good night, Helen."

CHAPTER 6

The thing that makes missing person cases so boring is all the telephone interviews and note taking. You can spend days following a false lead before coming to that conclusion. You have to try to reconstruct the days and hours leading up to the disappearance. Paul and Hal were spending many hours at their desks with just such interviews. Paul, bored with it all, placed a call to his mother.

"Sorry, Mom, I've just been up to my eyeballs in work. I intended to call you this past weekend, but you know how it goes...Helen? Oh, she's okay. I saw her just yesterday... No, we aren't serious...Well, she's sweet and all, and yes, she's beautiful, but she just isn't the one, Mom...I know, I know I'm almost thirty...Look, Mom, I have to go. Work's piling up...Love you too. Bye.

Paul hated to call home. It was always the same. "When are you going to give me some grandchildren?" He looked at his watch. It was nearly six thirty. He told dispatch he would be out of the office and on his cell phone until midnight. He called Candice.

"Hello, Paul. I have my jeans on. Can we go bicycle riding?"

"I'm on my way. Pick you up in twenty minutes."

"I'll be out front with Herman."

As Paul pulled into the loading zone, he saw Candice waiting for him. She was dressed in formfitting jeans and a summer top, her gorgeous red hair glowing in the late afternoon sunlight. *God she's lovely*, he thought.

Herman held the car door for her and helped her with her seat belt. "Good afternoon, sir," he said to Paul.

"My name is Paul, Herman. Please call me Paul. Yes, it is a great afternoon!"

Herman touched the bill of his cap as he closed the door.

Paul pulled out into traffic and headed toward the abandoned airfield. He parked at the end and in the center of the runway. Candice opened her door and started to get out.

"Wait just a minute," Paul said. "Do you remember what you told me yesterday? The one thing you couldn't do?"

"Yes, I told you one of the many things I can't do is drive an automobile."

Paul went to her side of the car and helped her out. He led her to the driver's side. "Get in," he instructed, placing her hand on the entryway handle. He helped her into the driver's seat. "Put on your seat belt and place your hands on the steering wheel. That's this thing right here. Okay, I'm going to adjust your seat now. There, is that more comfortable? Now, reach forward with you right foot. Do you feel that pedal? That's the brake pedal. Now just to the right of that is the accelerator. Put your right foot on that. That's right the small pedal there. Now you'll push that pedal towards the floor when you want to pick up speed and release it when you want to slow down. You push the brake pedal to slow down quicker or when you want to come to a complete stop. I'm going to get into the passenger seat now," Paul told her.

"Wait! What are you doing, Paul?"

"I'm giving you a driving lesson," he said. "You'll understand in just a few minutes."

After he was seated, he continued his instructions. "Let me have your right hand. This is called the gearshift lever. It's placed all the way forward in Park right now. Wrap your fingers around the gearshift lever. You feel that small lever on the front of it? You have to squeeze that whenever you want to change the position of the gearshift lever. As you pull the gearshift lever towards the rear of the vehicle, the first position that you'll feel is Reverse. We won't be backing today, so you can skip that position. The next position is called Neutral. This position allows your engine to run without the transmission being engaged. We'll skip that position today. The third position is called Drive. That's the one we'll be using today. There are three other positions, but we won't concern ourselves with them either. The lever is in Park now, you want to move it how many positions to place it in Drive?"

"Three. But, Paul—"

"Three. That's correct. Now let me have your right hand again. This is the ignition switch. Place your right foot on the brake pedal. Now put your hand on mine. Feel it as I start the engine. See how I released the key as soon as it started? Now you try. Perfect. Okay, now our engine is running. Keep your foot on the brake pedal and move the gearshift lever into Drive. Feel that? That was the transmission going into Reverse. The engine sounded as if it sped up as you shifted into Neutral. There, now we are in Drive. Take your foot off of the brake pedal and put it on the accelerator. Now push the accelerator slowly until you feel the car begin to move. The farther you push it towards the floor, the faster the car will go." Paul reached across her and opened her window. "Hear that Candice? You are driving."

"Oh! I'm so excited I'm trembling!"

"Okay, now I want you to drive slowly like this for a while and get the feel of the steering. Turn the steering wheel a few degrees first to one side and then to the other. How does that feel? Don't worry, this runway is long and wide, I won't let you hit anything. Now steer a little to the right. Yes, right there. Now gradually push the accelerator until we pick up some more speed. At the higher speeds, a quick turn of the steering wheel can turn us over so be aware of that. Can you hear the wind rushing by? You're speeding along at thirty miles an hour. Do you want to go faster?"

"Yes!" she said, as she pushed the accelerator harder. They were soon traveling at more than forty miles per hour. "How fast am I going now?"

"Forty-five."

"I'm driving, Paul! I'm driving!"

"Okay, now slow down. Slow down some more. I want you to turn around, and you're going a little too fast. Slower, slower, okay, now turn whichever way seems easiest to you. When I give you the word, just let go of the steering wheel, and it will straighten itself out. Now! Okay, you need to steer just a little to the left to get back in the center of the runway again. There, now you can drive us back to where we started."

Candice, feeling the exhilaration of mastering something she thought she would never be able to do, was soon speeding down the runway in the opposite direction.

"You're closing in on sixty miles per hour," Paul warned. "You should start slowing down now. We don't want to run out of runway."

She slowed, turned the car around, and with only a few suggested corrections on the car's position on the runway, she was soon speeding in the other direction. They continued this procedure for several laps before Candice slowed, turned the car around, and braked to a stop.

"Put the gearshift lever in Park and turn off the ignition," Paul instructed.

"That was so much fun!" she said excitedly. "I actually drove a car! Oh, I love you for this, Paul."

Paul put his left arm around her shoulders and pulled her toward him. She turned to face him. He placed his right hand gently under her chin, tilting her face up, and kissed her passionately on the lips. She responded in kind. "I can see you don't need any instructions in that area," he said.

Candice touched his face with both of her hands, taking her time tracing his mouth, his nose, his eyes, his eyebrows, his ears and hair. "You are even better-looking than I imagined," she said. "Is there more you want to teach me?"

"Yes," he whispered, "but not here in this vehicle. Not at this time."

They sat holding hands. He was staring at her, and she sat facing in his direction. After several moments of silence, he said apologetically, "I'm sorry you didn't get to ride your bicycle today. It's getting dark outside, and remember, I told you we sighted people are disadvantaged in the dark."

"Tomorrow, Paul?"

"Yes, maybe we can ride in the morning. I can pick you up around seven thirty. We can eat breakfast somewhere and then go riding. Is there anything else you've always wanted to do?"

"I think I'm content with the three gifts you've given me in the past two days."

"Three? Oh, you're counting the rose."

"No, that would be four. I was referring to riding a bicycle, driving a car, and kissing a prince."

"I missed seeing you kiss a prince," Paul said.

"Why, did you have your eyes closed?" She smiled. She touched his face again. "I'm so happy, Paul. Please don't ever make me sad."

"I'm going to kiss you again now," he said. He held her tenderly for a few minutes before releasing her seat belt and changing places with her.

Paul hardly slept; he was so anxious to see Candice again. He was pulling his car into the loading zone in front of her apartment ten minutes before the agreed upon time. Herman had not yet taken his post. Paul got out and hurried inside to the elevators. He paused. Should he go up and surprise her or wait for her there in the lobby? While he was deciding, he saw the light come on, calling for an elevator to the eighth floor. He decided to wait. Sure enough, very soon, the elevator door opened, and she stepped out, holding her telescopic cane in front of her.

"Can I be of some assistance, ma'am?" Paul asked, taking her hand.

"Yes, thank you, kind sir," she replied, grinning and taking his arm.

He bent and kissed her softly on the cheek. "You are so beautiful this morning."

She retracted her cane and put it into the fanny pack she was wearing with the pack in front. "Are we going to Mamacita's again this morning?"

"Yes, that's what I'd planned. Would you rather go to some other place?"

"Oh, no. I was hoping we would go back there. I love the atmosphere."

Paul held the door for her and watched as she buckled herself in. "Are you sure you don't want me to drive?" she teased.

"Do you remember the way to Mamacita's?"

"No. I guess it is better that you drive. Are you wearing perfume, Paul?"

"No. Oh, I'll bet your smelling the flowers in the rear seat. I brought you a small pot of colorful lupines. Do you like their smell?"

"Yes, they are quite fragrant."

They enjoyed their breakfast and one another's company for nearly an hour before heading to the airfield. Paul parked at the end of the runway as before and took the bicycles from the top of the car. Candice was quick to straddle her bicycle and was anxious to get started.

Paul stood beside her and positioned her bicycle so that it was headed in the correct direction. "This old runway is over a mile and a quarter in length. We are going to ride to the end and back. No short laps this morning. Is that okay with you?"

"Come on and stop stalling," she said as she started pedaling down the runway.

Paul jumped on his bicycle and rode after her. As they rode along side by side, they talked and laughed. Occasionally, Paul would give her a slight course change so they could stay near the center of the runway. Although they were riding at a moderate speed, they had soon reached the end of the runway. Paul instructed her to make a turn, and they headed back.

"Let's stop here a minute," Candice said as she braked to a stop. "I need a drink." She pulled a bottle of water from her pack and took several swallows.

"I carry a water bottle on my bicycle," Paul told her. I didn't think to outfit your bicycle with one. I apologize for being so thoughtless. Of course, you wouldn't want to drink from my bottle."

"Don't be silly. I brought this for both of us. If I'd let you drink from my bottle, then surely, you must agree I wouldn't hesitate to drink from yours."

"This has got to be the strangest conversation of my life!" Paul told her. "Shall we continue our ride?"

They rode close together for over two hours, talking and laughing and falling in love. Eventually, they had to end the ride so they could return to their separate lives.

Candice stood by her bicycle while Paul strapped his to the cartop carrier. Then she listened attentively as he strapped hers onto the carrier. As she started to climb into the car, Paul suddenly took her hand. She turned toward him as he kissed her passionately. She touched his face lovingly. They kissed again.

"Let me get in by myself," she told him. "I'm familiar with your vehicle by now." She climbed in, closed the door, and buckled herself into the seat. "I wish we had time for another driving lesson."

"Maybe tomorrow."

They were soon back at her apartment building. Paul was carrying the pot of flowers and holding her hand as they approached the elevator. "I've got just enough time to see you to your door," Paul told her.

"You can't come in for just a minute? Let me fix you a sandwich?"

"Another time maybe. Do you swim, Candice?"

"Yes, why do you ask?"

"I have a yearly pass to the pool in a private club near the station. I thought we could take a dip there after I get off work tonight. It will be after midnight. Would you like to do that? Do you have a suit?"

"Yes, I do have a suit, but I haven't had it on in a long time. I'm not sure it still fits. If it does, I would love to go swimming with you."

They had reached her door. She entered her pass code, and as she opened her door, she once again extended an invitation to him to stay for a sandwich. Instead, Paul gathered her into his arms and kissed her long and lovingly. "I'll call you before I come by tonight."

With all the sudden happy things happening in her life, Candice felt the urge to share her happiness with someone else. She had told Bo how happy she was, but that didn't seem enough. She opened a container of yogurt and called her mother.

"Candice, how great to hear from you. How are you, my dear?"

"Mother," she said excitedly, "how did you know when you were in love with Daddy?"

"I don't know exactly. I just knew. He was handsome and charming and made me feel so very special. Why do you ask, dear?"

"Mother, I'm in love! He's handsome and charming and makes me feel very special! Not only that, I just get goose bumps when he touches me. He's taught me to ride a bicycle and let me drive his car!"

"Wait a minute, Candice. Has there been a miracle that you didn't tell me about?"

"Yes, Mother, and his name is Paul! No, I haven't regained my sight, but he gives me such pleasure in so many other ways!"

"I don't want to hear about your sex life, Candice!"

"I'm not talking about that. I still haven't ever experienced that kind of physical love, Mother. I may always be a virgin. I'm talking about the thrills I get by just being close to Paul, listening to him talk and laugh, riding a bicycle next to him, speeding along behind the wheel of his car."

"I'm still trying to picture you driving. How did you pull that off?"

"He took me to an old abandoned airfield runway. Told me what to do and let me do it. I drove around out there for hours. I got his car up to sixty miles per hour."

"I'm having this Paul person arrested for endangering my daughter's life."

"I was in no danger, Mother. And guess what? Paul is a police detective, so you'd be asking them to arrest one of their own. Can't you just be happy for me?"

"I am happy for you, darling, but I worry too. When do you think your father and I will get to meet Paul?"

"I don't know. We haven't discussed our families as yet. I'll talk to him about it when I see him tonight."

"What dangerous things are the two of you doing tonight?"

"We're just going swimming. I really do love him, Mother. I've never been so happy."

"I love you, Candice. Please be careful. Bye now.

"Bye, Mother. I love you too."

CHAPTER 7

Paul and Hal ran down every lead, but to no avail. They were sitting at their desks, going over everything when Paul opined, "This guy isn't a missing person. He is a fugitive! Thousands in debt, records of multiple trips to Las Vegas and Henderson, a wife and a mistress. I think the bank where he worked should do an audit on all the accounts he was responsible for. I bet some of those with little or no action in the past year are almost if not completely depleted."

"I got a recent picture from the guy's mistress and circulated it to all the TV outlets," Hal advised. "I think it's going national tonight on all of the major networks."

"Good job," Paul said. "The only way we're going to find this guy is if someone sees him and calls in. I guess we could haunt the Las Vegas and Henderson casinos for a chance to see him. Do you think we could get the captain to send us to Vegas for a couple weeks all expenses paid?"

"Dream on!" Hal said. "Hey, what's up with you and Helen?"

"We're in one of our cooldown periods," Paul replied.

"I saw Marisa again last night. Met her dad, Tony, and her Uncle Guido. She isn't Spanish or Cuban like I thought. Turns out they're Italian. I think they're connected," Hal said.

"Every Italian isn't a member of the mob, Hal," Paul replied.

"Well, Tony and Guido don't care for Marisa's old man either. I hung out with 'em, had some beer, played some pool."

"I'm happy for you. Maybe Marisa's husband won't kill you after all. I really wasn't looking forward to training another rookie."

Near the end of his shift, Paul called Candice. "Did you find a suit?" he asked.

"Yes," she told him. "It's a little tight in places, but I think it will do. I seemed to have gained weight in the chest area since I last wore it."

"I forgot to ask. Will the chlorine in the water hurt your—"

"My eyes, Paul? No more than yours."

"I'll pick you up at your door about twelve twenty. There's a place at the pool where we can change, but why don't you just wear your suit under your dress?"

Paul had a suit in the pool locker room, but there was no one in the pool area that late at night, and he didn't want to leave Candice alone by the side of the pool. As he helped her out of her dress, he remarked at her loveliness in the one-piece suit. He quickly removed his clothes before helping her to the pool ladder. As she pushed away from the ladder into the pool, Paul dived into the water, coming up very near her. Candice busied herself by becoming familiar with the size and shape of the pool. After which, they swam laps. They treaded water in the deep end and dived from the side of the pool and the low board. They laughed and talked for over two hours before Paul climbed out of the pool and helped her out. He handed her a towel.

As she dried her hair, she told him, "I have a change of underwear in my purse. Is there somewhere I can change out of this wet suit?"

Paul led her to the women's locker room. He took her inside and introduced her to the showers, the lockers, the benches, the stalls, and the lavatories. "These rows of lockers may cause you some difficulty, so when you're dressed, just call me. I'll be just outside the door."

Paul toweled off and dressed. When she called, he went in, and taking her by the hand, led her out of the shower area. She held the wet suit out toward him. "I forgot to bring something to put this wet suit in," she said, "What did you do with yours?"

"I didn't wear one," he said as he took the wet suit from her hand and rolled it up in a dry towel.

She was silent for a while. "Why didn't you tell me we were going skinny-dipping?" she teased.

"Am I to believe that you would have swum naked with me if you'd only known?"

"You'll never know now, will you?"

"Well, the next time we come swimming, you'll have another chance to do the skinny-dipping thing. But I don't promise to keep my eyes closed."

"Then I will not promise to keep my hands to myself!" Candice said.

He took her hands and pulled her to him, kissing her tenderly on the mouth. He then led her to his car. As they headed toward her apartment, she remarked, "I talked to my mother today. She is anxious to meet you. She wants us to go up soon for a visit."

"Sure," Paul said. "I'd like to meet your family too. I'm sure we can work something out."

"Sunday after next is Mother's Day. Do you think we could go up there on Mother's Day?" Candice asked.

"That sounds like a very good day to meet them. What are they like? Is your Dad going to circle me with a firearm while your brothers sharpen their knives?"

Candice laughed. "No, my father is nothing like that, and I don't have any brothers or sisters."

"Whew," Paul said. "I was worried there for a while."

"How tall are you, Paul? You seem quite tall when you caress me."

"I'm a smidgen over six feet four inches in my bare feet. With these shoes, more like six feet five. I'm guessing you're five feet three inches."

"Exactly right."

"It's my job to observe and make sound conclusions."

They were at her door. She invited him in for the sandwich he had turned down earlier. He agreed to stay for a little while. He found the light switch and switched it on. Bo found her and nuzzled her hand. She spoke softly to Bo while she busied herself in the kitchen.

A short time later, she sat a plate down in front of Paul. "This is my own recipe for a muffuletta sandwich. I hope you like it. I use Italian bread, Italian olive salad, and extra thin slices of meats and provolone cheese. I still don't have any Pabst. I hope you like iced tea."

"Umm," Paul said as he bit into the muffuletta and tasted the savory mixture of the spices of the Italian olive salad meats and cheese. "I have never tasted anything like this in my life."

"You don't care about me, just my sandwich," she pretended to wail.

"This is *good*!" Paul said. "I can't think of the right superlative. I could eat one of these every night for the rest of my life if you were the one fixing it for me it!"

"I'm glad you like it," Candice said as she sat down beside him on the settee.

Paul finished his sandwich, washed it down with his iced tea, went to the kitchen, and poured himself another glass of tea. "Can I bring you something?" he asked.

"No, thank you. I'm fine, Paul. Please come back and sit here beside me."

He did as she asked and sat down. He put his arm around her shoulders, pulled her to him, and kissed her lovingly on her lips. She responded with more fervor than ever before. She drew her face away from his and put her hands on his face, gently feeling it over and over again.

"I love you, Paul," she told him. "I love you." She kissed him again passionately.

Paul was having some intense emotions of his own. He felt the urge to take their passionate kissing into the bedroom. Did he really love this woman, or was this just his carnal nature about to take over? He thought too much of her to lead her on. He enjoyed another few moments of passionate kissing before gently pushing her away.

"Don't you love me, Paul?" she asked.

"I think you're wonderful," he said. "I think about you every waking moment and dream of you at night. I dote on your accomplishments. Right now, I want to pick you up and carry you into your bed and make mad, passionate love to you. Yes, I think I love you, but is it the kind of love you need and deserve? That I don't know."

She snuggled against him. "You love me, Paul. I know you do."

They sat like that for only a few minutes before Paul stood, bent, and kissed her softly on her forehead. "It's late. I have to go. I'll call you later." He turned off the light and let himself out into the hall.

Paul was schooled in assembling a number of facts, assessing them, and coming up with a logical conclusion. That's what detective work entailed. But this time, he was stumped. Was he only interested in Candice so he could give her things like bicycle riding and driving? Watching her enjoy these things had been like a thrill he'd never felt before. Was he hesitant to declare his love for her because of the fear that he would someday find that her blindness could bring him a problem he couldn't solve? He tried to imagine every possible scenario where her being unable to see might affect their relationship. As long as he was part of these hypothetical situations, he did not see a problem. When he pictured her coping alone, he felt panic. He concluded that his innate desire to protect someone he claimed as his own was the stronger emotion. *This may be a tenet of love*, he thought, *but is it true love?* He knew he wanted to give that to Candice also. She deserved a true and unselfish love.

Paul eventually fell asleep only minutes before his radio alarm sounded. He turned it off and reset it for two hours later. When it sounded two hours later, he was still not ready to get up but dragged his tired body into the shower anyway.

"Man, you look like the part of the chicken they usually throw away!" Hal told Paul as he set coffee in front of him. "What did you do last night?"

"Nothing to write home about," Paul said. "Thanks for the coffee."

"Helen give you a hard time last night?" Hal asked.

"No. Forget me," Paul said. "Anything happen on Crimpton's picture?"

"Nothing yet," Hal answered. "The networks are going to keep running it."

"O'Keefe, Stewart, get in here!" Captain Bower bellowed.

Paul and Hal sauntered into the captain's office.

"While you two are loafing, I've got another two dozen cases that need looking into. Here, take your pick. The DA thinks we'll be ready for a prelim on the Hernandez case in a couple of weeks. You'll need to be available to testify. Any problem there?"

"No sir," Hal answered for the both of them.

"Oh hell, here!" the captain said, handing all of the folders to Paul. "Can't find the one you want, solve 'em all!" He waved them out of his office.

Paul put the stack of folders on his desk and started going through them. "Stolen tricycle, you can have that one. Weird moaning noises coming from a neighbor's garage late at night. Oh, here's an interesting one. A report of someone seeing a car speeding up and down the old abandoned airfield runway. I'll take that one."

Paul continued to try to keep his mind on his work, but he continually thought about Candice and their present situation. *I had no right to inject myself into her very stable and ordered life just to entertain myself with her successes,* he thought. If he should go along with her romantic ideas, it could lead to a situation, such as marriage and children, that could only complicate and burden her already difficult life. He imagined her, sightless, trying to chase a toddler. *The best thing for her,* he thought, *is for me to ease back out of her life while I still can.* He'd also need to do something about the promise to meet her parents. He was still deep in thought when the phone on his desk began to ring.

"Third precinct, Detective O'Keefe…Yes, ma'am…Your name please…You're sure it was Crimpton?…The Bellagio at the black-jack tables…What day was that?…What time of day?…Can you tell me what he was wearing?…Anything else you remember?… Do you have a number where I can reach you in the event I need to contact you later? Thank you very much, Miss Hastings."

"Hal," Paul called to his partner, "you know anybody in the Las Vegas Police Department?"

"Yes, as a matter of fact I do," Hal bragged. "Officer Renee Travis. Cute little blonde, neat figure, lots of laughs."

"I'm not looking for one of your girlfriends," Paul replied sarcastically. "I think we need someone to stake out the Bellagio. I just got an eyewitness report that Crimpton has been seen at the blackjack tables there."

"I'll run it by the captain. Maybe he'll send one of us out there for a couple of days," Hal said hopefully.

"You do that," Paul replied. "I'm going to take a lunch break."

Paul called the number to the switch board at Candice's apartment. He soon heard her sweet voice fill his ear.

"You didn't call me at all this morning," she said. "I had hoped you would take me driving again. Or at least bicycle riding. Are you okay, Paul?"

"Didn't sleep very well last night. Spent most of the night thinking about you, us, your folks—things like that."

"Have I ruined our relationship by saying I love you, Paul? I hope not because I am sure that what I feel is truly love."

"You may think you love me, but you haven't had time to really get to know me. You need to give us more time, Candice."

"Will I see you tonight, Paul? Will you come to my apartment?"

"I'm not sure."

"Then I'll meet you somewhere. Anywhere you wish. Why do you sound so cold, Paul?"

"No, I don't want you wandering all over the city at night. Look, maybe…I'll, okay, I'll come by your apartment for a little while after I check out tonight. I should be there a little after midnight. We'll talk then."

"Great, I'll fix you another muffuletta." She laughed softly. "I can't wait for you to get here!"

"I'll see you then."

"I love you, Paul."

Well, I shouldn't have tried to break it off with her over the phone, Paul thought. *I'll let her down gently tonight.*

As he approached her door later that night, Paul rehearsed his speech. He intended to tell her something like, "Hey, it has been fun," but as soon as she opened her door and saw her standing there, he became tongue-tied. She was dressed in an oxygen blue figure-hugging satin jumpsuit with bell-bottoms. That, and her red hair shimmering in the light she had turned on for him, caused him to take a second look. He stammered, "God, y-you are so beautiful! Right now, I'm at a disadvantage in the *light*."

"Are you hungry?" she said sweetly. "I have your sandwich prepared."

He pulled her to him. She quickly yielded her lithe body to his caress. He kissed her passionately! "I'm more hungry for this!" He held her tightly against him, kissing her again and again. Finally, he released her. "Okay, Candy," he said. "I surrender! You win. I'm crazy in love with you! I'm ready to accept your love and all that comes with it."

"You mean it, Paul? You really want me?"

"More than anything I've ever wanted in my entire life!"

"Then who was that on the phone earlier?" she asked sweetly.

"Just let me enjoy this for a little bit longer. We'll have plenty of time to be serious later." He pulled her to him again, kissing her lovingly. Just before their passion reached the point of no return, he released her and asked for his muffuletta.

Once Paul accepted the fact that he was totally in love with Candice, he put his entire self into his commitment. Fragrant flowers arrived at her door daily. They dined together every morning. They spent a part of every day either bicycling, swimming, or walking hand in hand in the park. On rare occasions, he would take her to the airfield to watch the enjoyment on her face as she drove up and down the runway.

"I'm just perfecting my driving skills," she would say.

On Mother's Day, he took her to her parents' home so he could meet the MacFarlanes. They were a couple in their late forties. Her mother, Marilyn, was smaller than Candice, about five feet two with blonde hair that was streaked with silver. She taught piano in her home. Her father, Richard, was a thin man about five feet ten inches tall, with slightly receding reddish-brown hair. He was wearing a pair of wire-rimmed glasses. He was an accredited architect with his own business. Her parents had many questions for the young couple.

After a pleasant and filling evening meal, Richard asked Paul if he would like to take a look at his new barbecue pit out in back. When they were sufficiently out of hearing distance of the two women, Richard asked, "What's the situation with you and Candice? Do you love her? Have the two of you discussed a future together?"

"I have to be truthful with you, sir. I think she is amazing. I know she is beautiful and intelligent and well, way out of my league. Seriously, it scares the hell out of me just thinking of what a future with her could be like."

"You mean because she's visually impaired?"

"Yes, sir, that's part of it, but more than that, I doubt my own abilities to give her everything she deserves. She is so knowledge-able and gifted and, yes, special in every way. And I'm, well, this."

"Have you asked her to marry you? Is that what the cold feet is all about?"

"No, I haven't. I want to ask her, but I'm not sure that I'm capable of making her as happy as I want her to be, as happy as she deserves to be."

"If you want my advice—and I'm going to give it to you any-way—I say you should ask her. And when she says yes—and she will say yes—you marry my little girl and love her just like you do today. Just love her, and everything else will fall into place."

Richard paused, watching for the desired reaction on Paul's face. "You see that beautiful blonde woman in the window there?" Richard continued. "I've loved her probably longer than you've been alive. We've been married for almost thirty years. Sometimes, all we had to live on was love. Keep that in mind, and you'll be all right. Now how about a game of yard darts?"

Inside, the two women were also talking of the young cou-ple's relationship.

"You're right, Candice. Paul is very handsome and charming. And I can see how happy he makes you. Also, it's plain to see that he adores you. Has he mentioned marriage?"

"No, we have never talked of it."

"Well, I won't be surprised when he does. Have you thought about what you'll say?"

"I'll say yes, of course. I love him so much, Mother. I've read hundreds of books where the characters fall in love, but until it happens to you, there is no way to understand it or to describe it."

"Have you thought about children?"

"No, I don't want to think about that right now. If Paul wants to marry me, I'm sure we'll talk about it sometime."

"Blindness is not hereditary, Candice! Just follow your heart, and everything will work out. You'll see. Now let's go join the men."

The conversation in the yard, once the ladies joined the men, turned to weather and current events. Soon the young couple said their good-byes and were on their way back to the city.

"What were you and my father talking about?" Candice wanted to know.

"Oh, lots of things. He thinks the White Sox have a chance at the pennant this year. What universe is he living in?"

"What else? Mother said you men really looked like you were discussing something serious out there."

"He threatened to kill me if I ever hurt you."

"Stop lying to me, Paul. I want to know!"

"Well, it was an implied threat. He said he thought you were really in love with me." Paul grinned. "But he thinks you're too young to marry."

"You talked to my father about marrying me?"

"In a manner of speaking."

"You asked my father for my hand in marriage, and you haven't asked me? What's going on, Paul?"

"I said, in a way, we talked of marriage. Why are you getting upset?"

"I just thought you asked the bride-to-be first, that's all."

"Well, Dick asked me if my intentions towards you were honorable, and of course, I lied and said yes."

"Oh," she said, reaching to touch his face. "That's what I thought!" she said as she felt his grinning face. "You've been teasing me."

"Guilty as charged," Paul said, kissing her outstretched hand.

It was less than a week later that Candice and Paul were walking down the sidewalk on the street that runs in front of the Truxton Tower Apartment building. Paul had told her he wanted her to go shopping with him.

"This looks like a neat store," Paul told her. "Let's go in here." He held her hand and led her to a counter toward the rear of the store.

"What kind of a store is it, Paul? Tell me what you see."

"Place your left hand here on the countertop," he told her, "and no peeking."

Paul signaled the salesman to silently measure her ring finger. The salesman held up the size 5 template. Paul then led her slowly along the counters until he saw what he was looking for. He pointed to it and the ring finger on Candice's hand. All the time, Paul was talking about the lighting, the colorful decorations, the manikins in the window—a constant chatter in an attempt to throw her off. The salesman nodded and placed a size 5 set on top of the counter for Paul to examine. Paul nodded and handed the set and his credit card to the salesman, who went to a cash register and rang up the sale. A few minutes later, Paul and Candice were walking along, headed back toward her apartment building.

"That was pathetic," Candice said. "Do you really think I didn't know what was going on back there?"

"You peeked!" Paul whined. "You spoiled my surprise!"

"I'm sorry. I promise to act surprised later."

In her apartment sometime later, they were sitting close together on the settee. Paul eased himself off of it and dropped down on his knees in front of Candice. He took her hand and softly asked her that all-important question. She took his face between her hands and feeling his seriousness, she whispered, "Yes."

Paul placed the ring on her finger. "You can look now," he told her.

She hurriedly felt the ring with her right hand. "So this is what it feels like," she said. Then, touching her breast just over her heart, she said, "And this is what it feels like to be engaged to be married!"

She reached for Paul with both hands. He obediently surrendered his face to her touch and her kisses.

CHAPTER 8

Paul was seated at his desk at the third precinct when the call came in. "This is Lieutenant Hawkins of the Henderson Police. We have your man, Boris Crimpton, in lockup here."

"That's great news," Paul said. "Are you holding him on any additional charges?"

"No, you can come and get him anytime. We picked him up at the Klondike Sunset Casino. He was drunk and making a scene about losing. He's been living on a houseboat on Lake Mead. Houseboat belongs to a wealthy widow woman. She claimed he was going to marry her."

"Another mistress!" Paul said. "Sounds like cards isn't the only way this joker is unlucky. Someone will be out to get him soon. Thank you, Lieutenant."

Paul made a verbal report to Captain Bower. "You want to go out to Henderson and get this perp, O'Keefe? Or would you rather I dispatched Stewart?"

"Let Hal go. He needs some time in the sun."

"Stewart!" the captain bellowed. "Get in here!"

When Hal returned, he was all smiles. "Guess you're going to have to find the missing tricycle all by yourself," he teased. "I have a plane to catch."

"Stay away from the roulette wheels," Paul warned him.

"No problem, partner. The only game of chance I'm going to play is with pretty Officer Renee Travis."

"What if Officer Travis has a new last name?"

"That won't stop old Hal!"

"One of these days, I'm going to have to visit you in the morgue!"

"Yeah, but I'll die happy."

"Get out of here," Paul ordered.

It was almost six before Paul took a break from his police duties. The first thing he did was call Candice. "Hi, Candy, honey, what are you doing?"

"I've been on the phone with my mother. She's helping me plan this amazing wedding!" Candice answered. She went on to describe everything in much detail—gowns, flowers, church, invitations, wedding cake, music, food, etc.

When she finally took a breath, Paul asked, "Am I invited?"

"We'll see," she told him with a smile in her voice.

"I've heard it said that the wedding is *all* about the bride."

"Yes, I'm going to be a bride, Paul! Something I thought I would only be able to read about and dream about. Thank you for this. I love you so much."

"It might not have happened if you would just look before you jump in front of someone's bicycle," he teased.

"Are you saying you would never marry me if I was sighted?"

"I guess so."

"Then my being blind is a miracle."

"I love you, Candy. You always think in the positive. I'll see you a little after midnight."

"Muffuletta sandwich, Paul?"

"Your sweet lips will be enough. Bye now." Paul pushed the Off button on his cell phone.

It was late afternoon of the following day. Paul sat and thought about what he must say to the next person he had to talk to. He disliked hurting people and was at a loss as to just how to approach this task. He checked out with dispatch, climbed into his car, and drove to Helen's house.

Helen's parents were sitting on the front porch and saw him when he got out of his car. "Helen's in the back by the pool," her father volunteered.

"Thank you," Paul answered. He opened the gate to the high wooden security fence and let himself into their backyard pool area.

Helen was lying topless by the pool, sunbathing in the late afternoon sun. When she saw him, she sat up smiling. "Paul, darling, I've been dying to hear from you. I was afraid some bad criminals had kidnapped you. You haven't called me since that night at Federico's. You aren't still sore at me about that, are you?"

"No, I'm not sore."

"I was about to turn onto my stomach. Will you put some of this lotion on my back?"

Paul sat down on the edge of her lounge and started applying the lotion.

"Listen, Helen, I have to tell you something." He paused.

"Why so glum, Paul? What do you need to tell me that would make you this hesitant?"

"It's just that…well, you know how fond I am of you. Listen, Helen, I'm getting married."

She lay there in silence for what seemed a very long time while he rubbed the lotion onto her skin. Finally, she replied, "This is very sudden. What happened? Did you get some bimbo pregnant? What about us, Paul? I thought we had something special."

"Look, Helen, you and I, we were never serious. We had a lot of good times. I've been trying to tell you for sometime that it's over. Can we at least be civil to each other? I love you dearly, Helen, but I'm not in love with you."

"Well, tell me about this other woman. How long have you been seeing her? Is she prettier than me?"

"I don't want to get into all of that right now, Helen. Maybe I'll send you an invitation."

"Don't bother!" she stood up, threw her top at him, and marched into the house.

Well, at least she didn't yell at me or threaten suicide, he thought. He said good-bye to Helen's parents before leaving.

That could have gone a lot better, Paul thought as he drove back to the precinct. *Helen is so bipolar. One day, she hates me the next day she doesn't. Who can live like that?*

He pulled into his parking space just as Hal was leaving. Hal waved his airline ticket at him. "Got to go home and pack." Hal grinned. "Want to drive me to the airport later?"

"What time?"

"My plane leaves at ten past eleven. I have to be there an hour before it leaves. Pick me up about nine thirty."

"Yeah, okay, I'll drive you. Pick you up in a little bit."

CHAPTER 9

The O'Keefe-MacFarlane wedding was far too extravagant in Paul's mind, but he overlooked it when he saw how excited and overjoyed his bride was. Candice was radiantly beautiful as he stood beside her holding her hand and reciting the vows. Their kiss, as the ceremony ended, was full of emotion and promise.

They honeymooned in Key West where Candice, with patient instructions from Paul, was seen water skiing, parasailing, and working the controls of both a rented personal watercraft and a sleek inboard motorboat.

While deep-sea fishing, she hooked into a massive marlin and worked hours trying to land it, finally passing the chore off to the boat crew. They brought it alongside and winched it out of the water just long enough for her to feel of it and have her picture taken with it before it was released to return to the sea.

They spent their nights walking on the sands, listening to the music of small Cuban combos in open-air restaurants or wrapped in each other's arms in their hotel room. Every day and every night, Candice was learning new and exciting things she never dreamed possible. As they lay together at sunrise early one morning, Paul whispered to her that the sun was just coming up.

"What does it look like, Paul? Please tell me. What do you see?"

Paul described for her the orange orb that appeared to be rising out of the sea. How the ocean in front of it had an orange hue. He described how some gulls in flight crossing in front of the sun appeared to be tiny and black. He explained that the sun seemed to be very close to them and quite large.

"It's almost as beautiful as the sight here next to me!" Paul whispered as he gently brushed some of her gorgeous red hair from her cheek.

Richard MacFarlane designed a custom home for them to be built not far from where he and Marilyn lived in the suburbs. While it was under construction, Candice and Paul continued to live in her tiny apartment in Truxton Tower. Although many of the features of the new home were similar to the arrangement of her present apartment, there was also more space and many built in conveniences that Candice would have to master before she would be completely comfortable in the new house. There was even a special room for Bo, with a dog door leading directly into the backyard.

On the date of their fourth month anniversary, Paul and Candice moved into their new home. Paul led her around the rooms, explaining where each item was located. Candice's analytical mind was fast at work calculating distances, steps, turns, sounds, and smells. She carried her telescopic cane with her as an added tool to her analysis. In mere days, she was maneuvering through the house without mishap. Paul watched with awe and pride.

One night, as they lay in bed, Paul pulled her near to him and cradled her soft body in his arms lovingly. As he kissed her softly, she whispered, "Paul, darling, you're going to be a daddy."

Paul propped himself up on one elbow and looked at her petite form. "Are you sure?" he asked.

"Yes," she said, "I'm quite sure."

Paul pulled her to him again, kissing her softly before lying back down on his back. "Wow!" he said. "It's hard to believe—me, a daddy, and you, a mama! That's amazing. That's just…fantastic!"

Candice snuggled against him. "When the baby comes," she said, "I'll have it all! You will have given me everything I ever dreamed of! I love you so much, Paul!"

Paul pulled her close, caressing her small soft body. "I love you too," he whispered.

Little Marilyn Candice O'Keefe was born early one spring morning nearly seven months later. The birds were singing sweeter; the flowers gave off more fragrant perfumes. The sky was bluer; the air was fresher. She had a covering of fine red hair on her tiny head and dark, almost-black eyes. She weighed in at exactly seven pounds.

Paul sat in the hospital room, feasting his eyes on his beautiful wife and daughter. He watched as their child snuggled to her mother's breast to take her first meal. Candice, wanting Paul to describe their infant daughter to her, said, "Tell me, Paul. Tell me. What do you see?"

"I see…heaven," Paul responded.

IT HAPPENED ON
THE INTERSTATE

HERBERT DURBIN

CHAPTER 1

It was already 3:30 p.m. when Dave left Barstow. They had been behind schedule in loading the refrigerated trailer in Fresno. Then construction on the highway in Bakersfield had put him even farther behind. The 55 mph California truck speed limit had also kept him from making any time. Dave knew the speed limit would jump to 70 mph when he hit Interstate 40, so in anticipation, he pushed the big Freightliner diesel to near 72 mph. It was still 144 miles to Needles and an additional 210 miles on to Flagstaff. There, he planned to fuel and rest a few minutes before continuing on east toward Albuquerque. He had a truckload of fresh produce headed for markets on the Eastern Seaboard. If nothing else got in his way, he would be in Flagstaff in another five and a half hours. Dave set his cruise control for 72 mph and relaxed as he maneuvered the semi onto the divided highway.

He passed the time by singing along with the artists on a country gold CD. It was just after 11:00 p.m., local time, when he pulled his truck up to the diesel pumps at the Flying J truck stop several miles past downtown Flagstaff.

While the tanks filled, he brought his logbook up to date. As he climbed down to top off the last tank, he noticed a shadowy figure moving quietly between his truck and the one beside it, checking door handles. Dave waited quietly in the shadow near the front wheel. When the figure started to sneak past the front of his truck, he quickly jumped out and grabbed him.

Dave immediately realized he was not struggling with a man, but instead was grappling with a noticeably supple female. She was flailing away with her arms and kicking with her feet as she tried to free herself from his grasp. Dave grabbed an arm and twisted it up behind her back while holding the other arm securely against her side. He picked her up off of the ground and held her tightly against himself while she continued to kick and try to twist free.

"Turn me loose," she yelled, trying to free her arm from his grasp.

"What are you up to sneaking around out here like this?" Dave asked her.

"I was trying to hitch a ride, if you must know!" she fumed. "Now let me go!"

Dave loosened his grip on her arm. "You might just try asking for a ride," he said as he eased her to the pavement while still maintaining his control.

"I did!" she answered curtly. "I've asked a dozen truckers, and they all said no! Company policy or something."

"Look," Dave said, "I'm going to turn you loose now. Then I'm going inside to pay up and get a sandwich. If you're still here wanting a lift when I get back, I'll take you a little way with me."

"Would you have enough money for two sandwiches?" she asked pitifully. "I've lost all of my money."

"Come on," Dave said, looking at her face for sincerity. "Let's go inside."

Dave paid for his fuel, ordered two meals, and went into the restroom to clean up and splash some water onto his face. He wanted to make Albuquerque tonight. When he returned, the woman was still at the table, just finishing her meal. Dave eased himself into the chair across from her and tore into his sandwich. The woman sat watching him. Dave swallowed, took a big swig of his drink, and asked, "What's your name, little one?"

"Please don't call me that. My name is Jodie."

"Well, Jodie, how far are you going? I'm headed east to Atlanta."

"East is good."

"How old are you? You aren't a runaway, are you?"

"I'm twenty-five," she stated.

"Do you have any bags here at the truck stop?" Dave inquired.

"No. Look, don't ask me so many questions."

"I'm trying to save myself some trouble," Dave informed her. "If you're a runaway or in trouble with the law or in some other kind of trouble, I could be setting myself up for a lot of grief. That's why the company drivers told you they couldn't let you ride along. I own my own rig, but I usually say no also. Do you want to tell me something to ease my mind?"

"I'm not a runaway, and I'm not in any trouble with the law. Feel better now?" she asked him.

Dave grinned and wiped his face with a napkin. He extended his hand. "Hi, Jodie, I'm Dave."

His big grin and her full stomach put Jodie at ease. She followed along beside him as he returned to his truck. "Get in and make yourself at home," he told her, lifting her into the cab. "I hope you like country music. All of my CDs are country gold—Hank Williams, Marty Robbins, Ernest Tubb, Eddy Arnold, Jim Reeves, Buck Owens, Conway Twitty, Loretta Lynn, stuff like that.

"Whatever," she said.

"I also have a Roy Orbison. You might like him."

As Dave drove the big rig back onto Interstate 40, Jodie settled down into her seat, watching the road ahead. Once Dave had the rig up to speed, he set the cruise control, settled back, and looked at his small passenger. She looked a lot younger than twenty-five. Her pretty little face was covered with entirely too much makeup. Her black hair was pulled back into a ponytail. Her large dark eyes, when she looked at him, reminded him of a lost puppy. She was wearing an SF Giants baseball cap, a high school letterman jacket and jeans. Her tan suede knee-high boots looked out of place with the rest of her attire. She was not carrying a purse.

"If you get tired," Dave said, "you can climb up there into the top bunk in the sleeper. The lower bunk is mine. Just drop the curtain if you want some privacy.

"Maybe later," she said. "Do you have anything to drink?"

"There's a small refer under that TV right behind you," Dave explained. "It has some bottled water in it. You can get me one too."

She unbuckled her seat belt and checked out the sleeper. A few minutes later, she returned to her seat, gave Dave a bottled water, buckled up, and opened her water. "You have a home away from home here, don't you?" she asked.

"It saves on hotel bills," Dave responded.

They were quiet for several miles. Finally, Dave broke the silence. "What are you running away from Jodie? Strict parents?"

"No, nothing like that."

"You don't have any luggage, no purse, nothing. I don't have to be a detective to know you left somewhere in a hurry without a plan. I'm not going to harm you, Jodie. I just need to know what I've gotten myself into."

"If you must know, I got tired of being a punching bag!" Jodie said. Then she fell silent again.

"Who would hit a little thing like you?" Dave asked.

Jodie sat silent for a long time. Finally, she sighed. "I'm tired," she said. "Are you sure it's okay for me to sleep up there in your bunk?"

"Sure," he said. "We'll be in Albuquerque about two thirty their time. Do you want me to wake you then?"

"I guess," she said sleepily.

The truck stop in Albuquerque was large. The building housed a chain restaurant and a large convenience store. There was also a lounge and shower area. Dave topped off his fuel tanks before waking Jodie.

"Rise and shine!" he called, sticking his head into the sleeper compartment.

"We're in Albuquerque already?" she asked.

"Yes, I'm just getting my overnight bag," Dave told her. "I'm going to get a shower and shave and change into some clean clothes. Wouldn't hurt you to visit the showers either. Here," Dave said, handing her some money, "this will get you into the showers."

"Thank you, but I don't have any shampoo or soap," she complained.

"Come on," Dave said. "Let's go shopping."

Dave had only intended to get her a few necessities, but by the time they got to the checkout register, she was carrying a small overnight bag, toilet articles, and a change of clothes.

"I can pay you back for all of this," Jodie promised.

Dave was waiting for her in the lounge just outside the shower area. He hardly recognized her. Her long black hair was now shiny and combed out. It framed her pretty little face, which was now devoid of any makeup. She was carrying her new overnight bag and a plastic bag containing the soiled clothing.

"This place has laundry facilities, but we've spent too much time here already," Dave explained. "It's going to be close to 8:00 a.m. by the time we reach Amarillo. Why don't you pick out a snack for you to eat later for your breakfast, and let's start moving."

Jodie picked up a small package of powdered sugar covered doughnuts, a package of chips, and an orange drink. Dave got his thermos filled with coffee. They were soon back on Interstate 40. The truck speed limit on interstate highways in New Mexico was seventy-five miles per hour, so Dave set his cruise control for seventy-seven.

Jodie sat back, opened her package of doughnuts, and began to eat happily. Dave concentrated on his driving. For a long while, they sat in silence.

Finally, Jodie remarked, "You remind me of my dad. He's big and usually kind, like you."

"When's the last time you saw him?" Dave asked.

"About seven years ago when I graduated high school. He didn't approve of my choice of boyfriends, and we argued about it."

"We dads tend to be very protective of our daughters," Dave told her.

"You have a daughter, Dave?"

"Yes, I have two children—a boy and a girl. My daughter is about your age. My son is a couple of years older. Do you have any siblings?" Dave asked.

"A younger brother. He's fourteen, I think." Jody replied. "Where is your family now?"

"My daughter is married, living in Katy, Texas," Dave answered. "That's a small town near Houston. My son is a partner in a Ford dealership in Panama City, Florida."

"And your wife?" Jodie inquired innocently.

"She left me for a real estate broker several years ago. Nicest thing she ever did for me. I had a fleet of ten trucks at the time. It was the biggest headache in the world! Working eighteen hours a day, seven days a week. Trying to make payroll, keep up with hauling contracts, fuel costs, FICA, workers' compensation costs, taxes, health care, retirement benefits. But by the time Maxine and her divorce lawyers got through with me, I was broke and homeless. So now all I have to worry about is me. And the occasional pretty hitchhiker." He grinned.

"I'm afraid my story is a lot more boring than yours," Jodie explained. "Right after my eighteenth birthday, I married the guy that me and my dad argued about. He turned out to be worse than even my dad thought. Jerry's a lazy, no-good, mind-numbed, pot-smoking bum. He lay around the house all day, smoking pot and watching porn while I worked. At night, he wanted me to clean up his messes, fix his supper, and be his whore. Anytime I refused, he'd beat me up. I was having a hard enough time earning enough to pay for the groceries, the rent and utilities, pay for the cable bill, and his drug habit. Then yesterday, on the way to meet his dealer, my old car broke down. He took my purse, and when he found that I had only $22 in it, he started yelling and cursing at me and started to come after me again. I just decided I'd had enough, so I kicked him in the nuts and ran. I ran until I got to the truck stop where you found me."

"Do you plan to go back home to your parents?" Dave asked.

"I don't know. I'm afraid Jerry will find me there," she told him.

"Since I picked you up near Flagstaff, I assume you were living somewhere near there," Dave surmised.

"We're renting a singlewide in Kachina Village," she told him. "I work as a cashier and sometimes waitress at the Subway there. At least I did until yesterday. I should probably call my supervisor."

"You might want to leave out the part about where you are and where you're headed," Dave suggested. "Old stoner Jerry might get the information. Where do your folks live?"

"Tucson. Dad's the sports editor for the paper there. You aren't thinking of turning me in to the police are you, Dave?"

"No," Dave promised. "I wouldn't do that, but don't you think you should be heading toward Tucson instead of east with me?"

"I don't want to hear my Dad say, 'I told you so'," Jodie said, with sadness in her voice.

"I'm betting he would be so glad to see his little girl that he wouldn't say anything like that," Dave encouraged her. "But what if he did? It's the truth, isn't it? He did try to protect you from a bad decision."

They continued the small talk for several miles. It was nearing sunup when Dave pulled into a rest area. "I'm going to get a couple of hours of shut-eye" he told her. "Driving into the rising sun always makes me sleepy."

"I have to go to the bathroom," Jodie said.

"Wait! I'll walk over with you," Dave told her. "These places aren't always safe for little girls."

"I'm not a little girl!" she said indignantly while climbing down out of the cab.

"I beg to differ," Dave said. "You may be an adult, but you can't argue about the little part."

"I hate when people make fun of my height," she said. "I'm five feet one and a half. That's almost five two!"

"Well, you'd still probably blow away in a stiff breeze," he told her. "How much do you weigh?"

"One hundred and one pounds if you must know!" Jodie said compellingly. "That's what I weighed at my last medical checkup."

They had reached the bathrooms. Dave waited just outside the door.

"Just scream if you need my help," he told her, "and I'll come running."

"Now it's my turn," he said, when she reappeared at the bathroom door. "Wait for me right here. And once again, just scream if you find yourself in trouble."

As they walked back to the truck a few minutes later, he told her he would be using the lower sleeper bunk, and she could either use the upper or just curl up on her seat. As Dave was about to climb into the sleeper, he handed her a blanket. "Here's an extra pillow too," he told her.

Dave had unsnapped his western-cut shirt and was taking it off when she stuck her head in and said, "You should teach me to drive this eighteen wheeler. Then you could sleep while I drive, and I could sleep while you drive."

"I'll think about it." Dave chuckled. "Now will you get out of my bedroom so I can undress?"

She laughed as she slid back down onto her seat.

She has a pretty laugh, Dave thought as he pulled off his engineering boots and his jeans. *I guess she hasn't always been sad and depressed.* In five minutes, he was snoring.

Dave's mental clock awakened him after two and a half hours. He sat up, pulled on his jeans, boots, and shirt, and crawled out of the sleeper. Jodie awoke, wiped the sleep from her eyes, and looked at him curiously.

"Time to get going," he told her. "I'm going to go wash my face and brush my teeth. You might want to do the same." He tousled her hair.

"Okay, Daddy," she said sarcastically, frowning and batting his hand away.

Dave smiled at her as he climbed down out of the cab and pulled her out after him.

"I'm still sleepy!" she complained peevishly. "And I'm hungry!"

"We'll be in Amarillo in about an hour," Dave told her. "We can get some breakfast there, and you can call your supervisor. You can sleep until we get there."

"Don't you have a cell phone?" she asked. "I could call my supervisor right now."

"No, I don't have a cell phone," Dave remarked. "I've never felt the need to constantly be connected to the rest of the world. In my opinion, cell phones are for needy people or those with extralarge egos."

"Your teasing me, aren't you? I've never met anyone who didn't have a cell phone," Jodie said.

"Well, I don't have one, and yet the sun still comes up every day," Dave replied.

As the rig left Amarillo an hour or so later, Dave checked his watch. "At this rate," he stated, "we won't get into Memphis before midnight. What did your supervisor say?"

"He wanted to know when I could be back," she explained. "When I couldn't tell him, he said he would have to replace me. He was nice and said to come in and see him if I ever got back to Kachina Village."

"Did you tell him where you are?" Dave wanted to know.

"No, I just told him I couldn't come in for a few days because of family problems," Jodie replied. "He said Jerry had been in looking for me and had demanded any pay I had coming. He didn't give it to Jerry. I told him I'd give him an address as soon as

I get one so he can mail it to me. I think he knew that Jerry and I are no longer together."

Dave was quiet for a while, watching the road and occasionally checking her face, which showed a lot of sadness. He decided to interrupt her thoughts.

"This pace will put us into Atlanta around eight tomorrow morning. We'll drop off the trailer, check into a motel, and sleep in a real bed. You can call your folks and explain everything. We'll spend the rest of the day in Atlanta. I'll check some truck depots and get a load going to San Diego. We'll spend another night there in Atlanta and get an early start on Wednesday. Using Interstate 10, I'll be going right through Tucson. I can drop you off at your parents' house if you'd like. I also plan to go through both Panama City and Katy on the way to see both of my kids. I'm looking forward to introducing you to my son."

"I'm sure he will think I'm just a little girl like you do," she said sarcastically. "If I just had some makeup!"

"You don't need any makeup to hide your pretty face," Dave told her. "But if you think you must, I'll loan you some money in Atlanta. You can get whatever you need there."

"What is your son's name, Dave?"

"David."

"Does he look like you?" Jodie asked, smiling.

"No," Dave told her. "He didn't get my handsome good looks. Poor kid has dark hair and brown eyes like you."

Jodie looked at him. She saw the grin on his face and the twinkle in his eye. She was sure he was being less than honest about his son's good looks. They had been in each other's company for only a few hours, yet she couldn't help liking this man. She felt comfortable and safe in his company.

"What about your daughter, Dave? Tell me about her."

"Her name is Abigail," Dave explained. "Abby has lighter-colored hair like me and blue eyes like me. Very pretty, like her mother Maxine was when she was that age."

"Do they know you are planning to visit them?" she asked.

"No," Dave replied.

"If you just had a cell phone, you could—"

"Don't start that again," he interrupted.

During the morning, they passed through Oklahoma City. They stopped for a quick meal at a travel stop in Okemah before crossing the remainder of Oklahoma. They passed just north of Fort Smith, Arkansas, during the afternoon hours, took the truck bypass just above North Little Rock, and finally arrived in Memphis just after midnight.

"You hungry?" Dave asked. "I know where there's a great barbeque place on US 78 just out of Memphis before we get to Interstate 22. You like hot, spicy foods?"

"Sometimes," Jodie answered. "But I've been in this moving truck, bouncing along for what seems like days now, and my stomach is a little queasy."

"Okay, well, they serve other things there, but the smells might get to you too. What do you suggest?" Dave asked her.

"I don't know," Jodie said hesitantly. "Can you find a restaurant where we can go inside and sit down? Maybe some soft scrambled eggs."

"Yeah, sure," Dave told her. "I know just the place. Breakfast twenty-four hours a day."

A few minutes later, the truck was idling in a truck parking space behind the restaurant. Dave picked up his logbook and quickly brought it up to date.

They took their time in the restaurant; Dave wanted her to feel solid ground under her feet for a while. He recalled how, when he was a young sailor so many years ago, it would often take hours for him to transfer from his sea legs to walking on terra firma when his ship made port. He had been riding that old truck so long that it hadn't so much as entered his mind that the constant motion could cause her discomfort.

"You feeling any better?" he asked her after about an hour. "Maybe we should get you some motion sickness pills. I think I saw a drugstore back there."

"I feel much better now. How much farther did you say it is to Atlanta?" Jodie asked.

"About six and a half hours," Dave explained. "Listen, Jodie, we haven't talked anymore about your destination. Do you plan to ride around with me for the rest of your life? Have you decided where you'd like me to drop you?"

"I really haven't thought about it," she answered. "I don't want to think about it. I like being here with you."

"I like you too, but you have to think about it," Dave admonished her. "Until you decide, you're welcome to ride along with me. I'm not going to kick you out anywhere."

After her stomach was full and she had paced around outside the restaurant for a while, Jodie declared she was ready to continue their journey.

They were soon picking up Interstate 20 in Birmingham and rolling on east to Atlanta. It was just after 8:00 a.m. when Dave parked the big rig in the truck parking area behind the upscale motel. He got them a luxury room with a pair of queen-size beds. As soon as Jodie was fast asleep in one of them, he quietly let himself out of the room and headed the truck to the depot.

"What happened?" the loading dock supervisor asked him. "We expected you last night."

"Don't ask!" Dave told him.

After they had finished their business and Dave had pocketed his paperwork, he asked, "Do you know of anything headed to San Diego in the next couple of days?"

"Why don't you try Dixie Paper?" the supervisor told him. "They sometimes have a load going to the naval supply depot."

"Thanks," Dave said. With a friendly wave, he was off.

He drove the big Freightliner tractor to the motel. He quietly let himself into their room. As he walked past the sleeping Jodie, he stopped for a few seconds and looked at her tiny form nestled so peacefully under the quilted spread. *How could anyone want to hurt that?* he thought. *I'd like to get my hands on that Jerry!* He picked up his overnight bag and went into the bath.

After a soothing shower, Dave pulled on his shorts and climbed into the other bed. He was soon in a deep and restful sleep.

CHAPTER 2

It was well past 1:00 p.m. when Dave awakened to Jodie's voice. "Do you know you sound like a freight train when you snore?"

Dave sat up, wiped the sleep from his eyes, and took in his surroundings. Jodie was dressed and had a tray of doughnuts and some cups of coffee nearby. "What time is it?" he asked.

"One thirty. I was just going to let you sleep all day, but your train noises were beginning to drown out the TV."

Dave reached for his jeans, pulled them on, and disappeared into the bath. After brushing his teeth and giving his face a close shave, he joined Jodie. "Is that coffee hot?" he asked as he put on his shirt and snapped it.

"Probably not. Here, let me warm it for you," she said as she placed it in the microwave.

"Thanks, Jodie. Where'd you get the doughnuts?"

"Across the street. I took some money from your wallet. I hope that's okay."

Dave looked at her. "Depends on how much you took."

She acted as if he had insulted her. "I took every red cent you had!" she said indignantly. "You want to frisk me?"

Dave grinned. "That might be impossible. I remember how you fought me when we first met. I'm sorry, Jodie, I'm sure everything you didn't need was returned. Can I get one of those chocolate-covered ones?"

She fixed him a paper plate with a chocolate-covered and a jelly-filled glazed doughnut and handed it and the heated coffee to him. He took the coffee and took a big swallow. "Umm, good!" he said. Then grinning, he continued, "Thanks, little one, I'm beginning to appreciate you being along on this trip."

Jodie relaxed, smiled at him, and replied, "I really just wanted to do something nice for you to pay you back for all you've done for me. I apologize for taking money out of your wallet without asking you first."

"Forget it," Dave told her. "I need to make a couple of phone calls. Then I think you should get in touch with your folks."

"I'm not sure I want to," Jodie said with a worried frown.

"Well, think about it while I take care of some business," Dave encouraged her.

"Okay," she told him, "I'll think about it."

Dave pulled a small black book out of his shirt pocket, picked up the phone, and dialed. "Mr. Rainey, Dave Wellborn, here…Do you have any trailer loads ready to go to San Diego? Okay, well, thank you very much."

Dave continued the same procedure for several more calls before connecting with a loaded trailer bound for the California markets. It was headed for Los Angeles, but Dave could still use Interstate 10 and go through Tucson as planned. Only this way, instead of splitting off onto Interstate 8 at Casa Grande, he could use Interstate 10 the entire distance from the Florida panhandle right into Los Angeles.

With that settled, Dave turned his attention to entertaining Jodie. "Have you ever been to Stone Mountain?" he asked her.

"I've never even heard of it," Jodie told him.

"Well, there's some hiking involved. You can't wear those high-heeled boots. Let's go get you a pair of good walking shoes."

The afternoon was filled with shopping and then hiking and picnicking at Stone Mountain. Eventually, they went by the depot, picked up their assigned trailer, stopped at a nice restaurant for a filling meal, and returned to the motel.

"You need to get to bed early tonight, Jodie. We're rolling out at four in the morning. I want to be clear of Atlanta before the traffic gets too congested."

"And I want to get to sleep before you start your train imitations!" she teased. "Did you call your son?"

"No," Dave replied. "We'll drop by his work tomorrow. If he's in, we'll stay a few minutes. If not, I'll catch him next time around. We only have seventy-two hours to get this load to California. Have you decided what to do about your folks? Do you want to call them and tell them you're on your way?"

"When will we be there? I mean, when do we get to Tucson?" Jodie inquired.

"Sometime Friday," Dave told her. "I'll know about what time once we get back on the road after we leave Abby's place there in Katy."

Jodie was sitting on the edge of her bed, sorting through her new things. "Thank you for the makeup, new shoes, new purse, the jeans, and blouse, but especially for the underwear and socks. Would you go with me to the laundry room so I can wash everything?"

"Sure." Dave grinned. "Can't take a chance on you getting lost. I've gotten too used to you pestering me."

By the time they finished the washing and drying, it was later than Dave had planned. They hurried to get ready for bed. As he turned out the last light, he addressed Jodie. "Enjoy your last night in this luxurious bed. You'll be using the sleeper till we get to your mom and dad's place. Good night, little one."

Jodie smiled to herself. She was beginning to like the name when Dave said it. It was like it was their very own secret. "Good night, Big Dave! she replied.

Dave grinned, rolled on to his side in hopes he wouldn't snore so loudly, and soon drifted off to sleep.

As requested, the telephone rang to announce their early morning call. They washed up, quickly dressed, and checked out. By 4:00 a.m., they were rolling out of the motel parking lot.

While Dave was busy maneuvering the semi through the streets of Atlanta and out onto the highway, Jodie was studying his face. He had a kind face, wrinkled by years of worry and the burdens of responsibility. Still, she was sure the other lines were from smiles and laughter. His wavy sandy-colored hair was streaked with silver. His blue eyes always seemed to smile at her when he looked her way. Jodie felt a strong urge just to reach out and touch his big hand. She had become very fond of this large man. She reached across the empty space between their seats and patted his forearm. Dave responded by reaching over and patting her on the head.

"I like you too," he said.

They rode in silence for several miles. Finally, Jodie broke the silence. "Is it okay if I ask you how old you are?" she said.

"Believe it or not," Dave said, "I'm only forty-eight. I'll bet you thought I was at least eighty."

"No, I didn't," Jodie answered him. "I just thought you were older than my dad, that's all."

"Would you pour me another cup of coffee please?" Dave requested.

Jodie picked up the thermos and poured a cup about two-thirds full and handed it to him. "I'm sorry I have to tell you this, but I'm getting hungry again."

"For a little girl, you sure do eat a lot! We'll stop down near La Grange for breakfast. There's a diner there that I know about. Pretty waitress by the name of Amy." Dave grinned widely. "Have you ever eaten grits, Jodie?"

"What are grits?" she asked, wide eyed.

"A little surprise made from corn," Dave explained.

Within the hour, Dave and Jodie were entering Cisco's Café on the outskirts of La Grange. They were able to get a table in the area where Amy was busy with several other customers. Dave picked up a menu and showed Jodie the several combinations of breakfast orders. "All of them come with grits," he told her.

Amy came hurriedly to their table, approaching from behind Dave's left shoulder, and didn't recognize him at first. "Coffee?" she asked.

"Please," Dave said, turning the cup right side up on its saucer. He turned toward Amy as she poured his coffee. Her eyes were on her coffee pouring.

"How about you, young lady?" Amy asked Jodie.

"No, thank you," Jodie said. "Can I please have a glass of orange juice?"

"Sure," Amy said as she set her coffee pot down on the table and took out her pad. "Have you decided—Big Dave! Is that really you? What a nice surprise! Who is this? Your daughter?"

Dave grinned widely. "This is Jodie, a friend of mine. Jodie, this is Amy."

They engaged in the usual greetings when people have not seen each other in a long time, or who have just met for the first time. Finally, Amy said, "I guess you'll want your usual, Dave. What about you, Jodie?"

"What's Dave's usual?" Jodie asked, looking at Amy inquiringly.

"Three scrambled, bacon, grits, gravy, and biscuits," Amy replied.

"I can't eat all of that." Jodie looked at the menu again. "Give me the number five," she said.

"How do you want your eggs?" Amy asked her.

"Soft scrambled," Jodie replied.

"I'll be right back," Amy said, picking up her coffee pot and filling Dave's cup again.

She brought their breakfasts and made several other trips to their table. During one quick stop to freshen Dave's coffee, she asked, "How long will you be in town? I get off at two today. Can I see you then?"

"Sorry, Amy, I'm hauling a load to LA. I'm in a little bit of a rush," Dave explained.

Amy leaned over so she could whisper in his ear. "You fancy the young ones now, Dave?" she asked while nodding toward Jodie.

"Just a friend, Amy," Dave told her. "I'll try to stop and see you on my next trip. Maybe we can get together then."

Later, as Dave paid the tab with a large bill, he gave Amy a large tip from his change, picked up Jodie's purse, and deposited the remainder of his change in it.

"What's that for?" Jodie asked him.

"Just a little telephone money," Dave told her. "You never know when you'll need to make a call."

"I couldn't call you anyway. But if you had a cell phone..."

Dave looked at her disapprovingly.

"I know," she said. "Don't mention cell phones."

As they pulled into traffic a few minutes later, Jodie asked, "What's the story with you and Amy? Is she your secret lover?"

"Our relationship isn't anyone's business except ours," Dave told her. "I can tell you this much, she is one of the best waitresses in the world. She wouldn't have to write anything down if she didn't need it for the cooks. She remembers everyone's orders, even years later."

"She didn't look that pretty to me," Jodie told him. "You said she was pretty."

"She is!" Dave said emphatically. "There's a lot more to people than their facade."

"Well, she's a lot older than you!" Jodie stated with authority.

"Wrong again!" Dave said. "She may be two or three years older. Look, I've known Amy for about twenty years now. I met her when she was about thirty. She has a little house up on West Point Lake. She can catch and skin more catfish than any man I know."

"Did your wife know about her?" Jodie asked him.

"There wasn't anything to know," Dave explained. "I have acquaintances all over these United States."

He was quiet for several minutes. Jodie studied his face and thought he must be remembering some of the good times with Amy. Suddenly, he spoke. "We are going to cross the Chattahoochee River at Columbus and cross back into Alabama for a few miles. We should be in Florida in about three hours. I think we'll get to David's place a little before ten o'clock."

Jodie was busy counting on her fingers. "Before you picked me up in Flagstaff," she said, "I had only been to four states—Arizona, California, Nevada, and New Mexico. Since I've been riding with you, I've added seven more, and Florida will be the eighth."

"You'll also get to add Louisiana to your list before we get you back to your home," Dave advised her.

They picked up US 431 at Columbus, Georgia, crossed the Chattahoochee River, and headed southwest into Dothan, Alabama, where they picked up US 231. A few miles farther, they were crossing the Florida state line. They stayed on US 231 to where it crosses US 98 in downtown Panama City. Dave made a right turn onto US 98, and just a few blocks later, he was maneuvering his rig onto the back lot of the huge Cates and Wellborn Ford dealership.

"Here we are!" Dave announced to Jodie. "Let's go see if David is in."

"Your son is a partner in this place?" Jodie asked with wonder.

"Yep," Dave said proudly. "It keeps him pretty busy."

They entered the front doors and walked through a large show room with many new automobiles. As Jodie stopped to admire a shiny new yellow Ford Thunderbird, a saleswoman quickly approached.

"I'm Linda. Can I show you this Thunderbird?" she asked them.

"Yes," Dave told her, crossing his arms. "Mr. Wellborn said the young lady could have this one at no charge."

"I'll have to check that out with Mr. Wellborn," Linda said, frowning slightly and turning to leave.

They waited beside the Thunderbird for a few minutes. Finally, Jodie saw a tall strikingly handsome young man in an expensive-looking suit coming their way. The serious look on his face suddenly changed as he saw her and Dave. His pace quickened, and as he reached them, he grabbed Dave's right hand and hugged him with his left arm.

"Dad!" he said, "what brings you here?" Then looking at Jodie, he said, "And who's the attractive lady here with you?"

Dave introduced David and Jodie. David took them back to his office where they could sit and converse more easily. He talked them into staying until after lunch.

"Before we go to lunch, Dad," David said excitedly, "there's something I want you to see."

David told his secretary he would be out for a while, and they all three got into a new Lincoln Town Car. David drove them to a house in Biltmore Beach. The yard backed up to Grand Lagoon and had a very nice pier leading out into the water.

"I'm buying it!" he told Dave. "We should close on it next week. What do you think, Dad?"

Dave stood on the pier and looked out across the water of the lagoon. "I think you need a big boat!" he said.

"It's just too wonderful for words," Jodie said, practically running from room to room. "What does your wife think about it?"

David smiled at her. "I'm not married," he explained.

"Oh, then what does your girlfriend think about it?" Jodie persisted.

"I see where this is going." David smiled at her. "There is no one of a serious nature in my life at this time. Does that satisfy your curiosity?"

Jodie blushed and tried to hide it behind her prettiest smile.

Later, during lunch at a very fancy restaurant, Dave was almost entirely left out of the conversation as the two young people continued to flirt and get to know each other. Jodie told David her last name was Underwood, something Dave had failed to ascertain. Because of the sudden attraction to each other and because neither wanted the lunch to end, it was well past 2:00 p.m. before they returned to the dealership.

David gave Jodie his card and asked her to keep in touch. Jodie told him she was between addresses but would contact him with her new one as soon as possible. When Jodie excused herself to go to the bathroom, David confronted his father.

"What's the story here, Dad? How do you know Jodie? She's too special to be one of your girlfriends."

"I'd resent that if I thought you were serious," Dave replied. "No, she's just a little friend that was looking for some nonjudgmental fatherly affection, and I was the lucky one she chose for the job. Anything else you want to know about her, you'll have to get from her. I will tell you this much though, I'm very fond of that little girl, and anyone who tries to hurt her will have to go through me!"

"I'm glad you're looking out for her, Dad."

As Jodie approached, Dave and David shook hands and hugged once again. Jodie reached up and gave David a hug and kissed him softly on the cheek. She followed along beside Dave as they went back to the truck. In less than an hour, they were back on Interstate 10 heading west.

Jodie had been sitting quietly for a long time. She took out the business card David had given her and began studying it. "David R. Wellborn, GM.," she said aloud. "What does the GM stand for, Dave?"

"General manager," Dave explained. "David wears many hats. He buys, sells, hires, and fires."

"That must be a lot of responsibility," Jodie mused. "What does the R stand for?"

"R?" Dave asked. "What R?"

"David R," Jodie replied.

"Oh," Dave said. "That stands for Riley. That's David's middle name."

"David Riley Wellborn, General Manager," Jodie said, still looking at the card. "You lied to me, Dave. You said David wasn't good-looking. He's very handsome! And he's taller than you."

"Sound's like someone has a big crush on my boy. Do you want me to turn this rig around and take you back to Panama City?" Dave asked.

Jodie blushed. "I'm just saying he wasn't at all what I expected. From what you told me, I was expecting a troll."

"Yeah." Dave grinned. "He's a cute little kid. He always was."

"How old is David?" she asked.

"Umm, let me see." Dave said, stroking his chin. "Maxine and I got married when I was twenty-one. David was born the next year. I think that makes him either twenty-six or twenty-seven."

"You don't know the ages of your children?" Jodie asked.

"I could figure it out it I needed to," he replied. "Why? Is it important to you?"

"No, it's not. I was just asking." She put the card into her purse. "I sure wish I had a cell phone."

"I wish you had one too!" Dave replied with a certain amount of irritation in his voice. Then after a short pause, he continued in a more normal tone. "You told David your last name was Underwood. What is your maiden name?"

"That is my maiden name. And it's the name I'll use till I can get rid of Jerry and his name! I never liked the name Ludlow. Jodie Ludlow. Yuk!"

The highway took them across a long bridge over Escambia Bay near Pensacola, Florida, and then over an even longer bridge over Mobile Bay where off to the left Jodie could see the battleship USS *Alabama*.

"Can we get closer to the ship?" Jodie begged.

"Maybe next time," Dave promised. "This rig is too big to take onto those roads."

They crossed the rest of the lower parts of Alabama and Mississippi and were soon crossing the Louisiana state line. At Slidell, Dave took Interstate 12, bypassing New Orleans, and followed it to the point where it converged with Interstate 10 again near Baton Rouge. It was 8:30 p.m. when Dave pulled the truck into a space near Bellue's Cajun and Creole Cuisine, a five-star restaurant in Baton Rouge.

"You ever eaten Cajun food?" he asked Jodie as he set the brakes.

"No," she replied.

"Well, you're in for a treat!" Dave told her. "I have to warn you though, some of it can be very hot and spicy. I'll try to steer you towards the foods that are less spicy."

They were an odd-looking couple as they entered the room that night. Dave stood six foot six and weighed two hundred and forty pounds while Jodie was just over five feet and weighed slightly more than one hundred pounds. His gray-blond hair and light blue eyes were also in stark contrast with her shiny black hair and big brown eyes.

They were soon seated at a table, where during the next hour, Dave got Jodie to try many new and different foods. Jodie, enjoying the attention, threw caution to the wind and tried everything. They were laughing and having so much fun that neither wanted the evening to end. It was just after 10:00 p.m. when Dave pulled them back to reality.

"That was so much fun!" Jodie chortled as they walked to the truck. "I just wish David had been here."

Dave reached over and put his hand on her far shoulder and pulled her against his side for a momentary fatherly hug. "I'm really glad you're along on this trip, little one," he told her.

Jodie's smile was a happy one. She took his big arm in both her hands and leaned her head against it. "Me too," she said. "You make me feel all warm and safe."

"It's pretty late, and we've been up since four this morning. There's a very nice rest area about half the way to Lafayette. I'm going to pull in there for a few hours," Dave told her. "We're only about five hours from Katy. If we drive all night, we'll get there too early to visit Abigail."

An hour later, Dave was wheeling the big rig into a rest area truck parking space. Jodi washed up while Dave stood guard outside the door of the restroom. Dave walked her back to the truck and locked her inside before he did his bedtime hygiene routine. A few minutes later, when he climbed into the tractor, he found Jodie fast asleep in the upper bunk. Dave stood there in a slightly stooped position for several minutes, watching her sleep before climbing into his bunk. Just before drifting off to sleep, he found himself thinking about how fond he had become of this little hitchhiker.

CHAPTER 3

It was midmorning when Dave pulled the rig up in front of his daughter's house in Katy. He climbed out, and with Jodie close behind him, approached the front door of the large ranch style house. After repeatedly ringing the doorbell and waiting, the door finally opened.

"Dad! Come in!" Abigail said, surprise and enthusiasm in her voice.

Dave stooped to give her a hug and kiss. Then he pushed her away to arms' length and, holding on to her shoulders, said, "What's this? Did you swallow a watermelon seed?"

"Yes, I'm pregnant!" Abigail smiled. "I would have told you sooner, but I never know where you are."

"I've been telling him he needs a cell phone!" Jodie interjected.

"This is my friend, Jodie," Dave said. "Jodie, this is my daughter, Abigail."

"Pleased to meet you, Jodie. Call me Abby. Y'all come on in. Can I get you something to drink? Iced tea? Lemonade?"

"Sure, I'd love some lemonade," Jodie said. "Abby, can I use your bathroom?"

"Right down that hall, second door on the right."

"How's Mark?" Dave asked as Abby handed him a glass of tea.

"Mark's fine," she told him. "He's taking a flight to Hawaii. I'm sure he'll be sorry he missed you. Oh, did I tell you he's no longer copilot? He's been moved to first seat!" She paused and looked at him. "Who's the young woman, Dad?"

"Just a friend," Dave told her. "So when is the baby due? Do you know if you are having a boy or a girl?"

"In about four more months. It's a boy," Abigail answered. "Stop changing the subject. Who is this Jodie? Am I about to get another mother who is obviously younger than me?"

"Of course not!" Dave stated, as if annoyed with her question. "She's just a friend riding along with me to keep me company!"

Jodie came back into the room just then, and they had to drop the subject. Abigail asked them to stay the rest of the day and have supper with her and Mark. Dave explained he was under obligation to deliver the contents of the trailer to the wholesaler in LA by Saturday noon. After a short three-hour visit which included a nice lunch with Abigail, Dave and Jodie returned to the truck and were soon speeding down Interstate 10 toward San Antonio.

Dave guided the truck onto the Anderson Loop as they neared San Antonio. Twenty minutes later, he was pulling into the outer edge of a parking lot in front of a strip mall just off of the loop.

"Come along," he told Jodie. "I'm going to need your expertise."

The store they entered had several displays of small mobile communication devices. "Pick out one for you and one for me," he told her. "Just how does this all work?" he asked the salesclerk.

Jodie took her time assessing the needs of each of them. Dave would need something simple with hardly any additional features. She, on the other hand, wanted the total package. Dave signed the program papers and got a fistful of instructions.

As they returned to the truck, he was still totally confused about how to use the small thin rectangular device he had been given. "Where's the mouthpiece? Where do I put my ear? How do you dial this thing?"

"Don't worry," Jodie encouraged him. "I'll teach you how to use it."

Jodie was as happy as he had ever seen her. Dave drove them back up onto the loop, and they were soon entering west bound Interstate 10. She was busy unwrapping her new cell phone and charging it. She was bouncing around in her seat, talking rapidly, when all of a sudden, she unbuckled her seat belt and stepped across the space between their seats and gave Dave a big hug and kissed him on the cheek.

"Thank you so much, Dave! I'm going to pay you back for everything one of these days when I get my life all straightened out. You'll see."

Dave was grinning and enjoying her youthful exuberance. Soon enough, he had to turn his thoughts to his schedule. They had lost time in Panama City. Lost more time in Katy, and now they had lost another hour in San Antonio. He calculated that it would be 10:00 p.m. by the time they reached Fort Stockton. They would have to fuel and use the truck stop there to get a sandwich. If he got right back on the road soon afterward and drove all night, they could make Tucson by 7:00 a.m. Jodie's folks should be up by that time. *Even so,* Dave thought, *I won't be able to make LA before 1:00 p.m. Pacific Coast time. That's an hour later than I planned.*

Jodie was checking the charge on her new touch screen phone every few minutes. Finally, she told Dave it had fully charged. She plugged Dave's phone into the outlet so it could be charged. She immediately took David's card from her purse and dialed his number.

"Hi, David. Guess who this is?" Dave heard her say. "No, silly, It's Jodie! Jodie Underwood! Did you already forget about me? How many women named Jodie do you know?...I'm calling from Dave's truck...My new touch screen phone!...Am too!...Dave got it for me today!...I don't know, somewhere in Texas...Just a minute...Dave says we're just past Sonora."

They continued to talk for several minutes. Jodie turned toward her window and started talking in a softer voice. Dave couldn't hear anymore of the conversation. Eventually, she turned forward again, and he heard her say, "I miss you too. Good-bye David."

"You haven't got anymore excuses for not calling your folks," Dave said.

"I don't remember their number," Jodie replied.

"I don't believe you," Dave said.

"Oh, okay! What should I tell them?" she asked him.

"I don't care," Dave replied, "but you should try to find out if someone will be there in the morning when I drop you off. I'm not leaving you on their doorstep. I want to see the people I'm leaving you with."

"Can't I just stay with you?"

"No! Listen, little one, I've become quite fond of you over the past few days, but if you want us to continue like this, you need to get a commercial license and some experience behind the steering wheel of a big rig! Now make your call!"

"The way you treat me," she whined, "you must think you're my daddy!"

"You're stalling!" Dave said.

"Oh, all right!" She dialed a number and waited. "Hello, Mama," Dave heard her say softly. "It's me, Jodie. I'm coming home, Mama. I'll be there in the morning sometime after seven."

They talked for only a short time. Jodie didn't get to talk to her father. After they finished their conversation, Jodie sighed deeply, slid down in her seat, and became very quiet. Dave left her alone with her thoughts for several miles, glancing her way every few minutes.

"You okay, Jodie?" he finally asked.

"Yes," she said, her voice just above a whisper, "I'm fine."

Dave had been taking advantage of the light traffic and seventy-five-mile-per-hour Texas truck speed limit and was pulling up to the pumps at Fort Stockton at 9:40 p.m. He filled the tanks and brought his logbook up to date. The truck stop was well-lighted inside and out, and after a short argument with Jodie, he finally consented to let her go inside alone to get them something to eat while he tended to the truck. They were back on the road in record time.

About midnight, Jodie said she was sleepy and climbed into her bunk. By 2:00 a.m. the Freightliner was passing through El Paso. It was 3:45 a.m. when it sped past the lights of Deming, New Mexico. An hour later, it was passing on the highway just south of Lordsburg. By 6:45 a.m., they were entering the outskirts of Tucson, Arizona. Dave took the exit at South Craycroft Road leading to the Triple T Truck Stop adjacent to Omar's Hi-Way Chef Restaurant. He pulled into one of the truck parking spots, set his brakes, and just sat there for a few minutes relaxing before waking Jodie.

"Time to get up, little one," he called.

Jodie yawned and stretched. "Where are we?" she asked.

"Truck stop on the outskirts of Tucson. You need to take your bag and get cleaned up. I think we should probably get some breakfast too. I don't want to drop in on your folks all hungry."

Silently, Jodie did as Dave suggested. They walked to the truck stop restrooms without saying a word. Later, they walked together to the restaurant without talking. They ordered breakfast before Jodie finally broke the silence.

"You promised me you wouldn't just kick me out somewhere. Now that's just what you are about to do."

"I understand you're apprehensive about going home after all this time, but it will give you a base to work from while you deal with your divorce," Dave told her. "And now, thanks to your constant nagging, I'll be just a cell phone call away."

Jodie smiled. "That is a comforting thought," she said.

"I think if you give your folks a chance, they'll be more forgiving and understanding than you want to believe," Dave told her, smiling warmly.

Dave took an invoice out of his pocket as they waited for their breakfast then took out his new cell phone. "Show me how to work this thing," he said. "I need to call this number in Los Angeles."

Jodie took the phone, dialed the number, then handed it back to him. "It's ringing," she said. "Just hold it up to your ear and talk normally."

As soon as Dave heard someone on the line, he asked for receiving. After another wait, he finally got to talk to the right person. Dave explained he was at a truck stop on the east side of Tucson and would be about three hours late delivering his load.

"Pretty neat!" he said. "I didn't even have to look for a phone booth. Now how do I hang this thing up?"

Jodie smiled prettily. "Just push this little button right here. Now aren't you glad you have me along?"

Dave smiled at her. "It has been very nice having you along, Jodie. I'm going to miss you something terrible!"

It was just before 8:00 a.m. when Dave was able to locate the Underwood home, a moderate-sized house in the San Gabriel area of Tucson. He parked the truck at the curb out front and climbed down. He waited for Jodie to get her things, helped her out of the cab, then walked beside her as she hesitantly walked toward the house.

They were several feet from the front porch, walking side by side, when a tall skinny man with long shaggy hair, an immature beard, and dirty clothes suddenly came toward them, swearing. "There you are, you little bitch," he yelled, reaching for Jodie. "Where the hell have you been?"

Before the man could reach Jodie, Dave quickly grabbed him by the back of his neck, burying the tips of his fingers and thumb into the flesh. He lifted him off of the ground with his large muscular right arm and flung him backward. As the man hit the ground, Dave turned and stood over him, his arms hanging loosely at his sides. "Get up, you piece of filth! I'd like nothing better than to pound you into dust!"

The frightened man scooted backward along the ground, trying to put some distance between himself and Dave. Dave just followed, towering over him. "Keep out of this, you big brute," he whimpered. "She's my old lady, and I can do whatever I want."

This was a bit too much for Dave. He was tired of waiting for him to stand up. He reached down, grabbed him by the dirty shirt front, and pulled him to his feet. Dave lifted him till his scraggly bearded face was close to his. Then in a low menacing voice, Dave said, "So you're Jerry. Well, listen to me, you little SOB. If you ever go near Jodie again, if you ever touch Jodie again"—Dave's voice was growing louder—"if you ever so much as talk to Jodie again—" Dave didn't finish. He just shoved Jerry away so forcefully that he landed hard on his back, crying out in pain.

Dave watched as Jerry got painfully to his feet and hurried away before he turned his attention to Jodie. She was standing on the porch with Mr. and Mrs. Underwood. Dave approached, smiled broadly, and stuck out his hand toward Mr. Underwood who was nearest to him. "Dave Wellborn," he said.

"Curtis Underwood," Jodie's father said, shaking Dave's hand, "and this is my wife Josephine."

"Pleased to meet you," Dave told him. Then, taking Mrs. Underwood's hand, he told her the same thing.

"Please call me Jo," she said.

They all went into the house where they talked casually for sometime. Finally, Dave told them he had to be on his way. "I'm about three hours behind schedule already," he told them.

Jodie followed him outside. She grabbed his hand and held on to it as he started down the porch steps. By the time he reached the third step, their eyes were on the same level. She pulled on his hand. "Wait!" she said.

He turned, looking into her lost puppy-dog eyes. "I have to go now, little one," he said softly. "You'll be okay now."

Jodie put her arms around his neck and hugged him tightly. "Will I ever see you again?"

"Yes, and that's a promise!" He wrapped one of his big arms around her, kissed her gently on the cheek, pushed her gently away, then turned and walked to the idling Freightliner.

Jodie watched until he was out of sight before joining her parents inside the house.

Dave was soon rolling down Interstate 10. He picked up Interstate 8, heading west at Casa Grande, then turned north on Arizona 85 at Gila Bend, bypassing Phoenix and returning to Interstate 10 just above Buckeye. The miles and hours rolled by. Not long after passing through Indio, California, he started driving in more congested traffic. He didn't get to the depot in Los Angeles until just before 4:00 p.m. After dropping off his trailer and completing his paperwork, Dave realized just how tired he was.

He headed to Long Beach and got a motel room not far from the container piers. After a relaxing shower, he sat down on the side of the bed and dialed Jodie's number.

Jodie answered on the second ring. "Hello."

"Hi, little one," Dave said, his voice sounding almost paternal. "I missed you today."

"I missed you too!" Jodie replied.

She sounds so much older than her years, Dave thought. Out loud, he asked, "How did things go with you and your folks?"

"We've been busy today. My dad has been very loving and understanding. He hired an attorney for me. The attorney is in the process of getting a restraining order against Jerry, and he's filing papers to dissolve the marriage. I think that's the word he used. They still have to find Jerry to serve the papers on him, but Mr. and Mrs. Ludlow have been very helpful. They said they will let us know the next time Jerry comes home."

"I'm happy for you, Jodie," Dave said. "The sooner you get him out of your life, the sooner you can move on to something better."

"When will you be coming back through Tucson?" Jodie asked. "When will I get to see you again?"

"I don't know, honey. Why would you want to see an old crust like me anyway?"

"Because I miss you, Big Dave."

"Ah, little one, I know just what you mean. I'm very fond of you too." There was silence on the line before Dave finally broke in. "Okay, Jody, I'll try to make Tucson one of my stops both going and coming from now on. I need to get some sleep now. I'll see you soon."

CHAPTER 4

It was just after 4:00 a.m. the following morning when Dave pulled away from the container port in Long Beach, towing two trailers headed for Philadelphia. The fastest route, and the one with less mileage, would not take him anywhere near Tucson, but Dave had made a promise. At the rest area just before Blythe, Dave made a restroom stop and then called Jodie's cell phone. He told her he was pulling two trailers and didn't want to pull them into the San Gabriel residential area. He asked if she could meet him for lunch at Omar's Hi-Way Chef Restaurant at noon.

"Bring your folks if you'd like," he told her.

"My dad's at work, but my mom might come with me."

For the next four and a half hours, Dave kept the Freightliner's tires humming as he sped toward Tucson and his special little friend. It was only 11:40 a.m. when he pulled off of the interstate and into a parking space north of the Triple T Truck Stop just east of Tucson. He set his brakes and checked his trailers and all twenty-six tires before walking swiftly to the restaurant.

Dave walked eagerly, yet slowly, from the door, checking each booth for Jodie and her mother. Finally, he saw her. She was wearing her SF Giants baseball cap, her ponytail threaded through the back of it. She had on her high school letterman jacket and her new jeans. Beside her in the booth, instead of her mother, he saw a small suitcase made from fabric. Dave slid into the seat opposite of her. He reached out and took her hands.

"Hi, little one," he said, grinning.

"Do you ever pick up hitchhikers?" Jodie asked him sweetly.

"I have a policy against it," Dave said.

"I don't take up much space, and I can pour coffee from a thermos at high speeds!"

"I'll think on it while I eat my lunch." Dave smiled.

After the waitress took their order and went to turn it in Jodie started again. "I can fill diesel truck tanks and keep a logbook. I can answer cell phone calls, place cell phone calls, make sandwiches, and make up a bunk all at high speeds."

"Okay, little one," Dave conceded, smiling broadly. "I'll take you as far as Benson! That's about forty-five minutes down the road. If you work out, maybe I'll take you a little farther."

As the Freightliner pulled into traffic on Interstate 10 an hour later, Dave asked, "Are your folks really okay with you traveling around the country with me?"

"My mom helped me pack and drove me to the restaurant!"

"And your dad?" Dave asked with concern in his voice.

"He was so happy that I'm getting away from Jerry," Jodie explained, "that he would have consented to almost anything. Besides, I convinced him I'm not at all attracted to you sexually."

"You're not? Now that's a blow to my ego." Dave grinned. "Check the maps, Jodie. We'll want to take Interstate 20 from its beginning near Kent, Texas. Figure out the straightest route from there to Philly. There's a long straight run from the rest area just this side of Sierra Blanca to the one the other side of Van Horn. If you're positive this is what you want to do, I'll let you take the wheel when we get to the Sierra Blanca rest area."

"Really, Dave? With two trailers?"

"The main differences between one and two trailers," Dave instructed, "is the distance required in passing and the procedure in backing, and of course, you have to be aware of the extra weight which requires a longer stopping distance. You won't be backing, and I'll guide you through any passing we have to do. Do you want to try it?"

"I don't know," Jodie said hesitantly.

"Well, you have about six hours to think about it," Dave told her.

"I'm going to put in a Loretta Lynn CD. I want to hear 'Wings upon Your Horns' and 'Blue Kentucky Girl.' Is that okay, Dave?" Jodie asked.

"Sure, play anything you want." He smiled at her.

As they sped along, the state of Arizona was soon behind them, and they were crossing the high desert of Southern New Mexico. Over the strains of country music, Dave pointed out the most notable landmarks—the ghost town of Steins, the three peaks to the south of the highway known as Tres Hermanas, the towering mountain peak to the north known as Cookes Peak, the wolf's eye in the peak of the Florida Mountains. Dave found it pleasant and rewarding to finally have someone to share his passion with. Someone who seemed to also appreciate all the natural beauty of the open road. Jodie was taking it all in as if her mind was a movie camera.

It was just before 6:00 p.m. when they reached the Socorro, Texas, exit and Dave pulled into the truck port at the Petro Shopping Center. While Dave tended to one side tank, Jodie tended to the other. Dave let her pull the truck forward into a parking space and set the brakes before they climbed down and went inside the restaurant for their supper. While they waited to be served, Dave listened to her youthful plans. He was amazed at how much her life had taken a turn for the better since the night he first tussled with her in the dark in front of his truck. She was much more self-assured. She seemed older and wiser somehow. Eventually, they ate and were soon back on their way across Texas.

Seventy miles farther down Interstate 10, Dave pulled into a rest area. "Your turn!" he told Jodie.

Jodie didn't hesitate. She climbed into the driver's seat and adjusted it to fit her tiny person. Dave helped her adjust the big side mirrors before climbing into the passenger seat.

"Okay," he said, "check your mirrors. When you're sure it's safe, release the brake, shift into first gear, ease down on the throttle, and slowly release the clutch. When the tachometer gets to about midrange, push the clutch in just far enough to break torque then shift to second. Continue that procedure until you get to sixth. For seventh through twelfth, push that button and shift through the same six positions."

Dave sat back and watched his small companion go through the maneuvers he had described for her. She was such a quick study, but he could also see the tension in her face.

"You're crowding the line on this side," he told her once. "Watch your mirrors on this side. You'll get the hang of it. I want you to stay below sixty-five. You're a natural, Jodie! You're doing just great, honey."

The distance between the rest areas was a little less than fifty miles. Jodie was driving slowly enough that she didn't have to overtake another vehicle. A mile before the Van Horn rest area, Dave told her to start slowing down and downshifting. "I want us to be just barely rolling when we enter the rest area," Dave instructed her. "We have a lot of weight here, and often, there are small children in the area. You're doing fine. Now pull alongside the curb up there and stop behind that other truck. Good. Now shift into neutral and set your brakes."

As Jodie set the brakes, she lifted her hands from the wheel, and they suddenly began to shake uncontrollably. She looked at Dave wide-eyed. "I'm trembling all over," she told him.

"That's just the adrenaline," he said, reaching and taking her hands in his. "You did great! I'm very proud of you, little one!" He pulled her out of her seat and gave her a big hug. Then he reached into the refrigerator and got them both a bottle of water. "Here," he said, "let's drink a toast!"

"My mouth is awfully dry," she confessed.

After they checked their load and the tires, Dave reset the mirrors and climbed into the truck. He adjusted his seat. Jodie climbed in and settled into her seat.

"I want you to notice something," Dave told her. "You parked just a little too close to the truck in front of us. It doesn't look like he's prepared to move, so I'll need to back just a few feet. When you back one of these trucks, it's all in the mirrors. But as you could see when you were behind the wheel, there is a lot of space directly behind the truck that you can't ever see. I need you to climb down and go back there and watch for me. Stay where you can see my eyes in the mirrors. That way, you can be sure that I can see your signals."

Jodie did as Dave instructed, and soon, they were back to highway speed. Jodie took out her phone and dialed David's number.

"David, this is Jodie...Jodie Underwood, don't start that again...No, I'm not in Tucson, I'm in Dave's truck about thirty miles from Kent, Texas...We're headed to Philadelphia. Dave just took over the driving. I was driving before that...Was too... Here, Dave, tell him."

She held her phone against Dave's head. "That right, son. She drove us from the other side of Sierra Blanca to the rest area this side of Van Horn...Well, look it up! Here's Jodie."

"See, I told you!...I don't know. I just made him bring me...I wanted to get back to Florida to see you...I hope so too, but it's up to Dave." Jodie giggled at something he said, and a few minutes later she told him good-bye. She leaned back in her seat, smiling.

"While you're making calls," Dave said, "call your folks and tell them you're okay. I wouldn't mention the driving lesson however."

Before she dialed her folks, she told Dave they would soon be coming to the highway junction of Interstates 10 and 20 and that he wanted to take Interstate 20 toward Pecos. Dave knew the junction by heart, but he wanted Jodie to learn to read the maps and feel the importance of being the navigator, so he said, "Thank you, little one. I'll keep an eye out for Interstate 20."

"They served Jerry with the papers, and he signed them," Jodie told Dave after she completed the call to her mother. "I can be free of him in sixty days! I just have to make one visit to the courthouse in Tucson on the sixty-first day to file the papers."

"Another toast," Dave said, picking up his bottle of water. They laughed and toasted the end of Jodie's long nightmare.

Just before 10:00 p.m., Dave pulled the truck into a parking space at the truck stop on the east side of Pecos, Texas. They had a light meal, hit the showers, and were soon back in the truck, crawling into their separate bunks. Dave was slowly beginning to relax his tired back and shoulders, thinking about the day ahead, when Jodie interrupted his thoughts.

"Do you think we will be able to visit David this trip?" she inquired.

"Depends on what we can find in Philadelphia," Dave said sleepily.

"You know what you need, Dave?" Jodie asked him sweetly.

"A good night's sleep?" he asked.

"No," she informed him, "you need a dispatcher. Someone to find and coordinate the loads, so you don't have to spend so much time looking for something at each destination."

"I've been working out of my little black book for a long time now," Dave told her. "I can usually find something within a couple of days. I like my independence. Besides, I can't afford to hire a dispatcher."

"I work really cheap," Jodie said excitedly, hanging her head over the side of her bunk.

"I was a happy, carefree, independent trucker until I picked up this little energetic meddler of a hitchhiker! Now I can't even get a peaceful night's sleep!" Dave complained. "Go to sleep!"

Jodie laid back in her bunk, smiling. "Good night, you old grouch," she said.

"Good night, little one," Dave responded.

They awakened early, had some breakfast, and were soon back on the road. Jodie mapped out the day's travel then asked Dave for his little black book. She made a number of calls using numbers she found in the book. Finally, she turned to Dave, and holding up a piece of paper, she announced their itinerary. She explained to him that when they dropped off their trailers in Philadelphia, they would be picking up a trailer bound for Chicago. After dropping off that trailer, they would proceed to the Chicago Ford assembly plant, where they would pick up a load of Ford Taurus and Explorer automobiles bound for the Cates and Wellborn Ford distributor in Panama City, Florida. "And I've been on the job for less than one day," she bragged.

"Oh, you're just wonderful!" Dave mocked her. "You would do anything just to see David."

Jodie flashed him her cutest smile. "So?"

"Pour me a cup of coffee please. Where are we going to get a payload from Panama City?"

Jodie handed him a cup of coffee. "Can you give me a couple a minutes to find us something? We haven't yet delivered the two we're towing!"

"Before you became my employee, you were a very nice, very sweet person," Dave jokingly complained. "I think I'll fire you so you'll be nice to me again."

Jodie unbuckled her seat belt, stepped across the space between them, and kissed him on the cheek. As she sat back down and buckled up, she said, "If I'm your employee, I'd like to hear my list of duties and how much you'll be paying me for each. I would also like to hear what's in the benefits package!"

"Oh!" Dave groaned. "I knew there was a good reason to *never* pick up a hitchhiker."

They continued the verbal jousting as they passed through Monahans, Odessa, and Midland. Eventually, Dave grew tired of the banter and fell silent. Jodie went back to studying her maps.

"We need to take Interstate 30 from Dallas to Little Rock," Jodie told Dave. "I think, timewise, Weatherford should be our lunch break."

"That's good planning," Dave told her, "and there is a very nice clean truck stop there."

"That should put us into Memphis about 9:30 p.m. their time. Do you want to rest there, or try to make it to Nashville?" she asked.

"I think the truck stop just east of Memphis would be a good place to hang 'em up for today."

As planned, they made the stop in Weatherford, cruised across Arkansas, crossed the Mississippi River at Memphis, and were soon parked for the night. They had cleaned up, and Dave was in his bunk, waiting for Jodie to run down. She was brushing her hair and getting ready to put it up for the night.

"You are so very pretty, Jodie. I'm glad you didn't have children with that—"

"We couldn't," she told him. "I was having a problem with missed and irregular periods one time, and I thought I might be pregnant. My gynecologist told me that it was almost impossible for me to get pregnant with someone like Jerry because of his excessive use of illegal drugs, especially marijuana. She told me it often causes sterilization in men."

"I'm glad of that!" Dave told her.

"I didn't tell her how many times during our fights that I kicked him there," Jodie explained.

"Someone that empty between the ears should be rendered impotent!" Dave snarled.

Then he lay there and watched her getting ready for bed. The extralong white T-shirt she was wearing as a gown, when silhouetted against the lights outside the window, allowed Dave to see just how perfect her tiny figure was. *God, I wish I was twenty years younger!* he thought. "Good night, little one," he said. He rolled onto his side, facing away from her, and tried to erase the image of her sexy form from his mind.

As Jodie climbed up and onto the bunk over him, she purposely dragged her toes across his back to tickle and tease him. "Good night, Dave," she said.

The close proximity of two people being confined to a small space for hours or days at a time can have different affects. On ships and submarines, men often become close friends, hated enemies, or just indifferent to one another. The same could be said for the confines of a moving semitractor.

In the case of Big Dave Wellborn, he was falling in love with the tiny Jodie Underwood whom, he presumed, could never be claimed as his own. On the other hand, Jodie Underwood thought of him as a close friend that she was very fond of. He was more like a father figure to her. After all, he was much older than she and was, in a way, her employer and mentor.

Although she often teased and flirted with him, it was all very innocent on her part. It was her way of telling him how fond she was of him without saying it. He flirted with her too. Only, his flirting seemed much more serious to her. She thought at times he looked at her like he was about to grab her and kiss her aggressively, but he never did. He was always so steady emotionally. His occasional hugs were brief and tender.

All Jodie knew up to this time, other than her father's caress and kisses, was the volatile, so-called love making of Jerry Ludwig. He only held her long enough to pleasure himself, never tenderly, never lovingly like she wanted and needed.

Jodie had a fantasy that David was just a much younger version of Big Dave. She assumed that she could have all the patience, care, and doting that she received from Dave, only from the much younger and more handsome David.

They had picked up Interstate 40 at Little Rock, Arkansas, and were now following it to Knoxville. There, Jodie had them taking Interstate 81 all the way into Philadelphia. Her 5:00 a.m.

reveille had them on the road early, and she predicted they would be outside the Philadelphia truck depot before 10:00 p.m.

Dave could have easily driven the route by rote, but he loved seeing how industriously Jodie tackled the job of logistics. He continued to compliment her on her management of their travels. He loved to see her smile with pride when he bragged on her. He loved to see her happy and smiling for any reason. His fondness for her seemed to grow more fervent with each passing mile.

They dropped their trailers at the terminal in Philadelphia. Jodie watched intently as Dave backed the rear trailer into place.

"For the second trailer," Dave instructed her, "it's just like looking into the mirror and backing a car."

"That was perfect!" Jodie remarked with awe. "Will I ever be able to do that?"

"Yes, of course," Dave told her as they climbed out and detached the rear trailer.

Dave positioned the next trailer in front of the space where it was to be unloaded. "For this one," he told her, "you watch your mirrors and turn your front wheels in the opposite direction you would turn when backing a car."

"That seems like it would be harder to do than the other one," she remarked.

The trailer going to Chicago was at the same Philadelphia terminal, and they were soon connected and leaving the terminal for a nearby motel.

"I'm tired of that sleeper," Dave declared. "Tonight, I want a hot shower and a soft bed. And you've earned a good night's sleep too! We're having room service and sleeping late. We have two days to get to Chicago, and it only takes thirteen hours. What do you say, little one?"

"Umm, that's going to put us into Panama City a day later than my plan," she said.

"But you are still the boss."

While Jody waited for the food to come, Dave was in the shower. Once again, it was Dave who crawled into bed first. He was trying to keep his mind off of her sexy tiny body when she came over and sat down next to him on the side of his bed.

"When are you going to give me another driving lesson?" she asked diffidently. "Maybe with just one trailer, I won't get so tense."

"Look, Jodie," Dave said, "you sitting here like this in your nightgown and all makes me tense! Could you sit over there?"

Jodie got up, turned, and sat on her bed. She pressed her knees together, and placing her hands with entwined fingers on her lap, she smiled at him alluringly. "Why, Dave, I didn't know you could still have feelings like that."

"Like I've told you before, I'm not as old as I look. Now listen, Jodie. I don't intend to give you anymore driving lessons. There are hundreds of good driving schools all over this country. In three weeks, you can graduate with a commercial license that will let you drive a big rig anywhere in these United States. I'll pay for your school and make you my partner when you graduate. Now quit sitting there looking so doggoned sexy. I need to get some sleep!" He turned onto his side, away from her.

Jodie got up, patted him on the shoulder, bent, and kissed him on the cheek before climbing into her bed and turning off the lamp.

"Are there any schools near Panama City?" she asked.

"Yes," Dave said quietly, "two or three in the Jacksonville area, another one near Dothan, Alabama. Why?"

"You know why. Maybe I could visit David on the weekends."

"Good night, Jodie!"

Dave hated the feeling of being jealous of his own son, but he couldn't help feeling the way he did. Since he first allowed her into his truck and into his life, he had felt it was his obligation to protect her and take care of her needs. Somehow, during all the nearness he had become much more attracted to her than accepted standards and morals allowed. He loved to see her smile, to hear her voice, to hear her giggle, even if it was at something David had said. He rolled back over and raised up on his elbows. For several minutes, he remained in that position, just looking at her small form lying in her bed beneath the sheet, her dark hair on the pillow surrounding her small, delicate face. Finally, he eased back onto the bed, sighed deeply, and rolled onto his side, facing away from her. He realized that, to him, she was unattainable.

CHAPTER 5

Dave awakened first and quietly dressed. He took the elevator to the lobby and helped himself to the coffee in the breakfast room. He poured a glass of orange juice, put several breakfast rolls on a plate, and carried them back to the room. As he let himself in, he noticed that Jodie's bed was empty and the bathroom door was closed. He set the plate of rolls and the glass of juice on the table. He turned on the TV to catch the weather then sat down to drink his coffee.

In a few minutes, Jodie joined him. She was dressed in a formfitting western-cut shirt and tight jeans. Her dark hair was hanging down her back in a single braid. She was, to Dave, extremely fascinating.

"I brought you some orange juice and a bear claw," Dave told her as he stared at her over his coffee cup.

"Thank you," Jodie said, smiling. "Why are you looking at me that way?"

"Because," Dave said, trying to keep his desire from showing, "you are just too doggoned lovely for words!"

"Thank you. Then you like my hair like this?" she asked.

"Yes, of course, but it's not the braid that makes you so attractive. It's the whole…package!"

Jodie blushed, sat down opposite of him, and ate a breakfast roll. She drank her orange juice without responding. Dave watched her eat for a few minutes then gathered up all his things and put them in his bag.

"Are you going to try to make Chicago today?" she asked.

"Yeah, thirteen hours is a pretty easy day," Dave answered her. "We'll off-load the trailer when we get there and bunk in the sleeper tonight. We'll pick up the cars tomorrow morning bright and early."

"I'll get on the phone and see what kind of load I can find us in the Panama City area."

"We might have to go empty from there to Jacksonville or Atlanta. What time is David expecting the load of cars?"

"I've been sending him text messages every day, several times a day, and he has never mentioned he was in a hurry. I'll ask him," she said, picking up her phone.

Dave watched as she held the phone in her hand and punched button after button with her tiny thumbs. She then laid the phone down and went back to her breakfast. She was putting all her things into her bag when she suddenly picked up the little cell phone, pushed a button, and told Dave, "He said he's not in any hurry for the cars, but he can't wait to see me."

"Let me see that," Dave said.

Jodie showed him the message on her phone.

"Amazing!" he said.

They were soon climbing into the rig and heading west toward Chicago. Jodie was intent with her logistics and had planned them a fuel and meal stop about half of the way to Chicago. They would be stopping south of Cleveland at the junction of Interstate Highways 80 and 71. The route she planned for them was new to Dave, so he was relying solely on her recommendations. Because of this, they found themselves eating at a diner that was not to Dave's liking.

The diner was dimly lit, and alcoholic drinks were being served. In the booth across from their table, Dave observed two big ugly earring-wearing men, both long-haired and tattooed, ogling Jodie. Dave was uncomfortable and rushed through his meal and pushed Jodie to do the same. As they left, they had to walk past the booth where the two men sat. Dave was following closely behind Jodie as they walked toward the checkout counter. Suddenly, one of the men grabbed Jodie by the wrist with one hand and by the butt with his other.

Dave's reaction was swift and harsh. He chopped the man violently in the throat with the outer edge of his flattened hand. As the man grabbed his throat and gasped for breath, Dave pulled Jodie behind him. He turned toward the second man just as he arose from the booth cursing Dave. Dave hit him in the forehead with the heel of his hand, knocking him backward into his seat. Before the man could react, Dave kicked him soundly in the chest, sending him back against the wall on the other side of the booth. Dave looked back at the first man who was still gasping for breath. He took Jodie by the hand, and placing her in front of him again, he walked them hurriedly to the cashier. Dave paid the check while occasionally looking behind him to see what the two men were doing.

Outside, he walked Jodie quickly to the truck, helped her inside, picked up his tire checking baton, and started back toward the diner. He hadn't reached the diner yet when he saw the two men coming out through the front doorway.

Dave was walking deliberately toward the two of them, slapping the baton against his left palm; his jaw was set, his face fixed in an angry scowl. The two men were climbing onto motorcycles when they saw Dave approaching menacingly. The one rubbing his throat held up his hand in a signal of surrender. The other, at first, started to challenge Dave, then thought better of it and climbed back onto his bike.

Dave stopped and watched as the two motorcycles roared away. He realized he was breathing heavily, and he could feel his heart pounding rapidly. He turned and walked slowly but deliberately back to the truck.

Back inside the truck, Dave turned his attention to Jodie. "Did that son of a bitch hurt you?" he asked.

"I'm fine," she said. "But you scared me! Were you going to kill those men, Dave?"

"They deserved killing just for what they wanted to do to you! And what they might have done if I hadn't been there to protect you!" Dave said, his jaws still tight with emotion.

"I don't ever want you angry with me," Jodie stated.

"You could never do anything to make me angry with you, little one," Dave said as he pulled the truck back onto the interstate. "Put on some Marty Robbins, the one with 'Devil Woman' on it."

Jodie put the CD into the slot and sat back and observed Dave. She had never seen a more frightening look on a man's face as the one she had witnessed when he was defending her. Now his face was relaxed as he softly sang along with the CD.

Suddenly, as the words, "Down the beach, I see what belongs to me," poured from the CD, Dave reached over and gently took her hand, holding it for several minutes. As the song ended, Dave looked at her lovingly, smiled, and released her hand.

If it wasn't for the fact that Dave was almost twice her age, it would have been obvious to Jodie that he was deeply in love with her. She continued to believe he was just a dear friend who would do anything to protect her. She enjoyed his fatherly attention and praise. This caused her to have a deep fondness for this large older man.

"Do you mind if I send David a text message about what happened tonight?" she asked Dave.

"It might just worry him. But you're a grown-up, tell him anything you want to. Tell him his cars will be there by 10:00 p.m. tomorrow."

"I think I'll call him instead," she replied.

Dave was listening to her talk to David on the phone with one ear and to Marty Robbins singing "El Paso" with the other. With Jodie so obviously enamored of David, the words of the song suddenly hit Dave like a blow between the eyes. "I was in love, but in vain, I could tell," Marty crooned. Dave looked over at Jodie who was so happily engaged in conversation with his son. He admitted the truth to himself. It was at that moment that Dave finally accepted the inevitable. He could never do more than love her from afar. He sighed deeply, ejected the CD, and turned off the player.

They were in Chicago earlier than planned. They delivered their load and were soon hooking up to the loaded automobile transport trailer at the Ford assembly plant in the Hegewisch area of Chicago. They slept in the truck on the assembly plant grounds that night. Shortly before 6:00 a.m. the following morning, Dave drove the loaded Freightliner out of the plant gate and was soon on Interstate 94 headed back toward Gary, Indiana. There they would take Interstate 65 south. According to Jodie, this would take them all the way to Montgomery, Alabama, where they would then take US 231 on into Panama City.

"I can do it with my eyes closed," Dave bragged.

"Please don't!" Jodie teased.

They made good time and were a little ahead of schedule when they pulled into a truck stop near Memphis during midday. Dave lifted Jodie down out of the truck as usual, but for the first time, he didn't hold her back with him as she hurried off to the restrooms. He was, in his own way, trying to turn her loose. He didn't worry any less and was relieved to see her tiny person as she joined him at the checkout counter.

Back on the road, Jodie made several calls and finally announced in a dejected manner that the nearest load she could get for their return trip to the West Coast was in Atlanta.

"One or two trailers?" Dave asked her. "We can make up the loss if we can get two."

"I'll call them back," Jodie replied. She took out her planner, and soon, she wrote something in it and held up her book. "We've got two!" she said with pride. "Both going to Phoenix."

"When do we have to pick them up?"

"The day after tomorrow. Should I get us something out of Phoenix coming this way?"

"Let's not get too far ahead," Dave said, watching her excitement. "Do you still want to be my partner and alternate driver?"

"I think it would be very exciting," she said, the anticipation showing plainly in her beautiful brown eyes.

"Okay," Dave said. "I'll have a partnership contract drawn up. Since I own the truck, I won't be able to split the earnings equally, but I'll be fair to you. Since I'll be getting the bigger piece of the pie, I'll be responsible for your meals and lodging while we're on the road. Meanwhile, you need to get to school and get that commercial license. There is a truck driving school in Tucson. You could be home every night."

"I don't see why we have to make a partnership agreement," Jodie said seriously. "Couldn't you just pay me so much per hour while I'm driving?"

"Then we get into another realm," Dave explained. "Employees are treated much differently than partners under our onerous and confusing tax system. I'd probably have to hire another employee just to do the paperwork. That's why I've been so content as my own boss all of these years. Do you understand now just how special you are to me, little one?"

Jodie just looked at him while she turned everything over in her mind. He was such a competent driver; he could sit there and talk about anything, yet he never lost his concentration on the surrounding traffic situation. His eyes were constantly moving from mirror to mirror and back to the traffic ahead. He seemed as relaxed behind the wheel as if he was at home in a recliner. Would she ever be able to be that confident in her abilities to drive? Probably not, but still she had a burning desire to try. She really wanted to be his partner, but she also realized that for her to become a partner, Dave was sacrificing a lot of his independence. Should she ask him to do that for her? She felt slightly self-conscious, reluctant to enter his area of expertise.

"Do you really think I have what it takes to be a good semi driver?" she asked.

"Yes, I do! I believe in you, Jodie."

The rest of the run from Memphis to Panama City was uneventful. Jodie spent some of the time sending text messages to David. Occasionally, she would let Dave in on the content of a message.

"David said he is going to remain at the office until we get there tonight," Jodie informed him. "He said he has rooms for us at a luxurious hotel just across the lagoon from his new house. He doesn't have his house furnished yet, but he has moved a bed into it, and he sleeps there."

"Rooms?" Dave asked. "We haven't needed rooms so far. Do you need a room to yourself, Jodie?"

"It would be nice to sleep somewhere away from your freight train noise," she answered.

"You just said you wanted to be partners with this old noisemaker. Now first chance you get, you abandon me. Do you realize I have only spent one night alone since I met you?"

"Poor Dave, all alone in a big old hotel room. How ever will you survive?" she teased him.

As promised, David was there to meet them. They left the truck where it was to be unloaded the following day. They all three piled into David's Lincoln and went out for a late supper. Once again, Dave felt totally left out as the two young people laughed and flirted, thoroughly enjoying one another's company.

It was after midnight when David escorted them up to their rooms. He told Dave good night at the door of his room then accompanied Jodie to a room down the hall. Dave watched from the door of his room as David disappeared into Jodie's room, carrying her bag. He fought a jealous urge to go pull his son out of Jodie's room.

"She's an adult woman!" Dave told himself. "And what she does and with whom is none of my business." He forced himself to enter his own room and close the door.

Dave didn't sleep very well that night. He couldn't keep the thought of what was probably happening just down the hall with the woman he loved from his tortured mind. Dave wanted to be the one holding her tiny sensuous body close to his while he showed her for the first time what tender, unselfish love making was like. He felt a terrible dislike for his own son for the first time in his life. He tossed and turned. There were no train-type snoring noises coming from Dave's room that night.

At daylight, he was up, shaved and showered and in his best clothes. He wandered down to the breakfast room and downed several cups of coffee. He thought about going up and knocking on Jodie's door but didn't think he could stand seeing David's grinning face. He wanted to call and check on Jodie, but he didn't think he could stand to hear David's voice if he was the one who picked up the phone. He just sat there drinking coffee, his heart aching. He couldn't remember a time, even in his teens, when he had felt this bad about losing the love of a woman.

"You're just weeks from your forty-ninth birthday," he told himself. "Time you did some growing up." Dave finished his coffee, sighed deeply, and returned to his room. He packed his bag and placed it on the end of the bed. He took a piece of notepaper and wrote a note to Jodie. He placed it in an envelope and put it in his pocket. He picked up his bag and quietly walked to Jodie's room. There, he slid the note under the door. He took the elevator to the lobby, checked out, and called a taxi.

Dave was at the Cates and Wellborn Ford dealership in time to supervise the unloading. Once the unloading was completed, he moved the trailer out of the way and parked at the far edge of the lot. He went inside to collect the paperwork.

"Mr. Wellborn will be in around noon," the secretary told him. "He had a very late night."

"Tell him I'm sorry I missed him," Dave told her. "I'm a working man. I have to pick up a load in Atlanta. Does he have to check the inventory, or can you cut me a check?"

"No, we can get you your check right away," she told him. "Mr. Cates is in the building. Have a seat. Have some coffee."

"Thank you," Dave answered.

Dave poured a small coffee and sat down. In five minutes, the secretary returned with his check. He thanked her and walked back to the truck. He checked around and found several of Jodie's things. He gathered them up and placed them in a plastic bag. He carried the bag inside to David office. The door to the office was locked, so he once again went to find the secretary.

"These things belong to Miss Underwood, Mr. Wellborn's friend," Dave explained. "Would you see to it that he gets them? He'll know where she is."

"Yes, sir," she replied. "I'll put them in his office right away."

"Thanks again for everything," Dave said as he turned and headed to the Freightliner.

He checked the time as he pulled onto US 95. It was 9:30 a.m. *I could be in La Grange by 2:00 p.m.,* he thought to himself. *Good time to catch Amy in a business lull. Maybe she'll have some time off. I don't need to be in Atlanta till tomorrow.*

At first, it was difficult to keep the Freightliner down to the speed limit with no weight on behind, but Dave soon mastered the change. As he passed through Dothan, he heard his cell phone ringing, but he wasn't going to pick it up while he was driving, even if he had known how to use it.

A little after 2:00 p.m., he was entering Cisco's. Amy, who was just coming from the rear of the café, saw him as he entered.

"Big Dave," she said with a smile, "did you come to pick me up, or do you want something to eat?"

"Both," Dave said with a grin.

"I'll be right back!" Amy promised.

A few minutes later, Amy set a plate down in front of him. It contained smothered pork chops, mashed potatoes, gravy, corn on the cob, and biscuits. She placed a large tossed green salad beside it, already covered with ranch dressing. She then slid into the booth across from him.

"I got off at two," she said. "Where's your little girlfriend?"

When he didn't answer, she went on carrying the conversation while he ate. She talked about her dogs, her house, and the fishing. Dave ate like a starving man. The food at Cisco's was so good that he always finished every bite.

"I'm stuffed," Dave said pushing his plate back. "We can get out of here as soon as you give me my ticket."

"Not today," Amy told him. "This one's on me. You want to follow me to my place or leave your truck here and ride with me? I'll have you back to your truck by five tomorrow morning. That's when I have to be here."

"Then I'll just ride with you."

They were at Amy's little house in twenty-five minutes. She parked in her carport and waited for Dave to open her car door for her. As he helped her out, he noticed how much closer the lake was to her house since the last time he had been there.

"Lake looks like it's up quite a bit," he offered.

Amy took his hand. "Did you come here to talk or to make love?" she asked him.

"I could use a friendly ear right now," Dave told her. "Can you believe I'm not in the mood for the other?"

"Big Dave, finally getting old? I don't believe it. Something is really bothering you. Okay, come on in and pour your heart out. I'm just going to put the dogs out."

Dave didn't really want to tell her about his broken heart, nor did he want a night of passion with Amy. He just wanted to be in the company of a good and loyal friend. Amy tried several times to get him to unburden his soul and several times to seduce him, but Dave was like a stone in his resolve to do neither. Eventually, they went out onto the dock and tried to catch a few fish. Before the night passed, Amy tried one more time to pique Dave's interest by leaving her bedroom door open while she undressed and changed for bed.

Dave called to her, "You are still a very sexy lady, Amy." Then to himself, he said, "Just not the one I want." He curled up on her couch but didn't sleep.

Jodie awoke around ten o'clock. She wondered why Dave hadn't called her. She cleaned up, put on her makeup, dressed, and dialed his cell phone. He didn't answer. She decided to check his room. As she started out the door, she discovered an envelope addressed to her on the floor just inside her door. Inside the envelope, she found a note from Dave.

"Dear Jodie," it began. "I didn't want to disturb you and your lover this morning. I have gone to pick up the trailers from Atlanta. If you still want to go to Phoenix with me after last night, meet me at the Love's Truck Stop at the junction of Interstate 10 and US 231 tomorrow. I'll be there around 11:00 a.m. I'll wait for you until noon. If you aren't there by that time, I will assume you no longer wish to be my partner. The enclosed cash is what I consider to be your pay through yesterday." It was signed simply with, "Dave."

Jodie dialed David's phone. When he answered, she felt some relief.

"Dave has gone off and left me!" she said, panic in her voice. "He just dumped me here and left! He left me a note, but it doesn't make any sense."

"Calm down, Jodi," David told her. "I'll be right there."

When David arrived, she was in the lobby with her bag. He waited for her to check out then took her across the street for a filling brunch. "Now, Jodie," he said, "tell me what this is all about."

Jodie handed him the note from his father. David read it over. "You had a lover in your room last night?" he asked.

"No! Not even in my dreams!" she stated emphatically.

"Then who is Dad talking about...Oh!" David said. "I get it! He saw me go into your room last night with your bag, and he just assumed the worst. Well, we should make Big Dave suffer for his naughty mind."

"What do you mean?" Jodie asked him innocently.

"My dad thinks I spent the night with you in your room," David explained. "We should just let him think that. When he's watching, we'll just carry on like two out of control lovers."

"No! I don't want Dave to think bad things about me. Your father has been nothing but kind to me. Two days ago, he almost killed two men just because one of them grabbed my ass. He has promised to take me on as his partner as soon as I get my commercial license. I love Dave as much as I love my own father. I need to tell him nothing happened last night!"

Jodie placed a call to Dave's cell phone every hour until late in the evening. It rang, but he didn't answer. What Jodie didn't know was that Dave was spending the afternoon and evening with Amy and had left his cell phone in his truck.

Amy let Dave out at his truck at 5:00 a.m. as promised. Before starting the big diesel, Dave made a routine check of everything. In the process, he noticed his cell phone in the utility basket with some CDs. "I need to learn how to use this thing," he told himself. He discovered there were thirteen missed calls, all from Jodie's number. He told himself that he should call her a little later when he was sure she would be up.

What if she just wants to tell me about her and David? She'll want me to be happy for her. I don't think I can do that. I know I should be happy for both of them, but I'm going to need more time, Dave thought.

As Dave connected onto the trailers, he thought about what he would say if he was instructing Jodie in this task. She had learned how to decouple but had never experienced the procedure for coupling two trailers.

Dave had bought his first rig just after being discharged from the navy. When David was still very young, he had often dreamed of having him ride along so he could teach him everything about the business. But David had never been interested in the long trips away from home or spending hours watching the world roll by at highway speeds. Dave thought he had replaced the dream of teaching his son with that of teaching Jodie. Now even that dream would not be realized. Dave felt despondent. Even the usual uplifting sounds from his Ernest Tubb CD couldn't pull him from his depression.

It was shortly after 11:00 a.m. when Dave made the turn into the Love's Truck Stop. As he made the loop, pulling his truck up to the pumps, he noticed David's Lincoln parked near the building. As he set the brakes, he saw the car door fly open and Jodie come running toward him. He climbed down to fuel his tanks just in time to catch her as she leaped into his arms. As he released her from his bear-like hug, Jodie began to scold him.

"You made me a promise that you would never just leave me by the side of the road, and now you've done it twice! Why did you leave me, Dave? You had me very worried and scared!"

"I thought that you and David—," he began.

"I know what you thought!" Jodie rebuked him. "Shame on you! What makes you think I'm that kind of woman?"

Dave was tongue-tied. He had jumped to conclusions based on very thin evidence. "I'm sorry, Jodie. I, I—"

"Let me have that nozzle," she demanded. "You go fill the other side!"

David arrived just then, carrying all of Jodie's things. He climbed into the truck and put them on the bunk. As he climbed down, he turned to his father.

"Good luck with that one," he said, nodding in Jodie's direction. They shook hands and hugged briefly before David returned to his car and drove away.

"Have you had lunch?" Dave called across to Jodie, trying to break the icy silence between them.

"No!" she replied coldly.

"Do you want to get some lunch here?" Dave asked cheerfully.

"I guess," Jodie answered with a little less hurt in her voice.

They finished their refueling. Jodie climbed into the driver side, adjusted the seat, and pulled the truck forward into a parking space. Dave just stood there and watched her. He was at the door to assist her from the truck after she had set the brakes. As he lifted her down, she actually smiled at him for a brief moment. Inside, they found a table and ordered lunch.

"I had to stay at the Thunderbird Motel last night," Jodie scolded as she ate her sandwich, "That place was noisy and not very nice! I was lonely and frightened."

"Uh, why didn't you stay at the place David got for you?" Dave asked softly.

"Because I wanted to use my own money," Jodie replied. "You already think I'm a kept woman!"

"I'll say it again," Dave said, hoping for her understanding. "I'm sorry, Jodie. Are you ever going to forgive me?"

"I don't know. What itinerary have you planned for today?" Jodie asked him, changing the subject.

"I don't have any," Dave replied. "I just thought I'd drive till I got tired."

"See," Jodie began, "you're lost without me, yet you still keep trying to run off and leave me! I'll make out the week's schedule as soon as we get back on the road. I had a lot of time on my hands yesterday, and I've been thinking. We need to trade the old Freightliner in on a powerful new Volvo FH16 700 with a modern, up-to-date sleeper. With that power, we can pull two trailers every time. It's supposed to be more fuel efficient too. We need to get the partnership papers finalized. I'll be in school the next three weeks, so I'll try to set up enough short trips during that time so you can do them without me. When I get my commercial license, I can plan us some longer trips. You can drive the night shifts, and I'll drive days."

Dave was smiling inside and out. Little One was back! And now she was in charge. He finished his meal, sat back in his chair, and watched her as she planned their future together; he watched her pretty face, her beautiful dark eyes sparkling excitedly, her small but perfect figure. He knew he could never possess her, but God, how he loved her!

EPILOGUE

Abigail and Mark had a baby boy who they named Mark David after the baby's father and grandfather.

Amy retired from Cisco's Café. She still lives in her house on West Point Lake where she fishes and is waitress to her dogs.

David continued as general manager of the Cates and Wellborn Ford dealership. He recently announced his engagement to his executive secretary. He and Jodie remain close friends.

Jodie completed truck driving school with high marks and received her Commercial Drivers License. She soon convinced Dave to trade in the old Freightliner for a new Volvo FH16 700.

Dave never got around to writing the partnership agreement. Instead, just six weeks after Jodie returned from truck driving school, she and Dave entered into a life-long partnership with a ceremony held in her parent's home in Tucson. They honeymooned in San Diego, Las Vegas, Denver, Kansas City and points east.

ACKNOWLEDGMENTS

Devil Woman written and performed by Marty Robbins 1962
El Paso written and performed by Marty Robbins 1959

Harry's memory and obvious misuse of some of the words to an old country song were based on: "That's Why I'm Walking" written by Melvin Endsley and Stonewall Jackson and recorded by Stonewall Jackson.